Forgotten Books

Hebrew and Babylonian Traditions

By

Morris Jastrow

1861 — 1921

Published by Forgotten Books 2012

Originally Published 1914

PIBN 1000047959

HEBREW AND BABYLONIAN TRADITIONS

To

WILLIAM WEST FRAZIER

A TRIBUTE

OF ESTEEM AND AFFECTION

PREFACE

WHEN the kind invitation was extended to me by the authorities of Oberlin College to become the Haskell Lecturer for 1913, I welcomed the oppor tunity to bring to a temporary close studies on the relationship between Hebrews and Babylonians that had occupied me, though with prolonged interrup tions, for a long term of years. Impressed by the fact that the civilisation of the Hebrews and Baby lonians moved along such different lines, despite the many features they had in common, I felt that the real problem involved in a comparative study of Hebrew and Babylonian folk-tales, beliefs, religious practices, and modes of thought was to determine the factor or factors that led to such entirely dif ferent issues in the case of the two peoples. Ar chæological research, in combination with the ascer tained and generally accepted results of biblical studies, had demonstrated the close bond existing between Hebrew and Babylonian traditions—to use a conveniently comprehensive term—beyond ques tion. It is idle at this stage to deny either the composite character of the stories in the early chap ters of Genesis, or the late date at which they must have received their present form; it is equally fu tile to deny the factor of evolution in the develop-

ment of religious ideas among the Hebrews. The
evidence is overwhelming; and whether we turn to
the legal sections of the Pentateuch, or to the his
torical records, or to the Prophets and Psalms, we
see everywhere the traces of a long-continued proc
ess of thought with many windings and turns, cul
minating in ethical monotheism, by which I mean
a view of divine government based on a spiritual
and ethical interpretation of the God-idea.

On the other hand, the rediscovery of Babylonia
and Assyria through the excavations conducted on
the sites of ancient cities in the Euphrates Valley
and along the banks of the Tigris has placed at
the disposal of students an enormous mass of ma
terial which has thrown much light on the origin
of the traditions and early beliefs of the Hebrews;
it has demonstrated that Hebrew history is unin
telligible without constant recourse to the data ob
tained from cuneiform literature. Hebrews and
Babylonians start out on their careers with much
in common; they share traditions regarding the
manner in which the world came into being, they
have common traditions regarding a disastrous Del
uge that swept over the part of the world known
to them. The source of the antediluvian chronology
of the Bible is to be sought in traditions current in
the Euphrates Valley; and there is a steady stream
of influence emanating more particularly from Baby
lonia from a very early period onward that helps
to maintain a close association with beliefs and
practices among the Hebrews up to the time when

the latter begin to move in an entirely different and novel direction. To be sure, there are other influences at work in the early history of the He brews besides those that are to be traced to Baby lonia and Assyria. Some of the tribes forming part of the confederacy of the Bene Israel had at one time much in common with the nomad Arabs, and all of them with the agricultural Canaanites whom they gradually dispossessed, but who passed on to the conquerors many of their religious practices. Egyptian culture also must have had some share in bringing about conditions that arose in Palestine, but Babylonia by virtue of early associations and by almost continuous contact, though closer at some periods than at others, is the most important ele ment in that phase of Hebrew life and thought with which we are concerned in this work.

Accepting the ascertained results of modern re search, the question, then, with which we are con fronted is to account for the tremendous influence exerted by Hebrew traditions in the form finally given to them, and to explain why the religious thought and practices of the Hebrews became, with the heritage of Greek and Roman culture, the foun dation structure on which the superstructure of modern civilisation has been erected. That fact is as undeniable as are the postulates of biblical crit icism and of archæological investigations.

Despite the many essays, monographs, and larger works that have appeared during the past three decades on the various phases of the relationship

existing between Hebrews and Babylonians, I feel
that there is room and need for a work like this
one, devoted primarily to pointing out the *differ
ences* between Babylonian myths, beliefs, and prac
tices, and the final form assumed by corresponding
Hebrew traditions, despite the circumstance that
these traditions are to be traced back to the same
source which gave rise to the Babylonian traditions
as we find them in the literature of Babylonia and
of the offshoot of Babylonia—Assyria.

This, then, is my purpose as set forth more fully
in the first chapter and as emphasised in all of the
chapters. It is quite likely that the book will not
be pleasing to "extremists," whether of the ultraconservative type, who present a resolute front
against departures from traditional views regarding
the books of the Old Testament, or of the equally
rigid ultra-unemotional type who, with a limited
historical horizon, are unable to enter sympathet
ically into the unfolding of the religious thought of
a people and are inclined to belittle the value of
religious beliefs as a factor in human evolution, for
fear of appearing to countenance a religious attitude
with which they themselves are not in accord. One
can readily understand how even learned and con
scientious scholars through a determination to cling
to certain views can acquire an attitude of mind
which prevents them from weighing evidence judi
ciously and fairly. This observation applies particu
larly to those who deceive themselves by imagining
that they are pursuing studies in an open-minded

spirit, whereas in reality they are merely seeking a
confirmation of views which they hold quite inde
pendently of their studies, and generally held antece
dent to any investigation.   But the observation may
be extended also to scholars of a more scientific type
who, in a spirit of reaction against views which they
have come to regard as untenable, fail to penetrate
into the depths of their subject because too much
absorbed in the externalities—in textual criticism, or
in investigations of special points without reference
to the necessary relationship of even the infinitesi
mal parts of a subject to the subject as a whole.

Whatever may be the verdict pronounced on the
method followed in my work and on the results
reached by me through this method, I feel that I
may assure my readers that I have approached the
many difficult and delicate themes included in this
work in a spirit of pure historical inquiry, and in
a frame of mind free from bias, without any predilec
tions for any special theological postulates.   Indeed,
I have aimed to keep my own position towards the
problems presented by the study of ancient relig
ions in the background, except in so far as my per
sonal creed includes a sympathetic attitude towards
the struggle of man everywhere and at all times to
reach out to an understanding of the mysteries by
which he is surrounded—mysteries that even in
early stages of culture are dimly perceived, and that
become more clearly defined and correspondingly
more profound as with enlarged experience and with
increasing knowledge man realises how much must

always remain for him within the shadow of the unknown and the unknowable—the dark impene trable territory beyond the border line, to which Job's paradox (10 : 22) may be applied, "where even light is as darkness."

Naturally, in a single course of five lectures only certain phases of the large topic could be treated. I chose those which seemed to be of greatest impor tance and which seemed best adapted to illustrate the different directions taken by Hebrew and Baby lonian traditions, namely, the views about Creation, the relationship existing between the Hebrew and Babylonian Sabbath, the unfolding of beliefs regard ing the after-life, and a survey of Hebrew and Baby lonian ethics. These aspects are sufficiently diverse to test the application of the main thesis in the investigation. Perhaps on another occasion I shall take up in the same way a comparative study of Hebrew and Babylonian legislation, of sacrificial rites, of divination practices, of marriage and funeral customs, and of the position of woman, all of which are calculated to illustrate the distinctive features of each of the two civilisations. Since, however, in the course of the subjects treated in the five chap ters, I had occasion to refer several times to the biblical and Babylonian narratives of the Deluge, I have thought it useful both on this account and because it was George Smith's discovery in 1872 of a fragment of the Babylonian Deluge story[1] that

[1] Read before the Society of Biblical Archæology at the memorable meeting on December 3, 1872, and published in the *Transactions* of the Society, vol. II, pp. 213–234.

originated the study of Babylonian and Hebrew traditions, to add in an appendix an analysis with copious extracts of the various versions of the Baby lonian tale regarding the great catastrophe that overwhelmed mankind, and then to set forth as an illustration of the modern method of biblical study the two accounts of the Deluge in Genesis that have been dovetailed into a continuous narra tive. Incidental remarks and a summary at the close of this Appendix will show how the point of view from which the ancient tradition is regarded in its transformed garb in Genesis is in keeping with the process to be detected in the biblical Creation stories and in other traditions, such as the tale of man's forfeiture of Paradise. I am particularly indebted to Dr. Arno Poebel for his kindness in placing at my disposal the advance sheets of his forthcoming publication of Sumerian texts contain ing the oldest known versions of both the Creation and Deluge myths of ancient Babylonia. These texts Dr. Poebel discovered among the tablets found at Nippur by the expedition of the University of Pennsylvania, and which are now in the Museum of Archæology of the University. Dr. Poebel has been actively at work since the summer of 1912 on the valuable material unearthed at Nippur, and his publication which is to appear in several volumes and which will greatly advance also our knowledge of Sumerian, the ancient non-Semitic speech of the Euphrates Valley, is being looked forward to with great interest. His generosity in allowing me to

utilise the results of his labours even before their
formal appearance has enabled me, in the Appendix,
to place before my readers the relationship of the
oldest Babylonian version of the Deluge to the
latest one as embodied in the Gilgamesh Epic—the
most notable literary production of Babylonia.

My thanks are also due, as on all former occasions,
to my wife, who has carefully read the whole of the
manuscript as well as the proofs. Traces of her
valuable suggestions are to be found on almost
every page. Realising her conscientious devotion
to a most unselfish task, I feel how inadequate the
mere word of acknowledgment is to convey my
feelings of gratitude towards her.

I am also under obligations to my dear friend
and colleague, Professor James A. Montgomery, of
the University of Pennsylvania, for his kindness in
reading a proof of the entire book, and in letting
me have the benefit of his valuable criticisms and
suggestions. My pupil, Dr. B. B. Charles, now in
structor of Semitic languages at the University of
Pennsylvania, kindly undertook to prepare the index
for the volume, and he has carried out the task in
the same careful manner that marked his work on
a former occasion. I feel deeply grateful to him
for transferring this task from my shoulders to his
more youthful ones. The lectures appear here in
an entirely revised and considerably enlarged form
from that originally given to them for oral delivery.
In order to adapt them to a reading public, I have
also in all except a few instances removed the ear-

marks of the lecture style, but I trust that if I shall be fortunate enough to have among my readers some who listened so sympathetically to the spoken word, they will recognise that the spirit has not been altered. They will also find questions which could be only partially discussed in the lectures more fully treated in the enlarged book. For me the week spent amidst the charming surroundings of Oberlin College while delivering the lectures will re main always a happy recollection. I feel under special obligations to Professor Albert T. Swing, on whom fell the burden of making the arrangements for these lectures, and who contributed so much to the pleasure of my stay.

Lastly, I regard it as a privilege to be permitted to dedicate this volume to a dear and highly es teemed friend, whose friendship has been a source of happiness and of strength to me during a long term of years.

MORRIS JASTROW, JR.

UNIVERSITY OF PENNSYLVANIA,
    December, 1913.

CONTENTS

HEBREW AND BABYLONIAN TRADITIONS

CHAPTER I

RELATIONS BETWEEN HEBREWS AND BABYLONIANS

I

IT will be my main aim in this investigation to set forth some of the aspects presented by a com parison of two civilisations that have much in com mon, that were developed by peoples belonging in part to the same stock, and that have both exer cised a wide influence, though in totally different directions. Despite many features in common, each of these civilisations went its own way, the one unfolding great political strength, supported by an elaborate military organisation, and producing, as outward expressions of this strength, monuments of gigantic proportions,—temples and palaces filled with works of art; it built great cities, created an extensive commerce, and made certain permanent contributions to the thought and achievements of mankind; the other, with little of outward display, politically insignificant, working out its destiny with apparently no thought of any extension of its influence beyond narrow boundaries, yet becoming one of the most potent factors in the religious history of mankind. The problem involved in a compari son between the Hebrew civilisation and the Eu- phratean culture, as we may briefly designate the Babylonian-Assyrian civilisation, since Assyria is merely an extension of the impulse that arose in the south and extended to the north, is to deter mine the point of separation between the two that led to such totally different issues. Why is it—we may properly ask—that with agreement in regard to many traditions, with religious ideas and prac tices that at one time bore a close resemblance to one another, with a general view of life, of divine government, of the fate of man after death, of prac tical ethics at the outset not sharply differentiated from one another, the courses taken by Hebrew and Babylonian traditions were so dissimilar. For it is to the different courses taken by this common stock of traditional ideas and practices that the contrast presented by Hebrews and Babylonians is to be traced—a contrast no less striking than the points of resemblance that once existed between the two civilisations. These resemblances have often been treated during the past decades, both in spe cial investigations and in general summaries. They have been discussed from various points of view: on the one hand, by critics whose aim appeared to have been to show the dependence of Hebrew ideas upon those of Babylonia and Assyria; and on the other, by those whose view-point was directed towards securing confirmation of the data presented by biblical records. I have little sympathy with either mode of treatment. To extend the claims of Babylonian-Assyrian civilisation so as to make Hebrew achievements merely a pale reflection of the picture presented by Euphratean culture is to forfeit the possibility of any real understanding of the spirit of Hebrew history, is to miss the point of that history, and to abandon the key that will en able us to solve the problem involved in the pro found influence exerted by the religious thought of the Hebrews. On the other hand, to press the apol ogetic attitude to the extent of assuming the un approachable quality of the entire Old Testament without distinguishing between incidental and es sential elements, and to carry on our historical re search merely with a purpose of finding a confir mation of preconceived points of view, is to place the Old Testament in a false light and to pursue a method that is both vicious and disingenuous. We must frankly and unreservedly take as our start ing-point in a comparative study of Babylonian and Hebrew traditions, the factor of evolution, by which I mean the assumption of a progress in re ligious thought, and apply that factor to Hebrew history precisely in the same manner and to the same degree as to the history of Babylonia and As syria. The Hebrews were subject to outside influ-] ences in precisely the same manner and to the same degree as were all other ethnic groups. They begin their career with the same mental equipment as

other nations; the differentiating factor in He
brew history is to be found in the outcome and not
in anything that has to do with its beginnings.
That history is unfolded under the same laws to
be observed elsewhere in the annals of a people.
What gives to the history of the Hebrews its unique
quality from a certain period is the introduction
of an element that, as an expression of the pecul
iar genius of the people, gradually changes the en
tire aspect of their attitude towards life. Gradual
growth must be assumed and not a sudden depar
ture from the normal—gradual growth in the polit
ical and social life and in the religious life as well.
We can trace this religious growth in the pages of
the Old Testament with the same definiteness that
we can follow the political and social unfolding of
the people, and even where our material is insuffi
cient for following this evolution in detail, we must
nevertheless assume such evolution or involve our
selves in hopeless difficulties from which we can
extract ourselves only by sophistry or by some
other form of vicious reasoning. It will therefore be
one of my aims to elucidate the special and pecul
iar element in Hebrew history which, manifesting
itself in diverse ways, leads to a wide deflection of
Hebrew traditions from their Babylonian counter
parts. Our comparative study will be directed
chiefly towards an elucidation of the ultimate
differences that arise between Hebrew and Baby
lonian points of view despite earlier and very
noticeable points of agreement; and I venture to

think that the real value of a comparative study
of any kind lies in bringing out differences. Only
a superficial view of comparisons stops at pointing
out resemblances.

Gradual growth involves survivals, that is to say,
indications of older views and customs carried over
into later periods. Evolution means not only trans
formations through historical processes, but a mix
ture of old and new. It will therefore be also
part of my purpose to trace the process of growth
in both Hebrew and Babylonian traditions, and to
show in how far older views were replaced, how far
they survived, and how, combined with new thought,
they gave rise to new religious practices.

II

It was to be foreseen at an early stage in the
exploration of Babylonian and Assyrian cities—the
work of the last seventy years[1]—and in the study
of the material unearthed, that the bearings of this
material upon Hebrew traditions, on Hebrew his
tory, and on Hebrew religious ideas would be mani
fold and important. Hebrew traditions carried back
the beginnings of the Hebrews to settlements in
the Euphrates Valley. Nay more, the first home
of mankind was fixed in this region, as is suffi
ciently evidenced by the mention of two rivers, the
Euphrates and Tigris, watering the Garden of Eden,

[1] A full account of these explorations will be found in chapter I of
a forthcoming work of the author, *The Civilization of Babylonia and
Assyria.*

where the first man and his consort were placed.
A writer intent upon giving an answer to two fun
damental questions, how mankind came to be dis
persed over the face of the globe, and why there
are so many different languages,[1] tells the curious
tale in the tenth chapter of Genesis—itself a com
bination of two stories, one about the building
of a city, the other of a high tower—which repre
sents the dispersion as radiating from the city of
Babylon in the land of Shinar (a general term for
the Euphrates Valley) as a centre, and the con
fusion of languages as a device of Yahweh to pre
vent the people from carrying out their design to
build the tower. The city of Babylon symbolised
for the writer the entire civilisation of the Euphra
tes Valley. The tower that the writer had in mind
was a characteristic feature of the sacred architec
ture in the Euphrates Valley—the staged construc
tion with broad terraces, heaped one above the other
in imitation of a mountain, with a winding road
leading to the top where the deity to whom the
tower was dedicated had his seat.[2] The story thus
not only takes us back to Babylonia, but represents
a characteristic protest of Old Testament writers
against Babylonish customs. It voices the feelings
of these writers towards Babylonia as a wicked place,
as a source of mankind's misfortunes and ills.

The contact between the Euphrates Valley and
Palestine is maintained in Hebrew traditions after

[1] See below, p. 56.
[2] See Jastrow, *Aspects of Belief and Practice in Babylonia and Assyria*,
pp. 282 *seq.*

the migration of the Terahites from Ur and Haran. Abraham sends his servant to his old home
in order to obtain a wife for his son from there—
an indication of the persistency of the tradition
which assumed close bonds between the Hebrew
settlements in Palestine and the Euphrates Valley.
From the Babylonian side we find this relationship
in the political sense confirmed; for an ancient con
queror, Sargon, who is to be placed somewhere
around 2600 B. C., extends his sway to the west
ern lands comprised under the name of Amurru,
which, in the broad sense, included Palestine. A
thousand years later we find the Babylonian lan
guage as the current medium of diplomatic exchange
between Palestine and Egypt. The reference to a
"cloak of Shinar" (Jos. 7 : 21) in the account of
the Hebrew conquest of Jericho is an interesting
testimony to commercial intercourse between Pal
estine and Babylonia; and I need hardly remind
you of the way in which Assyria and Babylonia
interfered with the fortunes of the Hebrew king
doms, from the middle of the ninth century on,
leading directly to the destruction of both. It was
therefore a moment of intense interest (though it
ought not to have been a surprise) when in the his
torical annals found in the remains of Babylonian
and Assyrian cities scholars began to read of these
political relations. Subsequently, traditions con
cerned with the Creation of the world and with a
disastrous Deluge that recalled the narratives in the
early chapters of Genesis began to come to light.

Interest in Babylonian-Assyrian research was in
creased when, on penetrating still deeper into the
religious literature and religious customs of Baby
lonia and Assyria, institutions and rites were re
vealed for which parallels could be found in the
pages of the Old Testament, including views re
garding life after death and hymns expressive of
ideas that reminded us of what was found in bib
lical psalms, and that were couched in phrases strik
ingly similar to biblical parlance. It is with this
material that we are chiefly concerned in this in
vestigation; but, in order to understand its real bear
ings, we must stop for a few moments to consider
the origin and character of Babylonian civilisation
which spread from the south—the Euphrates Val
ley—to the north, or to what was known as Assyria.
The impulse to the development of a high degree
of culture in the Euphrates Valley came from the
mixture of two heterogeneous races—Semites, whose
oldest designation appears to have been Akkadians,
and a non-Semitic people known as Sumerians, who
gave their name to the valley which survives, in a
somewhat distorted form, as Shinar in the book of
Genesis. Whether the Semites or the non-Semites
were the first settlers is a question which in the
present state of our knowledge cannot be deter
mined. The indications are—such, at least, is my
view[1]—that the Semites were the first to arrive and
there are reasons for believing that they came from
the northeastern or northwestern region known as

---

[1] Following Eduard Meyer, *Sumerier und Semiten in Babylonien*, p. 111.

Amurru, though the majority of scholars still in
cline to central Arabia as the oldest centre from
which Semitic hordes first entered the valley. These
Semites, taking up a settled form of life in ex
change for earlier nomadic habits, cultivated the
soil and had probably made some advances on the
road to civilisation when the Sumerians, entering
either from the northwestern or from the northeast
ern mountainous districts, conquered the country.
What the state of Sumerian civilisation was at the
time is also a pure matter of conjecture. The con
querors must have been superior to the Semites, for
in the oldest period to which our sources at present
take us, we find the Sumerians in more or less com
plete control. The language of the oldest historical
inscriptions is Sumerian, the commercial documents
down to about 2000 B. C. are likewise largely in
Sumerian. To this oldest period belong Sumerian
votive inscriptions, Sumerian hymns and lamenta
tions, rituals appealing to the gods to desist from
their wrath which had manifested itself in some po
litical catastrophe or in havoc wrought by destruc
tive storms; and it is a fair inference that the
script developing from a pictorial or hieroglyphic
form of writing was the invention of the Sumerians,
though developed with Semitic co-operation. For,
even in this earliest period, Semitic influences may
be detected. We find Semitic names and Semitic
words in very early inscriptions. The Sumerians
brought their gods with them but, as always hap
pened in the case of conquests in early days, the

conquerors also adopted the gods of the region into
which they came and transformed the character of
their own deities to conform to the new conditions
by which they were surrounded.   One of the oldest
centres of Sumerian settlements that acquired the
rank of a religious as well as of a political capital
was Nippur.   The patron deity of Nippur, Enlil
(or Ellil), was brought there by the Sumerians from
their mountain homes, and, like most gods who have
their seat on mountain tops, was a personification
of the storms and tempests, of the thunder and the
lightning.   Transferred to a valley in which agri
culture was the mainstay of the population, Enlil
was associated with an earlier deity, Enmasht[1]—
commonly spoken of as Ninib—who presided over
vegetation and the fertility of the soil.   Enlil, as
the god of the conquerors, becomes the father, and
Enmasht the son.   This relationship merely mir
rors the superiority of the newcomer who takes on
the traits of Enmasht, and as the head of the pan
theon receives the attributes most needed by a
deity in whose hands the welfare of an agricultural
population lay.   In this way then and in various
others, the religion of the Sumerians is transformed
through adaptation to their new surroundings, a
transformation that extends to the adoption into
their pantheon of deities already worshipped in the
district to which they had come, and which carries
with it the adoption of religious rites, festivals, and
forms of appeal suitable to agricultural communi-

[1] See Clay, *Amurru*, p. 121.

ties. Both elements of the population, therefore, contribute to the further unfolding of religious ideas and customs, just as the general advance in civili sation is due to mutual co-operation and mutual influence, although the one element remained for a long time the predominating factor. The result is a Sumero-Akkadian civilisation arising from the stimulus of one ethnic group meeting another. The observation has general application that a high order of civilisation arises only through the com bination of two or more ethnic factors. The mix ture of races because of this mutual stimulus al ways produces a higher type of culture than is brought about by a race that holds itself aloof from others. An absolutely pure race probably does not exist. If it did, it is safe to predict that it would not proceed far along the road of civilisation with out dying of inanition. The great and the greatest achievements of mankind in the domain of cul ture, in government, in art, in literature, in philo sophic thought, and in scholarship have been ac complished by the mixed races—by the Greeks with the admixture of Asiatic elements; by the Romans with the admixture of the Etruscans as the for eign mass to leaven the Italic stock; by the Egyp tians, a mixture of Hamitic and Semitic groups. Even among the ancient Hebrews we encounter the admixture of foreign groups which include Hittite elements. The Pentateuchal Codes protest against the commingling with the "seven" nations as they are conventionally termed, with an insistency that proves the extent to which the admixture had proceeded.

The predominance of the Sumerian e.ement begins to wane about the middle of the third millennium B. C., perhaps already some centuries earlier. The impending change in control manifests itself at first by the breaking up of the Euphrates Valley into separate districts, each grouped around some city— as a political and religious centre—no one of which seemed strong enough to hold the others under its control.[1]   At most, we now find one or the other of these districts or states exercising a jurisdiction over some adjoining one, and this for a limited period, to be followed by a reversal that brings a rival state more prominently forward.   The strug gle comes to a head in a more sharply accentuated rivalry between Sumerian and Akkadian settle ments, the former found chiefly in the more south ern sections, the latter more towards the north, though the geographical division is not absolute. Sargon, with his capital at Agade, a city not far from Babylon, is the first Semite to establish a strong empire; it is he who apparently introduces the policy of world-conquest which becomes the aim of Babylonian and more particularly of Assyr ian rulers.   Sargon spreads his victorious arms in all directions and founds a real empire, though of short duration—a kingdom of "the four quarters of the world," as it is officially designated.   The in-

---

[1] See, for this early period, L. W. King, *A History of Sumer and Akkad* (London, 1910).

dependence and extension of the rule of Sargon and of his immediate successors is a symptom of the strength that the Semites had acquired, and though a reaction bringing the Sumerians back to power for almost two centuries sets in, still the impend ing change was inevitable; and about the year 2000 B. C. a union of the states of the Euphrates Val ley was brought about through a great conqueror, the Semite Hammurapi[1] who establishes his centre at Babylon, and with whom the Semitic conquest of the Euphrates Valley becomes complete. The civilisation, however, had received its stamp from the mixture of Sumerian and Akkadian elements, with merely a transfer of the predominance of the non-Semitic element to the Semitic contingent.

III

It is about the time of Hammurapi that we may with probability fix the migration of the Terahites, first from Ur to Haran and thence to the north west, entering Palestine by way of a descent along the eastern banks of the Jordan. The fourteenth chapter of Genesis, in which Amraphel, King of Shi nar (i. e., of Babylonia), and Abraham are introduced as contemporaries, is generally regarded—and I think correctly—as a very late addition to the nar ratives of Genesis.[2] Despite this, it embodies a re markable store of historical tradition which is either based on very old oral sources or rests on the di-

---

[1] Or Hammurabi, though the writing with *p* is more correct.
[2] See, *e. g.*, Skinner's *Commentary on Genesis*, pp. 271–6.

rect use of written historical sources. Amraphel is
none other than Hammurapi, and the spread of
Semitic control under this great conqueror fits in
well with the movement of Semitic groups from
Babylonia to the west. The migration of the Tera-
hite group to which Abraham belongs is part of this
movement. The later Jewish rabbis of the Talmudic period were fond of spinning out the tales
of Abraham's relations to Babylonia and the Baby
lonians,[1] implied in the sojourn at Ur and Haran;
and while the stories themselves are purely fanci
ful, how Terah, the father of Abraham, was a man
ufacturer of idols, how the son gradually realised
the futility of idol-worship and argued with his en
vironment against the personification of the powers
of nature as the basis of religious worship, yet the
initiative for these tales is the deep-grained recol
lection on the part of some of the tribes that
eventually formed the group of the Bene Israel of
a close affiliation between themselves and the in
habitants of the Euphrates Valley. Youthful mem
ories are tenacious in the case of a group as of an
individual. Association with Babylonians necessa
rily entailed an acceptance of Babylonian customs
and ideas and at least a partial absorption of Euphratean culture in its various manifestations. It is
therefore most reasonable to assume that the agree
ment between Hebrew and Babylonian traditions
regarding the Creation of the world and regarding
a great catastrophe that wiped out mankind is due

[1] See Louis Ginzberg, *Legends of the Jews*, vol. I, pp. 195–216.

to this early contact, just as on the other hand the
tradition which places the original habitat of man
kind in the Euphrates Valley and such tales as
that of the city and tower of Babylon represent a
sediment due to this same contact. It is a natural
process that leads a people to identify the recol
lections of its origin with the origin of the world;
and dim and confused as such recollections become
in the course of time, unless we assume some his
torical starting-point, we lose the possibility of find
ing a reasonable explanation for their existence and
persistence.

To account for the presence of nomadic groups
in the Euphrates Valley at the period to which we
are led back in tracing the migrations of tribes that
formed an element in the later confederation of
Hebrew tribes,[1] it is sufficient to recall that a higher
culture is always a source of attraction to those
who occupy a lower grade. Central and northern
Arabia formed at all times a great reservoir of no
madic Semitic hordes, the overflow from which
passed naturally into the Euphrates Valley which
lay open to invaders from almost all sides. Some
of these nomadic groups were permanently won
over to more settled conditions of life, and were
sooner or later assimilated to the Sumero-Akkadian

[1] I say "an element" because it is now certain that the Hebrews rep
resent the result of a mixture of various elements, including probably
Hittites as well as Arabs, entering Palestine without submitting to the
mediatory influence of Babylonian civilisation. This mixed character
of the confederation formed in the twelfth century by "Hebrew" tribes
accounts for the double strain of traditions and popular customs, one
directing us to Babylonia, the other to Arabia.

culture, while others continued to move forward
and backward and frequently became a menace to
the native population.[1] The pressure from the
south appears to have been followed at frequent
intervals by a further movement of these nomads
to the north. One of the goals of such a move
ment was Syria which was reached by following
the course of the Euphrates and its tributaries, and
as pressure followed upon pressure there ensued the
further descent towards the seacoast or into the
interior along the valley of the Jordan.

In return, there was also a movement from Syria
into both Babylonia and Assyria. Recent investiga
tions have shown that these Amorites, as the people
from the northwest were generally termed, consti
tute an important factor in the Babylonian-Assyrian
civilisation, leaving their traces in the names of
certain deities that form part of the pantheon and
in other phases of the Babylonian-Assyrian religion.[2]
There thus resulted a steady shifting of the popu
lation of the Euphrates Valley, and to account for
this, we must bear in mind that the same ease
which enabled those accustomed to nomadic life
to take on within a short time a veneer of culture
also facilitated the backward step to former condi
tions. Arabic history furnishes several instances
of tribes which, after some generations of settled

---

[1] In the historical inscriptions as well as in the legends of Babylonia
and Assyria these nomads are frequently referred to as Suti, and the
probable explanation of the name as the "southerners" is thus indica
tive of the region whence they came.

[2] See Clay, *Amurru, the Home of the Northern Semites* (Philadelphia,
1909).

life, abandoned their settlements to take up again the untrammelled existence of the desert and the wilderness.   Moreover, not all who were attracted towards the Euphrates Valley were won over to Babylonian culture.   The opportunity for plunder proved an equally forcible magnet.   These non-assimilating Bedouins likewise passed into Syria and thence to the south and southwest, and commin gling there with the body of the population, pastoral and agricultural, that had been subjected to Babylo nian influences, also became tainted with Babylonian ideas and traditions.   In short, the deeper we pene trate into the history of Babylonia, the more abun dant is the evidence pointing to the close connec tion between the Euphrates Valley and western Asia Minor in general.   A famous ruler of a Baby lonian state, Gudea of Lagash (c. 2400 B. C.), finds it perfectly natural to send his emissaries to the Lebanon range and to the Phœnician coast to ob tain wood and stone for his buildings and works of art,[1] just as, on the other hand, he obtains diorite from Magan and copper from Kimash.   He speaks of these districts as though they were outlying provinces of Babylonia, and we have already referred to the still earlier notice,[2] embodied in a collection of his torical omens, of Sargon of Agade carrying his tri umphant arms to Amurru and the "sea of the set ting sun," by which the Mediterranean is meant.[3] It is therefore to this early contact between Baby-

---

[1] See L. W. King, *History of Sumer and Akkad*, p. 263.
[2] Above, p. 7.   [3] King, *ib.*, p. 225.

lonia and the west that we must ascribe the decidedly Babylonian strain in Hebrew traditions.

To assume, as has sometimes been done, that the
agreement between Hebrew and Babylonian tradi
tions is due to a contact in the later historical pe
riods, culminating in the transfer of large sections
of the Jerusalem population and of the surround
ing districts to the Euphrates Valley, is, I think,
quite impossible. The people were in no mood to
assimilate ideas and customs from those who ap
peared to them in the light of ruthless destroyers;
but, quite apart from this, the leaven of the new
teachings introduced by the Hebrew Prophets had
by this time begun to work. The religious thought
of the masses was too advanced even in the eighth
century, when the prophetical movement sets in,
to take up traditions that arose among a people in
an early state of culture. The impression one re
ceives from the style of the narratives in the early
chapters of Genesis is that they are incorporated
because they had formed for many centuries part
and parcel of the life of the people. The stories
were too popular to be suppressed or crowded out;
they are therefore transformed and adapted to
new conditions. The mythical element is reduced,
as we shall see, to a minimum; the ethical spirit is
introduced, and the materialistic conception of
Creation is replaced by a superior monotheistic
interpretation of divine rule. Tales embodying pop
ular tradition of long standing are thus made to
appear in a new light. To be sure, there was a

steady stream of Babylonian influence into Pales
tine during the centuries in which Babylonia exer
cised some measure of control over political affairs
in the west—the period which resulted in making
Babylonian speech in the fifteenth century B. C., a
medium of official communication between gov
ernors of cities and districts in Palestine and Syria
and their Egyptian masters.   An adjacent civilisa
tion of a high order necessarily spreads its influ
ence in all directions, and Palestine was as little
able to escape this influence of Babylonian ideas,
Babylonian ways, and Babylonian views of life as
it could escape, on the other side, the influence of
the great civilisation that arose along the banks of
the Nile.   This contact between Palestine and Baby
lonia, strongest just before the formative period of
the Hebrew nation in the thirteenth or fourteenth
century B. C., and which waned with the union of
the confederated tribes into a monarchy about
1000 B. C., may be accounted as an important factor
in *maintaining* the early traditions in undisturbed
rigour; but even this period would be too late for the
first introduction of these traditions.

Moreover, the specific mention of Ur and Haran
as stopping places of the Terahites in their wander
ings which eventually brought them into Palestine,
lends a further support for the thesis of an early
contact to account for the agreement in Hebrew
and Babylonian traditions.   Both Ur and Haran
are old religious and important political centres, and
it is rather curious that in both the worship of the

moon-god, Sin, was predominant. This can hardly
be a coincidence, but instead of seeing in this cir
cumstance a trace of a lunar myth in connection
with Abraham, as some scholars are inclined to do,[1]
it seems more plausible to ascribe the juxtaposi
tion of Ur and Haran to the combination of two
traditions,[2] one of which embodies a recollection of
a movement from Ur, the other from Haran.   It
is quite in keeping with the character of traditions,
dimmed by the lapse of ages and revived in the
course of a literary process, to amalgamate events
separated from one another by longer or shorter
periods.   We may perhaps even go a step farther
and recognise in the mention of Ur and Haran a
recollection of two periods of early Babylonian his
tory in which Ur and Haran respectively exercised
a supremacy over the Babylonian states.   In re
gard to Ur we know that this was the case c. 2400
B. C., when the kings of Ur claimed sovereignty
over Sumer and Akkad, which had become the desig
nation for southern and northern Babylonia.   Of
the older history of Haran we know as yet very
little, but the existence of a sanctuary at the place
to which rulers of Babylonia and Assyria as late as
the seventh and sixth centuries[3] pay their respects
speaks in favour of the supposition that the place
at one time also enjoyed political pre-eminence, for

---

[1] See Jeremias, *Das Alte Testament im Lichte des alten Orients*, p. 332,
following the late Hugo Winckler's *Geschichte Israels*, II, pp. 23 *seq.*

[2] A similar view is taken by Gunkel, *Genesis*, p. 145, who, however,
regards Haran and Ur originally as variants.

[3] Johns, *An Assyrian Doomsday Book*, Introduction.

religion and rule are close allies in ancient Baby
lonia. Be this as it may, the specific character of
the tradition regarding the sojourn of the Terahites
in certain Babylonian centres justifies our confi
dence in its substantial correctness.

Looking upon Babylonia as their home, it was
almost inevitable that when the Hebrews came to
speculate upon the question of origins they should
hit upon the Euphrates Valley as at one time the
home of all mankind, and it is equally natural that
Hebrew writers should have fallen in line with the
Babylonian tradition which regarded the settlement
of the valley as the result of a movement vaguely
described as "from the east."[1] It is not, there
fore, as a real solution of the difficult problem of
the origin of the human race, which still perplexes
modern ethnologists, that the tradition has any
value, but as an illustration of the dependence of
Hebrew views upon the historical bond uniting He
brews with Babylonians. This dependence of itself
would not necessarily lead to agreement in regard
to another problem of "origins"—the origin of the
world; for not only does speculation on this prob
lem begin at an earlier period in the cultural devel
opment of a people than attempts to specify a place
as the original home of mankind, but it is precisely
in Creation myths that the individuality of a people
and the reflex of its immediate surroundings manifest
themselves. While there is, of course, a general
similarity between the Creation stories of people

[1] Gen. 11 : 2.

living in a state of primitive culture, this similar
ity affects chiefly the limitations of the primitive
intellect which cannot conceive of any *real* begin
ning. But apart from this, the *variations* of the man
ner in which the world is supposed to have been
set in motion constitute the striking feature of
primitive Creation myths. It would therefore have
been quite within the range of possibility for the
Hebrews to have produced a Creation myth of their
own, either before they found their way into Baby
lonia or after they had entered Palestine. But if
we encounter in the first two chapters of Genesis
Creation stories clearly modelled upon Babylonian
prototypes, the obvious conclusion is that the early
contact between Babylonians and Hebrews exerted
a profound religious as well as a social influence.
The only hypothesis, then, that meets the condi
tions involved is the one assuming a very early relig
ious influence exerted by Babylonian ideas upon
those who moved into the Euphrates Valley, and
which was maintained by that contact between
Babylonia and the Semitic settlements to the west
up to the borders of the Mediterranean, which, as we
have seen, was practically uninterrupted for several
millenniums.

If the biblical tradition which carries the history
of the Hebrews back to an old settlement in Baby
lonia has any value, it points to a deep and perma
nent impress made upon the people during their
"Babylonian" period. Had this not been the case
the tradition would not have survived. The com-

pilers of Genesis, to emphasise the point once more, are not a set of imaginative writers who spin out romances; they merely record what belongs to a common stock of knowledge, and their originality consists in the manner in which they transform the material. There would not have been any occasion for carrying Hebrew history back to the Euphrates Valley had this tradition not been so deeply em bodied in the minds of the populace that a history of the Hebrews, such as the first eight books of the Bible in their present form aim to be, would have been regarded as hopelessly defective without a no tice of the former settlement in the Euphrates dis trict of tribes from which the Hebrews reckoned their descent. We may furthermore conclude, unless we reject the tradition altogether, that the sojourn, whether at Ur, Haran, or elsewhere, was not a short one, not a mere passage of nomadic hordes on their way from Arabia to Syria, for again we must argue that in that case the tradition would not have sur vived with such persistency. There would have been no occasion for its surviving. A relatively permanent settlement, however, involves partial as similation to the ways of the country, and we are therefore safe in placing the Hebrews among the immigrants who drank deep of Babylonian culture, even though they relapsed into the life of pastoral nomads, when with other Semites they passed into Syria and Palestine.

We must distinguish however in our study of these traditions, between the traditions themselves

and the period when they assumed their final lit
erary shape. The stories in the early chapters of
Genesis, the account of Creation, the habitat of the
first human pair, the early fortunes of the human
race, the narrative of the Deluge, the wanderings of
the Terahites, their entrance into Palestine, are an
cient, forming part of a stock of traditions held in
common by Babylonians and Hebrews from time
immemorial, just as the stories of the patriarchs, of
the sojourn in Egypt, and of the Exodus are old,
strengthened by their currency through a long pe
riod during which they sank deep into the minds
and hearts of the populace. The stories themselves,
however, underwent modifications as the Hebrews
passed from the nomadic to the agricultural stage
of life, and from this again to the founding of cities,
to the unfolding of more advanced forms of govern
ment, to the elaboration of an official ritual, and the
establishment of priesthoods in various centres: in
Shiloh, in Nob, in Bethel, in Ramah, in Shechem,
and, above all, in Jerusalem. When these tradi
tions were submitted to the influence of the new
ideals set up by the Prophets, their original charac
ter was still further modified until in the postexilic
period they assumed their present literary shape.
It is this somewhat complicated and composite
character of the Hebrew traditions that lends to
them their fascination for the student whose task
it is to trace the process of growth, just as it is that
because in their final shape they reflect the advanced
Jewish thought, they make a religious and emo-

tional appeal to us at the present time, despite the recognition of their historical evolution. The tra ditions in their final form have stood the test of modern criticism which has taught us to look at them in a manner that enables them to convey a message even to the modern mind.[1]

IV

Accepting, then, the position that the Hebrews passed through a long period of probation, involv ing an evolutionary process before their religion reached the stage reflected in the books of the Old Testament in their final form, wherein does the pe culiar quality of Hebrew monotheism lie, or, in other words, what was the course taken by religious thought among the Hebrews that gives to Hebrew traditions, to Hebrew conceptions of life after death, to Hebrew views of sin, to Hebrew institu tions, to Hebrew ethics, to the Hebrew system of divine government, a direction that separates these traditions, conceptions, views, institutions, ethics, and system from the Babylonian counterparts with which at one time they had so much in common?

No elaborate proof is any longer required to show that at one time the Hebrews shared, to all prac tical intent, the religion of their surroundings. As a branch of the Semitic race, their religion during their

---

[1] A good illustration of the results to be obtained from a systematic study of the process through which the traditional lore of the Hebrews passed is to be seen in Hugo Gressmann's recent work, *Mose und seine Zeit* (Gottingen, 1913).

early sojourn in Palestine was that of the Semites
in general. The pages of the Old Testament are
full of indications that the Hebrews, like their fel
low Semites, attached a sacred significance to stones
at certain places, to trees, to wells, to mountain
tops. The most primitive type of the Semitic altar
is a stone in which the deity is supposed to dwell
or which is the deity himself. The "rock of the
dome," as the large stone within the chief mosque
at Jerusalem—the Haram esh-Sherif[1]—is called, rep
resents one of these ancient sacred stones, the sanc
tity of which reaches back far beyond the time
when the Hebrews took possession of Mount Zion,[2]
where the deity manifested itself because it was his
seat, that is, because he dwelled there. The He
brews took over the sacred rock at the time when
they dispossessed the Jebusites, who worshipped at
that place. Solomon built his temple there, because
the stone had made it a sacred site. Palestine was
full of such sacred stones. The stone on which Jacob
slept at Bethel was a sacred object. Jacob has a
vision of the deity there, because the stone is the
dwelling-place of the deity. He anoints the stone,
regards it as a *masseba* (which is the common designa
tion of stone pillars), because the deity is in it or
manifests himself through it. Viewed in this light, the
words which Jacob utters upon awakening, "Behold
Yahweh is in this place"—the Hebrew word *makom*
designates a holy spot—"and I knew it not" (Gen.

---

[1] Commonly, though erroneously, known as the Mosque of Omar.
[2] The name Moriah for the mount (II Chron. 3 : 1) represents a late
and unreliable tradition.

28 : 16), receive a significance superior, I think, to
the traditional interpretation. The oak or terebinth
at Mamre, associated with Abraham, is a sacred tree
—the dwelling-place of a deity who, therefore, ap
pears to Abraham at that place. Palestine is full
of sacred trees, regarded as such even by the Arab
population of the present day, who hang bits of
clothing and ornaments on such trees as a symbol
of their attachment.[1] Abraham and Isaac are asso
ciated with Beer-Sheba, where there was a well the
name of which, "the well of the oath," [2] or (through
a play on the word [3]) "the well of seven"—seven
being a sacred number—attests its sanctity. Kadesh, where the Hebrews remained for a period be
fore entering Palestine in their wanderings after the
Exodus from Egypt, is a sacred place. The name
"Kadesh" means "holy," and the wells there, no
doubt, represent the reason for the sanctity of the
place. Palestine has many such holy wells. The
deity dwells in the water as he does in stones and
trees. Mount Sinai, Mount Nebo, Mount Seir, and
Mount Zion—all represent dwelling-places of the
deity, and the Hebrews on entering Palestine ac
cepted the current views which associated deities
with mountain tops or high eminences. These places
became sacred spots in Hebrew history, because the
Hebrews fell in with the current religious thought
and practices of their fellow Semites. In the tradi-

---

[1] On the present-day survivals of old Semitic stone, tree, river, well,
cults, etc., see S. I. Curtiss, *Primitive Semitic Religion To-day* (Chicago,
1902), especially chapter VII.

[2] Gen. 21 : 31.　　　　　　　　[3] Gen. 26 : 33.

tions associated with sacred stones, with trees, with wells, and high eminences, we have, therefore, the survivals of Semitic religion at the nomadic stage. But the Semites advanced to settled life which is marked by the agricultural stage. The Canaanites, who occupied Palestine proper at the time of the Hebrew conquest, represented an agricultural pop ulation who had to be dispossessed by the con querors. For the Canaanites the old Semitic dei ties became the protectors of the soil, presiding over vegetation. In general, these protectors were viewed as personifications of the sun. Each centre had such a protector, who was called "Baal" or "lord" of the place. When the Hebrews became agriculturists they adopted the "Baals" of the Canaanites; but, associating Baal with their national or tribal deity, Yahweh, originally having his seat on Mount Sinai, or, according to other traditions,[1] on Mount Seir, the cult of Yahweh took on the forms of Baal wor ship. The festivals of the Hebrews became agricul tural feasts, coincident with the seasons of impor tance to tillers of the soil—the spring, summer, and the final harvest of the fall; and there is no longer any doubt that these festivals, as described in the Pentateuchal Codes and in incidental references in the historical books, were taken over from the Ca naanites. Offerings of first-fruits and of the flock were brought to the sanctuaries throughout the land, in imitation of the example set by the Canaanites.

[1] E. g., in the Song of Deborah (Judges 5 : 4), where Yahweh comes from Seir.

Yahweh becomes the "Baal" or "lord" of the soil, and the transfer of the traits of a Baal to Yahweh was made so naturally that down to the days of David we find the two terms, Baal and Yahweh, used almost interchangeably. The Canaanitish Baals had their altars and sanctuaries on eminences, known as *bamoth* or "high places," and it was on such places that the cult of Yahweh was carried on by the Hebrew agricultural population. The Hebrew Prophets and the historical books are our witnesses that the Hebrews adopted even the symbolical of fering of their children to Malik—another designa tion of Baal, which pious Hebrew writers distorted to Molech[1]—from the Canaanites; and it is signif icant that in the Priestly Code a provision is made for the redemption or ransom of the first-born through the payment of a certain sum (Num. 13:16). Such a provision assumes as a recognised custom the rite of devoting the first-born to the deity, and the purpose of the enactment to buy off this sacrifice which the deity may claim is to

---

[1] Molech represents an intentional disguise for Malik, brought about through the attachment of the vowels of a word, *bosheth*, meaning "shame," to the consonants of Malik, which gives us Molek. The later Hebrew writers to whom the name Baal was so obnoxious as to prompt them to avoid using it, went so far as to substitute Bosheth for Baal even in proper names, as, *e. g.*, Ish-Bosheth ("man of shame") for Ish-Baal ("man of Baal"). On the other hand, there was also devel oped a disposition to avoid names too sacred for ordinary use. This led to giving to the consonants J (or Y) H W H, which form the sacred name of Israel's deity, the vowels of Adonai meaning "lord," " master," resulting in the form Jehovah in place of Jahweh or Yahweh, which was the original pronunciation. See, on the history of this disguise, G. F. Moore's article in *Old Testament and Semitic Studies*, in memory of W. R. Harper, pp. 143–163, and the references there given.

abolish the older method of symbolically offering a
child to Malik by "passing him through the fire," [1]
itself probably a substitute of a more merciful age
for a former actual burning of the child. The under
lying principle enunciated in the dictum, "Every
first issue of the womb among men and cattle be
longs to Yahweh" (Lev. 13 : 2; Ex. 34 : 19), rep
resents a direct adoption of the Canaanitish prac
tice, and this is further borne out by the use of the
very same term, "and thou shalt cause every first-
born to pass through to Yahweh" (Ex. 13 : 12),
which elsewhere occurs in describing the "passing
through" of children to Malik (II Kings 16 : 3
[Ahaz]; II Kings 21: 6; II Chron. 33: 6 [Manasseh]).
The redemption through money means therefore
the abolition of the Canaanitish rite, but the re
tention of the principle underlying the rite.   In
order to justify the principle, the explanation is of
fered (Ex. 13 : 14): "If thy son should ask thee to
morrow, What is the meaning of this, thou shalt say
to him: With a strong hand Yahweh brought us out
of Egypt, out of the house of bondage. And when
Pharaoh hardened himself against sending us forth,
Yahweh killed every first-born in Egypt from the
first-born of man to the first-born of cattle. There
fore I sacrifice to Yahweh every first male issue of
the womb, and every first-born of my sons I redeem."

---

[1] The phrase to "pass through the fire" shows that the victim was
not actually burned, but merely brought into contact with the fire as the
sacred element and the symbol of Malik, the sun-god. The custom is
of the same order as jumping across the fire in connection with the Saint
John's festival of the midsummer solstice. See Frazer, *The Dying God*,
p. 262, and the footnote references there given.

This is clearly an endeavour to find a justification within Hebrew history for a rite which, by evidence furnished through the Old Testament itself, is part of the general religion of the Semites in Palestine. If any further evidence is desired to show how com pletely up to a relatively late period the Hebrews shared the religious practices of their neighbours, the frank statement of the royal chronicler (II Kings 21 : 3-8), about Manasseh's course will surely suf fice. "And he again built high places which his father Hezekiah had destroyed and he erected altars to Baal and he made an Asherah[1] as Ahab the King of Israel had done, and he bowed down to the host of heaven and worshipped them . . . and he built altars to all the hosts of heaven in the two courts of the house of Yahweh; and he caused his son to pass through the fire, and he practiced divination and magic and necromancy and he increased doing evil in the eyes of Yahweh to provocation and he set up the Asherah post which he had made in the house of which Yahweh said to David and to Solo mon his son, 'In this house and in Jerusalem which I choose of all the tribes of Israel I shall place my name forever.'"

Here you have the whole paraphernalia of the religion of the Semites, both that belonging to the more primitive type and to the more advanced type

[1] A post or pillar set up at the side of the altar, symbolising the female element in nature, as the altar—originally the stone which was both the dwelling of the deity and the deity himself—symbolised the male ele ment. The post may have originally been a tree. See the article "Asherah," in Hastings, *Dictionary of the Bible*, or in the *Encyclopædia Biblica*.

—Baal worship, tree worship, fire worship, astral worship, and divination of all kinds. In the refer ence to the hosts of heaven and to divination prac tices we may see traces of that steady stream of Babylonian influences in Palestine to which we have referred, and which represents the natural overflow of a civilisation constantly extending in scope and power. This influence was naturally not limited to the Hebrews. The astral-theological system, ac companied by recourse to the observation of the heavens as a means of ascertaining what the future had in store, led to an attitude towards the moon, planets, and stars which superimposed an additional layer over the cult of Baals and Asherahs through out Palestine. The references to the "host of heaven" increase as we approach the period of di rect interference on the part of the Assyrian and then of the neo-Babylonian empire in the affairs of the Hebrew kingdoms. The pages of the Old Testa ment—particularly the Books of Kings and the ora tions of the pre-exilic Prophets—are full of references to astrological practices and other modes of divina tion betraying Babylonian influence by the side of Canaanitish customs, just as the legal codes in their protest against these practices and customs betray the extent to which they were followed down to postexilic days.

In the passage that I have quoted we have, how ever, also the evidence that the turning-point in the history of the religion of the Hebrews was soon to come. The reign of Manasseh, which may be dated

as 697 to 642 B. C., is portrayed as a period of re
action from the religious reforms instituted by his
father, Hezekiah (726–698 B. C.), who is a contem
porary of Isaiah. The first step demanded by the
Hebrew Prophets, of whom Isaiah may be regarded
as the type, was the overthrow of the Canaanitish
or general Semitic practices. The protest voiced
by the Prophets against everything for which Manasseh stood was historically justified, for the religion
practised by the Hebrews after their conquest of
Palestine was an adaptation of agricultural cults
that they found awaiting them. They are correct
in their assumption that the practices during the
nomadic period were simpler and not overweighted,
as were those coincident with the agricultural stage,
with an elaborate ritual, marked by festival sea
sons, sacrifices and purification rites, but the ear
lier practices of the Hebrews were likewise such as
were shared by other Semitic groups living in the
nomadic stage of culture. Yahweh, as the tribal
deity of the Hebrews, differed in no essential par
ticular from other tribal deities of nomadic groups;
and the chief festival of this early period was a
sheep-shearing occasion at which a blood rite was
observed, resting on the old Semitic view of blood
as a symbol of life.[1] The point of departure in the
Hebrew religion from that of the Semitic in general
—in the nomadic stage and from the later agricul-

---

[1] This festival with some later modifications and with the superim
posed association with the Exodus from Egypt as a justification for its
existence as part of the genuine Yahweh cult, led to the Passover festi
val, the time of the ripening of the first barley in Palestine.

tural stage—did not come until the rise of a body
of men who set up a new ideal of divine government
of the universe, and with it as a necessary corollary
a new standard of religious conduct. Throwing
down the barriers of tribal limitations to the juris
diction of a deity, it was the Hebrew Prophets who
first prominently and emphatically brought forth
the view of a divine power conceived in spiritual
terms, who, in presiding over the universe and in
controlling the fates of nations and individuals, acts
from self-imposed laws of righteousness tempered
with mercy.   To be sure, centuries before the Proph
ets, who began to make their appearance in the
eighth century B. C., a great leader had arisen who
gave to the people a higher view of Yahweh than
that current of tribal deities among surrounding
nations, but the god of Moses was still essentially
the god of the Hebrews—in the same sense that
Kemosh was the god of Moab, and Milkom the god
of Ammon.   Nor were the people, then in the begin
ning of their national life which was ushered in
through the powerful personality of their leader in
a position to rise beyond the conception of a god
limited in jurisdiction to a group, and concerned
with that group as a father is for his own children.
But Moses—so much may be concluded from a
study of our sources[1]—had invested the national

[1] See Gressmann's admirable and important work (already referred
to above) *Mose und seine Zeit*, showing, as a result of a careful study
of the various layers in the traditions regarding Moses, the line of de
marcation between legendary accretions and historical facts, and thence
the steps leading to the idealisation of the great leader without reference
to facts.

Yahweh with certain ethical traits that differentiated him from other tribal deities and which paved the way for the fuller and more complete conception of the Prophets of a power of universal sway, working through righteousness and making for righteousness. The Decalogue in its original form[1] may be regarded as embodying Moses' conception of Yahweh and as furnishing in rough outlines the standards of life and conduct set up by him. The Yahweh of Moses is a god who punishes wrong-doing and who rewards good deeds. He is not to be worshipped by images; he demands that children should honour their parents, by which is meant the recognition of parental au thority; he puts his protest on theft and murder; he insists upon the preservation of the purity of family life, and he goes even further in condemn ing the longing for the possessions of another as a crime, as almost equal to the actual seizure. Such a sentiment marks the introduction of an ethical ideal superior to the conventional distinction be tween right and wrong, dictated merely by prac tical considerations. The development of this idea of divine government, however, reaches a point be yond which it cannot go, if the deity is to be thought of as bound by loyalty to a certain group or to a

---

[1] In the so-called Book of the Covenant (Ex. 21–24) as well as in tne Pentateuchal Codes, many of the enactments, at least in their oldest form, belong to the earliest period of Hebrew history and reflect, as, e. g., in the treatment of slaves, the social conditions correlative with the early tribal organisation such as may have existed in the days of Moses. We may therefore justly attribute to him a part of the legis lation which many centuries afterwards in its final shape, after passing through a long and complicated process of development, was to pass under his name. See further in chapter V.

certain place. The favouritism or special concern
for a particular people is in itself a limitation to the
ethical qualities of such a power. The step of re
moving the barriers of nationalism in the concep
tion of the divine was essential to the production
of that peculiar type of ethical monotheism which
marks the distinction between the religion of the
Hebrews in its early and tribal stage, and the later
religion which grows into Judaism in the proper
sense of the term.

The two centuries preceding the fall of Jerusalem
were critical ones in the religious history of the
Hebrews. They mark the preparation for Judaism.
The continuation of the process leads, during the
exilic period, to the definite formation of Judaism
as a religion embodying both the spirit and the con
tent of the messages of the Prophets. But this new
phase of religion which meant a complete break
with the normal course of the religion of the Sem
ites did not, on that account, involve a break with
past traditions. However it may be in modern
times and in our Occidental civilisations, in antiq
uity and in the Orient the past is never entirely
superseded by the present—it is carried along by
the tide into the present and assimilated to new con
ditions. Accordingly, when the new religious move
ment among the Hebrews took on a definite shape,
when the ideals of the Prophets as the soul of the new
religion had to be encased in a body, the old tradi
tions that had struck their roots deep into the life and
hearts of the people were taken up once more, and

under modified forms not only brought into accord with the new thought, but made the medium for con veying that thought. We shall have occasion to see at greater detail in the next chapter that many features in the biblical account of Creation—or rather in the two accounts that have been combined in the first two chapters of Genesis—are not at all original; they find their parallel in Babylonian versions and, like the latter, point to the real character of the tale as a nature-myth, symbolising the change of season from the winter to the spring. In the same way, in the two biblical accounts of the Deluge[1] that have been dovetailed into each other, the basis of the story is the yearly phenomenon of the rainy and stormy season which lasts in Babylonia for several months and during which time whole districts in the Euphrates Valley are submerged. Great havoc was caused by the rains and storms until the per fection of canal systems regulated the overflow of the Euphrates and Tigris, when what had been a curse was converted into a blessing and brought about that astonishing fertility for which Babylonia became famous. The Hebrew story of the Deluge

[1] See, e. g., Skinner's *Genesis*, pp. 147-150. Of the two accounts—that of the Jahwist and the one embodied in the Priestly Code—the former is the fuller and also the one that betrays more of the earlier features which we encounter again in the main Babylonian version; for, in Baby lonia, too, there were several versions. The exact enumeration of the duration of the Deluge until the earth reassumed a normal appearance and such features as the distinction between clean and unclean animals belong to the priestly account. The Jahwist uses seven (number of ani mals and intervals between sending out the raven, the dove, and the second dove) and forty (duration of storm) as round numbers, but the two accounts have been so closely intertwined that only by a close anal ysis can the two be separated from each other. See the Appendix.

recalls a particularly destructive season that had
made a profound impression, and the comparison with
the parallel story found on clay tablets of Ashurbanapal's library confirms this view of the local
setting of the tale that represents a nature-myth
of the same character as the underlying stratum
of the Babylonian and biblical Creation narratives.
But in the form assumed by the old traditions re
garding the Creation and the Deluge once held in
common by the Hebrews and Babylonians, the dis
tinguishing mark of the biblical narratives lies in
the reduction of the original mythical element to
a minimum. So thoroughly has this process been
carried out, that it was only through the discovery
of the parallel tales on cuneiform tablets that the
original character of the biblical Creation and Del
uge stories was revealed. The transformation in
the case of the Creation story has been even more
thorough than that of the Deluge. There remained
of the old tradition merely the skeleton outlines—
the description of primeval chaos, a certain logical
order in the process of creation, and in the sec.
ond biblical version a trace of the conception of a
deity making man as an artist moulds a form out
of clay. The story, retained partly because of its
popularity, partly because of that natural desire to
carry back history to beginnings, is in all other re
spects completely remodelled and becomes a sub
lime poem, furnishing in impressive diction the pic
ture of a great, spiritually conceived power creating
the universe by the mere utterance of his intent—

God wills and it comes to pass. That is the pur
pose which in its present form the story was in
tended to serve. The narrative of the order of Crea
tion becomes merely the illustration used in order
to bring out this conception of Deity, due to the
transformation that the view of divine government
underwent among the Hebrews through the influ
ence of the Prophets. The view of a divine Creator
is the main thing, the incidents—including such
questions as the order and the division into six days—
are secondary, aye, more than this, merely incidental.
The same reasoning may be applied to the story
of the Deluge, the real purport of which is not to
recount an old tradition of a destructive overflow
that wiped out mankind, but to account for the
special favour shown to Noah. He is singled out to
be saved because he is just. In the Babylonian
story Utnapishtim, or, as he is called in another
version, Khasisatra, and again in a third version,
recently discovered, Ziugiddu, described as a king,
is saved, but all that we are told is that he was a fa
vourite of Ea or of some other god who in a dream
revealed to him the intention of the gods. Thus
warned, he saves himself and his family and be
longings by taking refuge on a ship that he builds.
Corresponding to the picture of a divine Creator
conceived as a spiritual power and not as a mate
rialistic manifestation of some phenomenon of na
ture, we have in the biblical accounts of the Deluge
a distinctively ethical quality associated with that
Power—who rules by meting out justice, who pun-

ishes the wrong-doers and saves the righteous. The
two views—the conception of a supreme God ex
pressed in terms of spiritual power and the ethical
content of the monotheistic view of divine govern
ment of the universe—embody the main teachings
of the Prophets.   The same spirit is to be observed
in the biblical story of the fall of man, which will
be taken up in detail later on.[1]   The framework of
the tale, or rather of the two interwoven tales, is
primitive in character.   The serpent, as the wisest
of the animals, talking and acting as a human being;
a tree the fruit of which results in death; another
which is capable of endowing man with eternal life;
God described as walking about in the garden in
the cool of the evening; the intimate converse be
tween God and the first human pair—all are pictures
that belong to the naïvest folk-lore period of prim
itive culture.

But this biblical story is raised far above the
level of a primitive tale, as the nature-myth under
lying the story of the Deluge is removed into an
entirely different sphere, by their both being made
the medium for illustrating the dire consequences
of disobedience to the dictates of a God who de
mands adherence to His behests, that are promul
gated in man's interest.   Such transformations of
old tales that in themselves have no distinguishing
Hebrew features are again due to the totally trans
formed point of view of God's relationship to man
brought about by the teachings of the Prophets.

[1] See below, pp. 47 *seq.*

This may be confidently asserted despite the pes
simistic strain running through the tales that looks
upon work as a curse due to disobedience and that
declares man to be hopelessly inclined to evil.[1] The
Prophets not infrequently imply that man's lot on
earth is full of vexations and sorrows. The minor
note is often struck in the Psalms and in the later
liturgy of Judaism, just as a strong pessimistic strain
may be detected in mediæval Christianity, which
was inclined to look upon this sojourn as a vale
of tears. We need only recall the dominant pessi
mism in Buddhistic doctrines to be convinced that
the sadder undertone and even an attitude border
ing on despair are part and parcel of higher forms
of faith.

V

Primitive tales are thus retained and transformed.
They are given a new interpretation in the light of
the teachings of the Prophets whose discourses are
all so many melodies based on the one theme—the
dire results of disobedience. Israel's sin, by which
she lost her national independence and eventually
became a wanderer on the face of the earth—a Cain
with the mark of God on his brow is disobedience
to the commands of a Deity who, while the embodi
ment of right and justice tempered with love and
mercy, is yet a God intolerant of deliberate wrong
doing, which is inevitably followed by punishment.
Similarly, throughout the Pentateuch and the histor-

[1] See below, pp. 57 *seq.*

ical books proper the key-note is obedience. Abra
ham, the type of the perfect Hebrew, obeys the
commands of Elohim and is ready to sacrifice his
son, though no reason is assigned why this demand
is made of him. On the other hand, all misfortunes
are attributed to a single cause—disobedience to the
commands of Yahweh. The obedience must be
absolute. Hence in the significant twenty-eighth
chapter of Deuteronomy this theological principle is
summed up in the statement that all possible bless
ings will follow upon obedience, and all possible
curses be the fruit of disobedience. Hebrew his
tory, with its ups and downs and its final catas
trophe, is regarded by these biblical writers merely
as an illustration of this single principle. There is
nothing of this stern and yet exalted point of view
in the Babylonian-Assyrian theology which contin
ues to conceive the gods as strong, all-powerful,
but arbitrary, protecting their favourites whether
they merit it or not, accessible to flattery and bribes
in the form of homage and sacrifices, who may be
relied upon as aids if one only carries out the
forms of the ritual, and whose anger, made manifest
by disaster in war, by poor crops, by pestilence,
or by other misfortunes, is ascribed to neglect of
their cult or even to such trivial causes as an unin
tentional error in some ceremonial detail.

The Pentateuchal Codes, though as full of ritual
as are the incantation texts and the other branches
of religious literature of Babylonia and Assyria, are
demarcated by this same trait of stern ethical ideal-

ism. The older purely legal regulations for deter
mining the relationships of men to one another—
in commerce, in questions of life and property, in
marriage and family affairs—are modified in the
long process of development by the test of con
formity to the spirit of justice and righteousness
that finds its fullest expression in the utterances of
the Prophets. "Holy shall ye be, for holy am I,
Yahweh, your God," is the crisp formula of pro
phetic doctrines as characteristic of legalistic Judaism
as is the Mohammedan formula of "no God but
Allah, and Mohammed is his apostle" of Islamism,
or as is the trinitarian formula of traditional Chris
tianity. The aim of the law is to make the people
holy. It is this point of view that reconciles us in
a measure to the detailed and rather wearisome
sacrificial and ceremonial regulations of the Pentateuchal Codes—regulations which further amplified
by traditional customs not specifically provided for
in the codes and by further deductions from the
codes, changed the Judaism of the Prophets into a
vast legal compilation in which the spirit was in
constant danger of being stifled by the letter. There
is nothing particularly novel or particularly inspir
ing in the provisions of the Pentateuchal Codes for
the daily sacrifices, for the steadily increasing ani
mal and cereal offerings for the festal occasions,
or even in the provisions for offerings in the case
of sins unintentionally committed. Similar sacri
ficial codes were developed among many peoples by
a natural process, wherever the state encouraged

the growth of a temple administration extending its scope and power with the enlargement of the state. The food laws of the Priestly Code fall within the category of taboos, such as we encoun ter among primitive people everywhere. The reg ulations of "cleanliness" and "uncleanliness," for the one who has come into contact with a corpse, for the man with an unclean "issue," for the woman in her monthly sickness or who is recovering from childbirth, contain just the same minimal proportion of hygienic considerations and the same maximum of taboo and demonology that hold good for similar provisions in all other religious systems of the prim itive or of the more advanced types. The line of demarcation in these sections of the Pentateuchal Codes lies again in the endeavour to make the laws serve as the expression of certain ethical ideals. These same ideals led to humanitarian regulations regarding criminals and captives, regarding depend ent classes, and even regarding the treatment of trees and fields—which are a noteworthy feature more particularly of the Deuteronomic Code (Deut. 12–26), though also marked in the other codes. I hold no brief for the sacrificial and ceremonial mi nutiæ—so largely survivals of primitive customs and the symbolism natural to primitive views of nature and of the gods. They eventually proved an im pediment to the further unfolding of the teachings of the Prophets who protested so strongly against the dangers inherent in every ceremonial system. An impartial survey, however, demands the recogni-

tion that the Pentateuchal Codes breathe the genu
ine spirit of ethical monotheism that distinguishes
the Prophets. The attempt is clearly made in these
codes to conform ritualistic practice to the teach
ings of the Prophets, just as we have noted this
endeavour in the transformation and adaptation of
the early traditions regarding the creation of the
world, of the disastrous catastrophe that destroyed
mankind, or of the traditions accounting for man's
hard lot and for the presence of death in the world.

The spirit everywhere is the same. The entire Old
Testament is soaked with this spirit. The nation's
past is viewed and reviewed from the standpoint
of the ethical monotheism of the Prophets. The
stories of the Patriarchs—partly tribal traditions,
partly purely fanciful—are retold from this point
of view. Episodes are selected and episodes even
invented that might illustrate the teachings of Juda
ism as set forth in the writings of the Prophets.
Abraham, the traditional ancestor, we have seen,
becomes the type of the pious Jew. Isaac, Jacob,
and Joseph, to whom a variety of folk-tales are
attached—many of them not specifically Hebraic,
others embodying dimmed recollections of tribal
struggles, of intrigues and hostilities—are likewise
types made to conform in a greater or less degree
to the ideals brought to the highest point of per
fection in Abraham and Moses. The heroes of the
more clearly outlined historical periods, Samson,
Gideon, Saul, Samuel, David, and Solomon, are
idealised from this point of view, and so naïvely

idealised that their real character crops out in the stories told of them with such charm and power.[1] The historical sources of the northern and southern kingdoms are re-edited and rewritten to serve as illustrations of the key-note of the teachings of the Prophets that righteousness exalts a people and that all the misfortunes of Israel are due to a de parture from these teachings, which are carried back to the beginnings of the national life of the people and even beyond this to the very beginnings of time. Moses, Abraham, Noah, and Abel are viewed as personages who aimed to conform to the law of di vine obedience and who derived their strength by drinking of the never-failing well of righteousness. The change brought about in the religion of the Hebrews through the new factor introduced by the Prophets thus produced equally profound changes both in the general ethical ideals and in the religious institutions which were transformed and interpreted in accord with a faith centring around the doctrine of ethical monotheism. It is also a direct result of this phase of monotheism that the views regard ing life after death underwent most striking changes. At an earlier stage, the traditions among the He brews regarding the fate of a man after his earthly career is closed were hardly to be distinguished, as will be pointed out, from what we find among the Babylonians and Assyrians, the agreement being again due in part to early contact and in part to the possession of common traditions carried along

[1] See further in chapter V.

from the most primitive phases of culture. Into these traditions an ethical element having that spe cial flavour which is the unmistakable indication of the prophetical spirit is infused, and lo! the old tradition assumes a new aspect in which merely traces of earlier views remain, just enough to war rant us in predicating an evolution from the same traditions to which the Babylonians and Assyrians clung with but minor changes to the close of their long and eventful history.

VI

Let me, in conclusion, give you in more detailed manner a particularly striking illustration of the way in which a tradition belonging to a primitive order of thought, through the infusion of the ethical element and with a view of adapting it to an ethical conception of divine Providence in place of a merely physical view of the government of the universe, is so radically transformed among the Hebrews as to obscure the original identity with a Babylonian counterpart.

Among the myths found among the tablets of Ashurbanapal's library was a tale of a certain Adapa[1] who is endowed with great wisdom so that he be comes a leader of men. Ea, the god of humanity,

[1] See, for the full text so far as preserved, Ungnad-Gressmann, *Oriental- ische Texte und Bilder*, I, pp. 34–38. A fragment was also found among the tablets of the cuneiform archive discovered in 1887 in Tell-Amarna (Egypt). Unfortunately, the four fragments do not give us the story in full. For the interpretation, see also Jastrow, *Religion of Babylonia and Assyria*, pp. 544–555.

had lavished upon him all qualities except that of
eternal life.

> "Great understanding he[1] had granted him to reveal the fate of
>   the land;[2]
> Wisdom he had given him, but eternal life he had not given
>   him."

In Eridu, the city of Ea, this "wisest" of men,
who seems to have been accounted, like Gilgamesh[3]
and other heroes, as belonging to a minor order of
divine beings, ruled supreme, and, besides being wise,
he appears to have been perfect.

> "Without blemish, with pure hands, a priest (?) who observed
>   the laws of the gods."

He is represented also as a zealous provider for the
sanctuary at Eridu, baking bread, providing food
and drink for the temple, and catching fish in the
Persian Gulf—described as a "sea"—on or close to
which Eridu was situated. One day as he was fish
ing "for the lord," that is, for Ea's temple, the
south wind dipped him into the water, and in re
venge Adapa broke the wings of the south wind,
so that for seven days[4] no south wind blew. The
god Anu, the chief god of heaven, notices this, and
upon inquiring the reason of his vizier Ilabrat is
told:

> "My lord! Adapa has broken the wings of the south wind."

---

[1] Ea is probably meant.

[2] *I. e.*, to divine the future, an indication of great wisdom derived
directly from the gods.

[3] See below, p. 85 and the Appendix.

[4] Seven as a large and round number.

Anu, enraged, orders Ea to send his favourite to heaven to answer for his crime. Ea obeys and in structs Adapa how to conduct himself. He tells him to put on mourning garb. At the gate of Anu he will find two gods, Tammuz and Gishzida, who will ask:

"Why this appearance, Adapa? For whom dost thou wear a mourning garb?"

Adapa is to reply:

"Two gods have disappeared from our land, therefore do I ap· pear as I am."

He will then be asked who these gods are, and is to reply by mentioning the names of Tammuz and Gishzida, who will look at one another in amaze ment, and out of pity for Adapa will then intercede in his behalf with Anu. Ea continues his instruc tions as follows:

"When thou comest into the presence of Anu, they will offer thee food of death,—do not eat it;
They will offer thee water of death,—do not drink it;
They will offer thee a dress,—put it on;
They will offer thee oil,—anoint thyself with it.
The advice that I give thee do not neglect,
The word that I tell thee observe."

Everything happens as Ea had foretold. Adapa, in reply to Anu's query why he broke the wings of the south wind, tells him the south wind tried to sink him into the water and that his action was in re venge for this. His plea is apparently self-defence.

Then Tammuz and Gishzida plead with Anu on behalf of Adapa and the god's anger is appeased. He is reconciled to Ea's protection of Adapa.

> "He [*i. e.*, Ea] has made him strong, has given him a name.
> What can we do in addition?
> Bring him food of life that he may eat."

Adapa, remembering the counsel of Ea, who said that food and water of death would be offered to him, declines Anu's offer:

"Food of life they brought him—he did not eat;
Water of life they brought him—he did not drink;
A dress they brought him—he put it on;
Oil they brought him—he anointed himself;
When Anu saw this he was amazed;
'Now, Adapa, why didst thou not eat? Why didst thou not
    drink?
Now thou wilt not remain alive.'"

Adapa replies:

> "Ea, my lord, commanded, 'Do not eat, do not drink.'"

The remainder of the narrative is badly pre served and only so much is clear: that Adapa is sent back to earth, presumably to live the life of a mortal and eventually to die.

Owing to the fragmentary condition of the text, the interpretation of the story is encumbered with difficulties. I am inclined to believe that two in dependent tales have been combined in the narra tive, one a nature-myth symbolising the change of seasons, the other a tale intended to explain the

presence of death in the world. Tammuz and Gishzida are gods of vegetation.[1] Their removal from
earth marks the end of the summer season, when
decay sets in and nature puts on a mourning garb.
The south wind is the prevailing wind in tropical
climes during the summer and dry season. Its
ceasing to blow is therefore again indicative of
the summer's end. With these two elements of a
nature-myth, a story has been combined which, like
many similar stories among primitive peoples, is in
tended to explain the fact that men die. As will
be pointed out in the last chapter, primitive man
can only with difficulty bring himself to believe
that life should come to an absolute standstill. He
sees life in nature constantly being revived. Why
should man not revive and continue to live? We
owe to J. G. Frazer[2] the collection of a large num
ber of stories among Australian tribes and elsewhere,
all of which are told to account for the presence of
death in the world; and in many cases the eating
of some food is introduced into these tales as the
cause of death. So among some tribes the fact that
a remote ancestor ate bananas instead of river-
crabs[3] brought death into the world. The tale of
Adapa evidently belongs to this order. The com
bination with a nature-myth is due to a literary
process that is a characteristic feature of Baby-

---

[1] See Zimmern's monograph, *Der Babylonische Gott Tamuz* (Leipzig,
1911); and Jastrow, *Aspects of Belief and Practice in Babylonia and
Assyria*, pp. 343–350.

[2] *Belief in Immortality*, I, pp. 59–86.

[3] Frazer, *ib.*, I, p. 70.

Ionian literature.[1] It is not quite clear from the story of Adapa whether Ea did not wish his fa vourite who becomes a type of mankind in general to have immortal life, knowing that Anu would offer water and food of life, or whether he did not anticipate Anu's change of his original intent. The main thought is that man forfeited immortality by his own act. He had the chance of eating of the food of life and drinking of the water of life, but failed to avail himself of the opportunity. Hence death came into the world, and all mankind is doomed to die because of Adapa's unfortunate mistake.

Now the Hebrews must have known of this tale. Indeed it is not impossible, as Professor Sayce was the first to suggest, that the name Adapa, which can also be read Adawa, is identical with the He brew Adam which may have been intentionally modified so as to suggest the play upon the Hebrew word adamā, "earth," out of which according to the second version of Creation (Gen. 2 : 5–25), man is fashioned. Be this as it may be, a careful reading of the story of the fall of man shows that it has been modified from its original form and entirely recast. The narrative in its present form is some what confused owing to the introduction of two trees, the tree of knowledge of good and evil and the tree of life. The solution of the problem is sug gested by the twenty-second verse of chapter three, which reads as follows:

[1] See further illustrations of this mode of composition in Jastrow, *Religion of Babylonia and Assyria*, chapter XXIII.

"And Yahweh Elohim said, Behold man is become as one of us, knowing good and evil; and now lest he put forth his hand and take also of the tree of life and eat and live forever."

To avoid this contingency the first pair are re moved from the garden and Cherubim, represent ing some inferior order of divine beings, are placed to guard the approach to the tree of life.[1] It is evi dent from this that there was a tale current among the Hebrews according to which Yahweh Himself did not want man to live for ever. He is afraid that man may eat of the tree of life, as Ea may have been afraid that Adapa would eat of the food of life, and He prevents him from doing so. That is one type of stories current among primitive peoples, told to explain the presence of death in the world, stories in which some god or demon pur posely prevents man from eating the food that will give him everlasting life. Now, the story of Yah weh's permission to man to eat of all the trees of the garden with the exception of the tree in the midst of the garden, interpreted in the recast form as the tree of knowledge of good and evil, assumes that it was God's intention to keep man perma nently in the garden, there to enjoy life without

[1] The picture is suggested by the design, so frequently placed on seal cylinders and which is also a favourite subject of decoration on the sculptured walls of Assyrian palaces, of winged beings, standing in front of the tree of life, and marked as gods by the caps on their heads. See Jastrow, *Aspects of Belief and Practice in Babylonia and Assyria*, p. 367, and the explanation to Fig. 2 (Pl. 26), facing p. 318. Some rational istically inclined editor, offended by the reference to Cherubim, sug gested as a substitute "a flaming sword turning about" which, creep ing into the text, brought about the incongruous picture of Cherubim with flaming swords.

interruption. Death, according to this tale, comes into the world because man eats a fruit of some kind. It will not be considered too bold a conjecture, in view of the analogy presented by the story of Adapa, to assume that this fruit must have been the fruit of death or what amounts to the same thing the food of death. This part of the story then in its original form must have contained a caution not to eat of some fruit—as in the Adapa story—which would entail death. This is distinctly implied in the woman's speech to the serpent (Gen. 3 : 3): "But of the fruit of the tree which is in the midst of the garden, Elohim[1] said, 'Ye shall not eat of it or touch it, lest ye die.'" According to this the command of Yahweh in Gen. 2 : 16-17 must have originally read:

> "Of every tree of the garden thou mayest freely eat, but of the tree in the midst of the garden thou shalt not eat nor touch it, lest thou diest."

This would then form a parallel to Ea's order to Adapa not to eat of the food of death nor to drink of the water of death. The tree the fruit of which is not to be eaten must have been the tree of death. There were thus two tales known to the Hebrews: one of the tree of life of which God did not want man to eat, the other of the tree of death, the fruit of which was not to be eaten. We may go a step further. In the case of the second tale a deception

---

[1] The fact that Elohim is used here instead of Yahweh Elohim (orig inally Yahweh to which Elohim is attached) is also an indication of a different stratum.

is practised on man, just as Adapa is deceived. Ea tells him not to eat, but instead of the food of death and the water of death, the food of life and the water of life are offered to him. Adapa obeys Ea and forfeits immortality. In the biblical story the serpent, intended as a demon or evil spirit, tells the woman that the tree is not the tree of death but the tree of life. This is implied in the words of the serpent (Gen. 3 : 4-5), "Ye shall not die . . . ye shall be like Elohim," [1] which can only mean that if one eats of the fruit one will live for ever as Elohim. Man is deceived by some divine being, though of a lower order than the gods and thus loses the chance of everlasting life.

These two tales were combined, but in addition they were subjected to a process of radical transfor mation. The substitution of a tree of knowledge of good and evil for the tree of death seems to be an original feature in the modified Hebrew tradition. A tree of life and its counterpart, a tree of death, fall within the category of primitive conceptions; not so, however, a tree the fruit of which endows one with knowledge, with mature judgment, with wisdom. Such is clearly the meaning of the phrase "knowing good and evil," marking the change from the innocence and ignorance of the child to the full mental and physical vigour of the adult.[2] The writer

---

[1] Naturally, the speech of the serpent is not entirely preserved in its original form; it has been modified to meet the requirements of the transformed combined tale.

[2] The debilitated old man, therefore, as the child, is described as "with out knowledge of good and evil"; *e. g.*, II Sam. 19 : 36, where Barzilai says: "I am eighty years old, do I know good from evil?"

who introduces this tree is the same philosopher
who seeks to explain how mankind came to be scat
tered on the face of the globe and why people speak
different languages,[1] how the arts originated,[2] how
cities came to be built,[3] how people came to wear
clothes,[4] the reason for the strength of the marriage
bond.[5]   The tree of knowledge of good and evil is
therefore introduced to explain how man came to
be endowed with wisdom, to develop maturity of
intellect, to know how to cultivate the ground, to
provide for himself instead of having everything
furnished to him as in the Garden of Eden.   This
philosopher is also inclined to take a rather gloomy
view of things in this world, of the character and
position of man;   and we shall have occasion to
see[6] that he merits being called the father of pessi
mism.   The spread of people on the globe is, from
his point of view, a misfortune brought about as a
punishment for man's audacity in attempting to
build a tower that should reach up to the domain
of the gods.   Similarly, the fact that people speak
different languages so that one group does not un
derstand the other is regarded by our pessimistic
philosopher as an evil inflicted upon mankind so as

[1] These two questions are involved in the story of the building of the
city and tower, above, p. 6.

[2] Gen. 4 : 21–22.

[3] Gen. 4 : 17.

[4] Gen. 3 : 7–8.   The Hebrew word ordinarily translated "aprons"
means "loin cloths," the most primitive form of dress.   Originally, ac
cording to this author, the coverings were made of leaves (Gen. 3 : 7);
afterwards of skin (Gen. 3 : 21).   Our author thus shows his interest in
the evolution of dress.

[5] Gen. 2 : 23–24.   [6] Chapter V.

to prevent them from carrying out their mischievous purposes. Work, according to this thinker, is like wise a curse, a punishment sent to man because of disobedience by which he forfeited a life of ease and comfort in the primeval habitation. This author views human life with open eyes. He sees how full of hardships it is, how people must struggle to gain their daily bread, how women suffer in giving birth to offspring, whereas the animals seem to throw off their young without difficulty, and he concludes that the fate of man is imposed upon him as a consequence of his evil ways. Nor has he much hope of the future, for it is the same philosopher who makes Yahweh repent of having created man.[1] The Deluge is brought on because of man's wickedness; but, though the world was peopled anew of the seed of Noah, as offspring of the man who was "righteous and perfect in his generation" (Gen. 6 : 9), corrup tion again enters the world. Yahweh resolves never to bring on another Deluge, but merely because he recognises that it is not worth while to try to re form mankind, "because the inclination of the mind[2] of man is evil from his youth on." Man is a hope less sinner. Knowledge, too, is regarded as an evil. Man in a state of ignorance was innocent and happy, dwelling in a Paradise and having everything that his heart could desire without any effort on his part; but with knowledge, with maturity of intellect and physical vigour, came also the necessity to work and

[1] Gen. 6 : 6.
[2] The Hebrew uses "heart," but as the seat of the intellect.

struggle. The philosopher sees how the strength of
man leads him to tyrannise over a weaker brother,
how knowledge and skill are turned to evil purposes,
and how the struggle for life leads to incessant hos
tility. The greatest evil of all, however, to his
mind, seems to be woman. He is a misogynist, if
ever there was one, for he traces back to woman
the original act of disobedience which entails all
the misfortunes and miseries of human existence.
Woman is weak, weaker, at all events, than man.
Therefore the demon succeeds without difficulty in
deceiving her. Adam becomes the innocent victim
of her wiles.[1] There can be no doubt that the epi
sode in introducing a woman in the story intended
to explain the presence of death in the world is
conceived from this point of view, to prove that
woman is responsible for man's forfeiture of ever
lasting life. We have already had occasion to touch
upon this austere attitude towards life[2] which mani
fests itself in other ways in the pages of the Old
Testament, and we shall come back to it in the
last chapter. Here it is sufficient to have furnished
the proof that the change from the tree of death
to the tree of knowledge of good and evil is made
with a view of accounting for man's hard fate, end
ing after a constant struggle[3] in death. "Dust
thou art and unto dust shalt thou return." [4] The

---

[1] "Because thou didst hearken to the voice of thy wife" (Gen. 3 : 17)
—can misogyny go further?
[2] Above, pp. 41 *seq.*
[3] "In pain thou wilt eat bread all the days of thy life" (Gen. 3 : 17).
[4] Gen. 3 : 19.

whole character of the primitive tradition is changed
by this procedure, and only enough remains of the
original tale to justify us in carrying back the He
brew story of Adam's forfeiture of eternal life to
the same source that produced the tale of Adapa
—a story which, as we have seen, is quite independ
ent of the nature-myth with which it has been com
bined. This combination of a Babylonian folk-tale
with a nature-myth is as characteristic of the Baby
lonian mind as is the transformation of the Hebrew
tradition into a tale with an ethical substratum for
the development through which Hebrew thought
passed. The story of a Deity trying to prevent man
from eating of the tree of life was incompatible with
the later point of view, which we have endeavoured
to outline in this chapter and which we will have
occasion to amplify in the succeeding chapters. A
God who is pictured as a spiritual force, who is
above all else holy, who is enthroned in justice and
righteousness, free from all caprice, cannot possibly
be supposed to be afraid of man, just as little as
He can be conceived to be actuated by any hostil
ity towards man. This tale therefore is instinc
tively set aside and there merely remains of it the
faint trace in the verse to which attention has been
called,[1] so disguised moreover as to be almost un
recognisable as the *torso* of the primitive tale. The
other tale, about the tree of death—the tree in the
midst of the garden—was also too bald in its original
form to be incorporated in a collection of traditions

[1] Above, p. 53.

that were to be made the medium of illustrating the divine government of the universe by a power whose majesty reaches its climax in the picture of a Creator bringing the world into being by His mere command—His 'Word.'

The vitality of the primitive tradition was, how ever, strong enough to preserve some of its features, such as the deception practised upon man, the eat ing of a fruit as the explanation of death and the serpent as a symbol of an evil demon; but the main stress is laid in the spirit of the Prophets upon disobedience to the divine behest. The story, one cannot help feeling, would have been more impres sive had the sin of disobedience been portrayed in a more direct manner. Adam, as the type of man, should have been held up as the real sinner. The introduction of the woman as a medium between the serpent and the man carries the pessimism too far; it gives to the author's view of human existence an almost forbidding character, but nevertheless the main thought that disobedience is responsi ble for all the evils of the world stands out promi nently in the narrative in its present form. Through this element the primitive tale is lifted up into a higher region. Even its original character as fur nishing an explanation of death becomes secondary, and the story acquires the force of an impressive parable to illustrate the fundamental principle of the higher religion that brought about the wide de parture of so many other Hebrew traditions from their Babylonian counterparts—the principle of obedience to the will of a Power of universal scope, who guides mankind in love and mercy. Looked at in this light, we can overlook the trace of primi tive conceptions involved in picturing a serpent as a demon, a notion that is so prominent in primitive beliefs.[1] Viewed as a parable, we are reconciled even to the pessimistic strain running through the tale and which represents merely the extreme of the ethical aspect of life as revealed in the Prophets, who look upon life as a serious responsibility and who, while recognising the sinful nature of man, hold out the hope of salvation by an uncompro mising attachment to high ideals of conduct. Taken by itself, the transformation of a naïve tradition born of primitive beliefs into a parable of deep ethical import and of spiritual power, is thus a wit ness to the change in the attitude towards life. If this testimony can be confirmed by being shown to be in harmony also with the treatment accorded to other traditions which the Hebrews once held in common with the Babylonians, we shall have estab lished the thesis here maintained: that Hebrew and Babylonian traditions—using tradition in the larger sense, as embracing views and beliefs handed down as precious heirlooms from one generation to the

---

[1] On this view of the serpent and the reasons for the belief which sees a demon in a serpent, see Jastrow, *Religion Babyloniens und Assyriens*, II, pp. 775 *seq.* It is not impossible that the suggestion for the combina tion of man, woman, and serpent may have come from Babylonia. See the seal cylinder in Ward, *Seal Cylinders of Western Asia*, Fig. 388, por traying a man and woman (who appear to be gods) seated on either side of a tree—the tree of life—and a serpent in the background. To discuss the point involved, however, would carry us too far.

other—tend to diverge until finally, through the totally different direction taken by religious thought and ethical ideals among the Hebrews, we find these traditions so altered and recast as to show merely, through incidental "survivals," the path that leads us to Babylonia and Assyria as the centre from which they started out.

The main problem, then, involved in a study of Hebrew and Babylonian traditions, is to take note of the differences by the side of points of contact and to account for them. It is through these dif ferences that the specific quality of the Hebrew civ ilisation as distinguished from the Babylonian-As syrian is revealed. The resemblances are of value chiefly in pointing to a common ethnic stock to which both Babylonians and Assyrians and Hebrews belong—though it must always be borne in mind that Babylonians and Assyrians represent a mix ture of non-Semitic elements with Semites, and that the Hebrews are far from being a pure, unmixed Semitic race.[1]

Naturally, in a limited course the subject cannot be treated exhaustively. A selection must be made from the many phases that it presents, and only a number of the problems involved can be set forth. I choose therefore as illustrations of my main the sis such fundamental aspects as the study of the Hebrew and Babylonian views of Creation, the He-

---

[1] Ezekiel in a notable passage (16 : 3) reminds his people that "thy father was an Amorite, and thy mother a Hittite," an interesting refer ence to the mixed character of the Hebrews. See p. 15, note 1.

brew and Babylonian views of the Sabbath, the Hebrew and Babylonian views of life after death, and Hebrew and Babylonian ethics.[1] Through a consideration of these aspects we shall, I venture to hope, obtain a firm grasp of the important and fas cinating subject. The general plan will be in the case of each of these subjects, first to set forth the Babylonian traditions and points of view, follow ing their development so far as our material per mits us to do so, and then to set forth the course of development taken by the corresponding Hebrew traditions and points of view. In the course of the treatment the points of resemblance will suggest themselves to you without much effort on my part, while it will be my chief task to endeavour to inter pret the real and deeper significance of the points of difference. The method to be followed in the discussion will be the historical one, by which I mean that as a student of ancient civilisations I am actuated by no other motive than the desire to set forth the facts as I see them—frankly, with out bias or prejudice—but, I trust, with sympathy for the impressive struggle of mankind in its at tempt to penetrate the mystery by which it ever finds itself surrounded, and to attain to that modi cum of truth which it is within the power of the finite mind to grasp. The great lesson to be de rived from the historical study of religions—and this applies to the whole field as to every part of it—is that the goal of mankind is truth, even though

[1] In an appendix also Hebrew and Babylonian accounts of a Deluge.

it be that the search for truth will never end so long
as man survives; for truth is infinite, even as the
source of truth is infinite—aye, is the Infinite Him
self.

CHAPTER II

THE HEBREW AND BABYLONIAN ACCOUNTS OF CREATION

I

THE desire to trace things to their origin is so strong in man as to suggest the possibility of its being a deeply ingrained instinct. From the child's curiosity to see the wheels go round to the question, "what makes them go round?" is merely a step, and from this, again, to "who makes the wheels?" another step, and not a very large one. Curiosity is, indeed, the beginning of wisdom, and the most modern and most advanced scientific spirit is merely curiosity, plus the application of a proper method to satisfy it. Creation stories abound every where among people in a primitive state of culture, the stage of naïve curiosity, and from this stage they are carried over to the higher level, the stage of methodical inquiry, modified somewhat and trans formed to adapt them to higher points of view but in all essentials they are still the old stories, handed down from generation to generation by word of mouth until through the rise of the literary spirit they are given a definite form. The characters in these early endeavours to picture the universe coming into being are naturally the gods, and as the religious life, keeping pace with the social status and the political turmoils, becomes more definitely regulated, the gods assume a definite relationship to one another with variations in rank correspond ing to those which hold good for human society. Instead of an indefinite series of powers, represent ing the personification of the many forces mani festing themselves in nature and that condition man's welfare, we have a selection, and the powers so selected form a pantheon which becomes more or less systematically organised. At this stage Creation stories—one may say everywhere, for the exceptions if such there be are negligible—assume the character of a nature-myth, that is to say, a story of some occurrence in nature in which gods as actors personify the occurrence itself. The par ticular myth chosen will depend largely upon cli matic conditions. In tropical districts, suitable for man in the early stages of culture, the two seasons of the year, the rainy and the dry, generally sug gest by analogy the change from the rainy to the dry season as the beginning of the universe, or at all events, as the condition for the appearance of life in nature, of regularity and order as contrasted with the violence of storms and the destruction wrought during the rainy season, when forces of dis order seem to be in unbridled control. Such is the case with the various versions of Babylonian Crea tion myths that have been preserved, wholly or in part, but which appears most clearly in what may

be designated as the main version. This is the
story of a contest between the forces of evil and
lawlessness, symbolising the wintry and rainy sea
son, and the opponents of these forces endeavouring
to establish law and order.

We can now say with certainty that in each one
of the great religious centres of Babylonia sub
stantially the same story was told, with merely a
different arrangement of the actors on the stage.
The hero who triumphs in the contest with violent
forces is in each case the chief deity of a particular
centre. So in Nippur, which early acquired a sacred
position, it is Enlil, the patron of the city, who is
represented as quelling a general uprising of the
powers of nature. At Eridu, situated on or near
the Persian Gulf, it is a water deity, Ea. At Uruk
it is a solar deity, Anu; and, no doubt, at Sippar, the
chief city of the worship of Shamash (the general
designation of the sun), it was the sun-god who was
pictured as the conqueror. But these originally
distinct and early phases all gave way in time to
the claims of the god of the city of Babylon, Marduk, who, with the rise of Babylon as the political
capital of the entire Euphratean Valley, definitely
assumes the headship of the panthcon. In its final
and most elaborate form the Babylonian Creation
story thus becomes a pæan in praise of the power
of Marduk, who, endowed with the attributes of
all the other gods and thus surpassing any one of
them in strength and glory, is represented as accom
plishing a task in which others fail, or from which

they shrink. The local variations of the nature-myth are combined, but instead of any of the local gods, whether sun-deities or water-gods or storm-gods, succeeding in establishing order and in creating the universe, they are represented in this final version as having been foiled in the attempt and as proclaiming Marduk to be the only one who can overcome the chaotic condition produced through the rainy and stormy season. This condition was at an early date symbolised as the rule of a huge monster, with an army of minor but yet formidable monsters at her command.

II

Let us take up this story, which is known to us chiefly from fragments of clay tablets in the library of Ashurbanapal, King of Assyria (668–626 B. C.), though we also have some portions of it in neo-Babylonian tablets from some of the temples in the south, such as Babylon, Borsippa, and Sippar.[1] In addition to these we have much-distorted accounts in Greek writers, who quote as their source Berosus, a Chaldean priest who flourished in Babylonia towards the end of the fourth century, and who wrote a history of Babylonia and Assyria which is unfortunately lost. The story, which is poetic in form, begins as follows:

"When above, the heavens were not named,
Below, the terra firma was not called a name.

[1] See the complete publication of all the material, with a translation and commentary by L. W. King, *The Seven Tablets of Creation* (London, 1902. 2 vols.).

Apsu, first of their seed,
Mummu (and) Tiamat, producer of all of them,
Their waters were joined together,
Soil had not yet been marked off, shoot had not yet sprung up.

There was a time when none of the gods had as yet burst forth,
Not been called a name, fates had not been fixed;
Then were created the [twelve gods],
Lakhmu and Lakhamu burst forth.
Ages increased.
Anshar and Kishar were created and over them . . .
Days grew long—there came forth . . .
Anu, their son . . .
Anshar, (?) Anu . . .
Nudimmud whom his father [had begotten],
Abounding in wisdom, . . .
Exceedingly strong, . . .
Without a rival, . . .
Thus were established [the great gods]."

The attempt is evidently made here to set up a genealogy of the gods and we are fortunately in a position to supplement this enumeration through lists that have come down to us in the library of Ashurbanapal,[1] of powers or deities that are desig nated as the twenty-one male and female offspring of a divine progenitor symbolised as the heaven or the god of Heaven. To be sure, such lists repre sent the purely theoretical speculations of later priests or theologians, but they are nevertheless valuable as embodying traditions of ages when other gods than those which formed the object of wor ship in later times existed. In only a few cases do we know the nature of these early deities, but we

[1] Published in *Cuneiform Texts from Babylonian Tablets, etc., in the British Museum*, Parts XXIV–V.

are reminded in a general way of the similar geneal
ogies found in Hesiod's Theogony, giving us several
successive generations of deities who presided over
the Olympian pantheon. First in order are: Gaia
(Earth), and Uranos (Heaven), who produce the
Titans, the youngest of whom, Kronos, establishes
a new rule which in time is replaced by that of
Zeus, though not before many other series of gods
are brought forth through Kronos and Rhea. The
analogy between Hesiod's Theogony and that de
vised by Babylonian theologians can be carried
further, for in both cases the ultimate source to
which the powers—or, what amounts to the same
thing, the generations of gods—are traced back is
the heaven, the Uranos of Hesiod corresponding to
Anu in the Babylonian list. In Hesiod's Theogony
Kronos and Rhea, just as Zeus and Hera, represent
a divine pair. The male element in both instances
is again identical with the heavens, precisely as is
Uranos, the earliest progenitor of divine beings,
while Rhea and Hera as the female elements are
types of Gaia (the Earth), but become in both the
Babylonian and the Greek systems merely consorts
of the god of Heaven. The Babylonian lists of
divine pairs thus bring out the same thought as
found among the Greeks, only in a more definite
and clearer form. An (the sign for Heaven) and Ki
(Earth) are identified in these lists with Anum and
Antum, the divine pair, the god of Heaven and
his consort. In the same way the other pairs in
these lists, like Ib and Ninib, An-shar-gal and Ki-

shar-gal (*i. e.*, "the great universe of what is above" and "the great universe of what is below"), An-shar and Ki-shar, Du-ur and Da-ur, Lakhmu and Lakhamu, Alala and Belili, En-ur-ul-la and Nin-ur-ul-la, are merely so many designations of the same divine pair symbolised by the heaven as the male element, while the female element, originally the earth or that which is below, fades into a mere re flection of the male element and becomes the fe male companion of the god of Heaven. Hence the interchange in these names between the use of the element Ki, which means the earth, and Nin, which signifies the female element without further qualification.[1] The later stratum of thought is also shown by the divine pair to which these groups are traced back and which are no longer heaven and earth, but heaven and his heavenly consort, Anum and Antum, both being actually designated by the same sign—a star, as a symbol of the heavenly expanse.

All this points to the tendency both among the Greeks and Babylonians to give to the pantheon an astral character; in other words, to project the gods, quite independently of their original char acter, on to the heavens. We shall have occasion to refer to this later on.[2] I mention it here as an illustration of the frankly materialistic aspect of the Babylonian theology. This limitation in the conception of the divine involved the association

[1] The later male element corresponding to Nin is En.
[2] See chapter III.

of the manifestation of the divine with some sub
stantial, visible object. "The heavens proclaim
the glory of God," says the Psalmist,[1] in a sublime
burst of admiration at the beauty of the stars; for
the Babylonian the heavens proclaimed the gods
—*were* gods. Between the two conceptions lies the
difference between a spiritualistic and a material
istic faith, a view of divine government expressed
in poetical metaphors as a means of conveying ideas
for which ordinary language does not suffice, as
against the literal interpretation of the metaphor.
This materialistic aspect is the characteristic key
note of all the Babylonian Creation stories, and this
despite certain impressive features, particularly in
the Marduk epic, which we must not overlook. Let
us proceed with the account.

The Theogony of Hesiod assumes at the begin
ning of things, Chaos, apparently conceived as an
immeasurable empty space; then comes the triad
Earth (Gaia), the Depth (Tartaros), and Love
(Eros). Out of Chaos come Erebos and Night,
and from these, the Atmosphere (Ether) and Day
(Hemera). The process of creation was thus evolu
tion from darkness to light. This triad—Gaia,
Tartaros and Eros—has a counterpart in the specu
lations of the Babylonian theologians in Apsu,
Mummu, and Tiamat; but more consistently, or at
least more reasonably, than the Greek speculation,
Chaos is pictured as a time when water alone filled
all space. Apsu, antedating heaven and earth, is

the watery expanse. Tiamat, "the mother of all," associated with Apsu, is the watery deep, and Mummu, apparently the offspring of the two through the commingling of their waters, is again a term signifying water. It is a time of "water, water everywhere." A later attempt at differentiation makes Apsu the sweet, and Tiamat the bitter or salt waters, with Mummu as the generic designa tion for water without further specification. How ever this may be, Apsu and Tiamat, in the continu ation of the story, are represented in control, with Mummu as the messenger and an army of monsters as followers. The description of these monsters as "huge serpents, sharp of tooth and with merciless fangs, their bodies filled with poison instead of blood, dragons, raging hounds, scorpion-men, fish-men, devastating tempests, and fish-goats, all bear ing cruel weapons, and fearless of spirit," reminds us of the Cyclops and the Hekatocheiron (the hundred-handed monster), who in Hesiod's Theogony form part of the progeny of Gaia and Uranos by the side of the Titans. Berosus also, in his Babylonian history,[1] recalls these traditions of an age in which monstrous beings of hybrid form flourished. In Hesiod we do not learn, however, of any opposition between this army of monsters and the gods, whereas the main features of the Babylonian tale rest on a coming conflict between the two forces. The mon sters are not the creation of Anu and his consort, or

[1] See the translation of the passage in Cory, *Ancient Fragments*, p. 58; or Zimmern, *Keilinschriften und das Alte Testament*, pp. 488 *seq.*

of An (Heaven), and Ki (Earth), but the brood of
Apsu and Tiamat; and if we may follow Berosus,
who says that a woman named Homorka[1] presided
over this strange host, a version existed in which
the female element as the source of the monstrous
brood was alone introduced.

Apsu and Tiamat are disturbed through the
creation of the gods—Lakhmu, An-shar, Anu, Nudimmud and their consorts. They feel that with
the gods a new element has been introduced presag
ing the end of their own rule. The daybreak of a
new order is always coincident with the twilight
of the gods of the dissolving order, but the old does
not pass away without a severe struggle. Accord
ingly, Apsu and Tiamat decide to call upon their
forces for a desperate encounter for life and death.
We can detect in the description of the struggle
traces of several versions, each presumably belong
ing to a separate centre that have been combined
in accord with the regular principle of composition
in the ancient and later Orient, which in myths,
legends, and historical narratives is always and es
sentially a combination of existing traditions. Tak
ing the version however as it stands, the under
current of thought which betrays the higher spirit
of the priests in their remodelling of nature-myths
is the contest between the chaotic and lawless con-

[1] Homorka is a corruption of some Babylonian or Sumerian term.
Since in the course of the story a female being, Ummu-khubur, is intro
duced, pointing to a version in which she takes the place assigned to
Tiamat in our story, it may well be that we have here the original and
correct form of Homorka.

ditions symbolised by Apsu and Tiamat and their followers on the one hand, and order and higher law on the other, represented by the gods. The new order is the higher one, in which respect we again find an analogy with Hesiod who places the rule of Kronos on a higher plane than that of his father, while Zeus as the son of Kronos becomes the symbol of law and justice.

Apsu and Tiamat bewail the growing power of the gods: "By day I have no rest, at night I have no sleep; but I will wipe out their course; I will sweep them away; lamentations shall set in and after that we shall have rest again." Mummu comes to give counsel to Apsu and Tiamat, and the three plan a test of strength. There are indications at this point of the story that in an earlier version the gods selected Ea (or Nudimmud) to head the fight in their behalf.[1] Since Ea is the chief god of Eridu—probably the oldest of the sacred cities of Babylon—the prominence of Ea points to a version originating in this centre. If this be so, we may be sure that in this version Ea was celebrated as the vanquisher of Apsu and Tiamat. In another ver sion Anu was depicted as leader and victor, point ing to a form of the story that originated in Uruk, the seat of Anu worship; but Ea and Anu must yield their claims to a greater than either, to the favourite of all the gods who succeeds where others failed, who excels them all in strength and courage.

---

[1] See the writer's article, "The Composite Character of the Creation Story," in the *Noldeke Festschrift*, II, pp. 969–982.

This is Marduk, the chief god of Babylon. In his interest, and to add to his glory, all the other ver sions of the nature-myth are transformed so as to lead up to his triumph over chaos and lawlessness. Instead of Ea and Anu despatching the army of monsters, they are represented as succeeding merely in disposing of Apsu and Mummu, but Tiamat, the mother of the brood of monsters, remains at large.

As already suggested, Apsu, Mummu, and Tia mat are identical figures and represent the various names given to the same chief symbol of watery chaos in various centres but combined in the latest form of the story and placed in relationship to one another. In Babylon the name of the chief mon ster was Tiamat. She is, therefore, the one against whom Marduk in the final form of the tale directs his attack, but the story also implies that with Apsu and Mummu out of the way little has been accomplished, so long as Tiamat flourishes. Once more with true epic breadth the army of monsters, banded together at the side of Tiamat, are described in terms calculated to strike terror in the breast of the gods. Eleven monsters of especially terrific as pect are fashioned by Tiamat. She makes Kingu her consort and appoints him as the general of the army. To Kingu she assigns the command over all the gods and as a sign of his power hangs the tablets of destiny on his breast. The main thought of the story, as thus once more revealed, is to pic ture the opposition between the old and the new order, but with this nuance, that the new order has already proceeded far enough to place the gods in control and that only Tiamat remains to be over come. In her despair Tiamat takes the offensive and openly revolts, assuming the power of decreeing fates which, it is implied, already belongs to the new order about to triumph. Thus, as the story takes final shape, new features are introduced which, while adding also to the dramatic power, are of value chiefly because they reflect the thought and specula tion of the compilers.

Anshar, who presides over the assembly of the gods convened to take measures for quelling the re volt, calls upon his son Marduk to stand up against Tiamat.

> "The Lord rejoiced at the word of his father,
> He drew nigh and stood in Anshar's presence.
> Anshar looked on him and his heart was filled with joy,
> He kissed him on the lips and fear departed from him."

Marduk declares his readiness to go against Tia mat. Nay, he is impatient to trample her under foot, but exacts as a condition that in case of suc cess he shall be supreme in command.

> "'If I, your avenger,' he says to Anshar,
> 'Vanquish Tiamat and give you life,
> Then appoint an assembly, make my destiny supreme.
> In Upshukkinaku[1] seat yourselves joyfully.
> My word instead of yours shall decree fates.
> What I determine to bring about shall not be altered;
> The utterance of my lips shall not be taken back or super-
> seded.'"

---

[1] The mystical chamber of fate in which the gods meet for counsel and for decreeing destinies.

These lines reveal the aim of the story in its final form, namely, to explain and to justify the supreme rank accorded to Marduk as the head of the later Babylonian pantheon. He won his right to this claim by virtue of his power, and the claim is thus carried back in the poem to the beginning of time. The story of Creation becomes secondary to the pur pose of singing the praises of Marduk. Hence three of the seven tablets are taken up with a description of the preparation for the final conflict and with the conflict itself, ending in the complete discomfiture of Tiamat. The materialistic aspect of the old nature-myth is emphasised to such a degree in these three tablets as to border on vulgarity. The gods are so happy at the prospects of Marduk's victory that they gorge themselves at a banquet and become roaring drunk.

"They were greatly at ease, their liver was exalted,
For Marduk, their avenger, they decreed power."

Even before he sets out they address him as

"Marduk, thou art our avenger!
We give thee sovereignty over the whole universe.

.   .   .   .

Thy fate [i. e., thy power] be supreme among the gods!
For destroying and creating speak thou the word and it will be
    fulfilled."

As proof of his power he is told to command a garment to vanish, and it promptly disappears; and upon his command it reappears. He is hailed as

"Marduk is King!" Sceptre, throne, and ring are bestowed on him, and weapons are offered to him.

"Go and cut off the life of Tiamat
And let the wind carry her blood to remote places."

Marduk then arms himself with weapons which betray the naturalistic element of the original story. He provides a net with which to enclose Tiamat; he stations the winds as gods, so as to prevent her escape; various destructive winds are created by him and sent forth to arouse Tiamat. He then mounts his chariot, which is called "The Storm," and drives headlong towards the monster. In terror and dismay Tiamat utters her powerful charms, but they are of no avail. Undismayed, Marduk approaches.

"You and I," he shouts, "come, let us fight." Graphically the encounter is described. Tiamat in a rage opened her mouth, and Marduk drove in the evil wind which filled her belly. She gasps for breath, and Marduk, taking advantage of this moment, seizes the spear and bursts open her belly, severs her entrails and penetrates clear to her heart. The army of Tiamat flees in terror, but the monsters are all caught in Marduk's net and held prisoners.

Thus the opposition to the gods is overcome, and Marduk to symbolise his control takes from Kingu, the consort of Tiamat, the tablets of fate ("which were not rightfully Kingu's," the text adds) and hangs them on his own breast. With the triumph of Mar-

duk over Tiamat the story returns to its original
purpose, the account of Creation.

This account thus turns out to be a curious mix
ture of primitive notions such as are found in cos
mogonies of other peoples, with a more advanced
symbolism that leads Marduk, for example, to split
the flattened body of Tiamat in half and to use
one side of it as a covering for the heavens. He
draws a bolt across the expanse and stations a
watchman, so as to restrain the waters from gush
ing forth. This is a purely primitive conceit to ac
count for the control of the waters that come from
above. Water, as the primeval element, is still
everywhere as it was in the beginning, only under
control—below, through the bounds set to it; above,
through the expanse which is stretched like a cover
ing or curtain across the heavens. The same picture
of the waters above and below and of the expanse to
prevent the upper waters from escaping is found in
the biblical story; but combined with this naïve and
childlike conception there is in the Babylonian tale
the more advanced thought that through the sun of
the spring, symbolised by Marduk, the storms and
rains of winter are driven back to the heavens and
kept in control there like prisoners behind bolts
and bars under the surveillance of a watchman.

Still a third and likewise a relatively advanced
thought is woven into the primitive tale, one that
is closely bound up with Babylonian-Assyrian astral
mythology, according to which there is a perfect
correspondence between phenomena on earth and

the occurrences in heaven. The waters of the earth are regarded as united to one another. They en circle the earth which was conceived of as a float ing island, but these waters have their counterpart in the heavens. Marduk, accordingly, is repre- sented as measuring out space for the waters in heaven to correspond to the structure of the deep. Nudimmud, or Ea, as the god of the waters, is pro jected to the heavens and becomes the lord of the upper as well as of the lower waters, for whom a large mansion is constructed. The continuation of the story is even more astral in character. The heavens in Babylonian-Assyrian astrology were di vided into three large divisions, one assigned to Anu, the second to Enlil, and the third to Ea. These three gods constitute a triad that plays a great part in the theology of Babylonia and Assyria. Originally local deities, Anu is the sun-god whose centre of worship was in Uruk; Enlil, the chief god of Nippur and the head of the older Babylonian pantheon, is a storm-god who, however, also ab sorbs the attributes of solar and agricultural deities; while Ea, a water deity, had his centre at Eridu and presided over the Persian Gulf—the father of all the waters, from the Babylonian point of view. In time, and through a process which we cannot stop to consider here, these three gods are delocalised and become abstractions symbolising the three regions of the universe, the heaven above, the earth and the atmosphere immediately above it, and the waters around and under the earth—the same three divisions which we encounter in the Decalogue, where in evident allusion to the personification of the three divisions, the prohibition is emphasised against mak ing "any image of what is in the heaven above, on the earth beneath or in the waters under the earth" (Ex. 20:4; Deut. 5:8). Under the influence of as trological doctrines which transformed popular be liefs into a more systematic theology, Anu, Enlil, and Ea—as the three factors controlling the uni verse—are projected on to the heavens and become the three governors of the starry heavens, each hav ing a region of his own. The heavens then become the domain or, as the Babylonians called it, the "way" of Anu, Enlil, and Ea. All the great gods, irrespective of their origin, are projected on to the heavens—symbolised by stars. Marduk assigns places to these gods. Astrology forming the basis of the calendar, the year is divided into twelve months by Marduk and placed under the control of the stars. He fixes the courses of the planets; he places a gate at either end of the heavens. Through the one the sun was supposed to pass out in the morning and to enter through the other at night; he intrusts the night to the moon-god and regulates the phases of the moon. At this point, unfortu nately, the fifth tablet in which this work of Mar duk is detailed becomes defective, but enough re mains to warrant the assumption that the chief constellations are also established in their places in the heavens. Whether there was also included in the tablet an account of the creation of plants and verdure on the earth, as has been supposed by some scholars, is a point in regard to which no certain conclusions can be reached because of the defective condition of the tablet. Up to this point, then, we have only four themes: (1) the description of pri meval chaos; (2) a conflict between the older and the newer order; (3) the triumph and glorification of Marduk; (4) the regulation of the movements in the heavens or astral cosmogony, if this expression be allowed. A detailed plan of creation does not, therefore, appear to have been the main aim, at least of this version, of the Babylonian tale—and this despite the fact that in the sixth tablet the creation of man is introduced.

The point of view from which this work of crea tion is done is interesting. The gods are in full control. The older order represented by Apsu, Tia mat, Mummu, Kingu, Ummu-khubur has disap peared. The gods ought to be happy, but apparently are not. They are lonely in their solitary grandeur, just as Adam is represented as being lonely without a companion; but the loneliness of the gods is of a different order. The Babylonian could not conceive of gods without temples and worship. His view of divine government of the universe was limited by his conception of the gods themselves and their consorts. Creating their gods in their own image, the Babylonians, in common with other peoples of antiquity, endowed them with purely human attri butes and needs. Hence the gods have female con sorts and raise families. They are rulers, but as such they must not only have a kingdom to rule over like earthly kings, but they demand homage and tribute. What is the use of being a god if there is no one there to pay worship—if there are no temples in which offerings and sacrifices can be brought and homage paid? Strange as it may seem, the complaint of the gods to Marduk that they feel lonely, unhappy, and neglected because there is no one to worship them is assigned as the reason for the creation of man. It is provoking that the sixth tablet in which the creation of man is recounted breaks off at the most important juncture. Let us hope that a lucky chance will some day supply the missing sections without which our view of the Mar duk epic of necessity remains defective. The open ing lines read as follows:[1]

"Upon Marduk's hearing the utterance of the gods he was
    prompted to carry out [a clever plan].
He opened his mouth and unto Ea [he spake],
What he had conceived in his heart he revealed to him.
'My blood I will gather and bone [I will (take)],
I will set up man that man may . . .
I will create man to inhabit [the earth],
That the worship of the gods may be established, that shrines
    [may be built].
I will change the ways of the gods, I will alter.
Altogether shall they be honored, against evil [will they set
    their face].' "

What a contrast to the biblical account where man is created in the image of God to be the crown-

---

[1] The bracketed words indicate conjectural restorations of defective lines.

ing point of the universe, placed in an earthly Para
dise by the favour of the Almighty; whereas here
man exists because the gods are lonely and in their
vanity crave worship and adoration. An interest
ing feature, however, of the Babylonian narrative
which redeems it in a measure from its crude aspect
is the creation of man from the blood of Marduk
himself. This touch is confirmed by the account in
Berosus which, preserved for us through secondary
sources,[1] confirms the cuneiform account, though the
tradition has become somewhat distorted. Bel, as
Marduk is called in the extract from Berosus, see
ing that the earth was not cultivated, is represented
as cutting off his head or ordering one of the gods
to do so; and from the flowing blood mixed with
earth, man was created. Through this blood man
is brought into association with the gods—a link
is forged connecting man with the divine. We may
properly assume that this thought was in the mind
of the compilers of the Babylonian tale, and that it
reflected the view held of man's dignity, thus rising
supreme over the animal world. In so far man and
God are, as it were, placed on the same level; and
the association of the two plays a part in the Baby
lonian theology which, e. g., in the case of the hero
of the national epic, describes Gilgamesh as two-
thirds god and one-third man. The deification of
kings which we encounter at various points of Baby-

---

[1] Through Alex. Polyhistor and Nicholas of Damascus (sixth century
A. D.). See the translation in Cory's *Ancient Fragments*, p. 60; or
Zimmern, *Keilinschriften und das Alte Testament*, pp. 489 *seq.*

lonian history[1] is another expression of this relation
ship between gods and men, which is involved in
the doctrine that gives to man the blood of the
gods.

The Babylonian-Assyrian religion may be said to
revolve largely around the two ideas which we find
expressed in the sixth tablet of the Marduk epic—
the worship of the gods as one of the purposes for
which man exists, and the presence of a divine ele
ment in man, typified by the blood of Marduk which
is the life-giving quality of the god's own being. It
is a fair inference that the continuation of the sixth
tablet embraced an account of the creation of ani
mals—as given in the tradition of Berosus—and
perhaps also of plants. At all events, towards the
end of the tablet we see the gods assembled in Up-
shukkinaku—the great hall where the fates are de
termined. Marduk has snatched from Kingu the
tablets of fate and hung them around his own neck.
He is hailed as the great conqueror who has deliv
ered the gods from their opponents; and the seventh
and closing tablet of the series is taken up with the
enumeration of the fifty names bestowed upon Mar
duk—names that represent in part attributes to
indicate his manifold powers, in part other gods
whose essence and powers are transferred to him
as the one who absorbs the minor and most of the
major gods of the pantheon. Attached to each
name is an explanation of its meaning and applica-

---

[1] See on this King, *History of Sumer and Akkad*, pp. 251, 273 *seq.*,
298 *seq.*

tion. Asari, "the bestower of planting, the estab-
lisher of seeds, creator of grain and plants, causing
the green herbs to spring up"; Asari-alim, "revered
in the house of counsel"; Asari-alim-nunna, "the
mighty one, the light of the father who begat him,
who directs the commands of Anu, Enlil, and Ea";
Tutu, "who creates anew"; and so on through the
long list celebrating Marduk as the sun-god, as the
god of vegetation, as the creator of everything on
earth, and as the guide of the movements in the
heavens. He thus becomes in fact the god of heaven
and earth, "without a rival among the gods," as it
is expressly stated. Besides attributes of strength,
ethical qualities are also ascribed to him among the
titles heaped upon him. He is the subduer of the
disobedient, director of righteousness, the destroyer
of all the wicked; but the climax is reached when
the older heads of the pantheon—Enlil of Nippur,
and Ea of Eridu, whom Marduk supplants—bestow
their names upon him, and with their names their
very beings in accordance with the ideas anciently
associated with the name.[1]

> " ' The lord of the worlds,' father Enlil called him,
> The designation proclaimed by all the Igigi.[2]
> Ea heard it and his liver rejoiced.
> 'He whose name his father made glorious
> Shall be even as I—Ea be his name.
> The control of all decrees be his sphere.
> All my commands shall he make known.' "

[1] The name, according to the prevailing view in antiquity, is the es
sence of a being or object. To have a name is to exist; to wipe out
one's name is to destroy one.

[2] A name comprising a lower order of divine beings.

Thus the older version in which Ea is celebrated as the creator is combined with the new one. Ea is replaced by Marduk. The aim of the story— the celebration of the deeds of Marduk—is dis tinctly avowed in the epilogue attached to the nar rative, in which all are called upon to hold the fifty names in remembrance.

"Let the wise and the man of understanding consider them
  together,
  Let the father repeat them and teach them to his son,
  Let them resound in the ears of pastor and shepherd.
  May one rejoice in Marduk the lord of the gods,
  That his land may prosper—glory to him!
  His word stands firm, his command is unalterable,
  The utterance of his mouth no god alters.
  If he is enangered, his neck is not turned,
  If he is wroth, no god can oppose him.
  But wide is his heart, broad is his compassion."

These closing lines touch the high-water mark of religious thought in Babylonia and Assyria. They show that even in a materialistic conception of di vine government and despite the crude manner in which primitive traditions are handed down, the deeper religious note is sounded, and the aspiration of man to reach out to an understanding of the mysteries of life and of the universe finds an utter ance, even though it be a weak one.

III

There is another Babylonian version of the story of Creation[1] which likewise shows evidence of hav ing been adapted from an older form to serve the purposes of the priests of Babylon to add to the glory of Marduk, and about which a few words need to be said before we pass on to a consideration of the Hebrew accounts. It is important to note that in this second version—unfortunately preserved only in part—the same idea that the earth existed pri-v marily for the sake of the temples of the gods can be traced. As in the other version, the primitive state of things is pictured as a time when the waters covered everything, but the interesting touch is added that the dry land appears through the gath ering of the waters into a channel. In order to de scribe the primeval period the account begins by saying that no holy house, no house of the gods, no sacred place had been built. It continues as follows:

> "No reed had sprung up, no tree had been planted,
> No brick laid, no building erected,
> No house made, no city founded."

It will be observed that there is no direct refer ence to the fact that the earth did not exist. Its ex istence, indeed, appears to be assumed, only that it

[1] See King, *Seven Tablets of Creation*, II, pp. 130-9—a Sumerian original with an Akkadian translation.

is submerged through the waters which everywhere abound. The account then mentions three of the most ancient cities—Nippur, Uruk, and Eridu—and says that none of these three had been founded and their temples did not yet exist. Again, it will be observed, the association of city with temple, as though the one without the other were inconceivable. "All the land," the account continues, "was sea."

The adaptation of the older version to a form which would accord with the position of Marduk as the head of the pantheon is to be seen in the enumeration of the first places to appear after the waters had flowed into a channel, in consequence of which the dry land came into view. Eridu and Babylon take the place of Nippur, Uruk, and Eridu in the opening lines of this version. We might, indeed, have expected Babylon to be mentioned as the first city, but a concession is made to established tradition in joining Eridu with Babylon because of the close association between Marduk, the god of the city of Babylon, and Ea, the god of the much older city of Eridu. Marduk, despite his position at the head of the pantheon, is invariably and through all periods of history designated as the son of Ea, which points to the transfer of the Marduk cult from Eridu to Babylon. This transfer is also shown in the circumstance that the name of Ea's sanctuary at Eridu is identical with that of Marduk's temple at Babylon, called E-Sagila, the "lofty house." We therefore read in this second version:

"Then Eridu was established and E-Sagila built.
E-Sagila where in the midst of the deep the god Lugal-dulazagga
has his dwelling.
Babylon was built, E-Sagila completed.
The Anunnaki[1] together were created.
The holy city, the dwelling of their choice, they proclaimed as
supreme."

The purpose of these lines lies on the surface—
to justify the pre-eminent position occupied by the
city of Babylon, the sanctity of which is thus car
ried back to the very beginning of time. As in the
first version, mankind is created by Marduk for the
sake of the gods, though the purpose is put some
what differently in this version.

"In order that the gods may be induced to dwell in the dwelling place of their choice, he created mankind."

The gods proclaim Babylon as the city of their
choice, but in order to induce them to retain this
preference for all times, mankind is created to render
them the homage and tribute that will keep them in
a happy frame of mind, favourably disposed for all
time towards the city of their heart. At this point
the most interesting feature of the second version
is introduced. A distinct reference is made to an
earlier form of the story in which Marduk is the
creator but in association with a goddess Aruru.
In order to combine Marduk with Aruru the old
version is modified to read:

[1] Another name to comprise a lower order of divine beings like the
Igigi (above, p. 87). As a means of differentiating between the two,
the Anunnaki are represented as the spirits of the earth, and the Igigi
as the spirits of heaven.

"The goddess Aruru, together with him, created the seed of
    mankind."

We have not, as yet, been able to ascertain in
what centre this goddess Aruru was worshipped. We
come across her occasionally in the religious litera
ture, but generally as the consort of Marduk. The
circumstance, however, that in this second version
her name appears first and that it is she who, to
gether with Marduk (and not vice versa), creates
mankind is most significant as a proof that in the
older form of the story the prominent part in the
creation of mankind, at least, and probably also in
the creation of animals, was played by the personi
fication of the female principle in nature. There
now follows in a systematic though brief form the
account of the creation of animals and of verdure.

"Cattle of the field, living creatures were created in the field.
    (Tigris and Euphrates were created and placed in position;
    Good names were given to them.)[1]
    Grass, reed, . . . were created.
    The verdure of the field was created."

The composite character of the account is revealed
in the following lines, showing evidently a variant
account with an interesting distinction between wild
and domesticated animals:

"Lands, marshes and steppes,[2] . . .
    The wild cow and her young, the wild calf,
        the ewe and her young, the lamb of the stall,
    Gardens and woods,
    Goat and wild mountain goat."

[1] These two lines represent, I believe, a later insertion.
[2] The exact meaning of two further terms for plant life escapes us.

It is not necessary for our purposes to consider the problems involved in this compilation in detail. We may content ourselves with the general state ment that in the older forms of this second version the beginning is made with the creation of mankind in order that he may worship the gods; that this creation was brought about by the goddess Aruru, who also brings into being the beasts of the field and the living creatures of the field. Then, in order to make the earth habitable, reeds are formed, trees created, bricks laid, buildings set up, houses erected, cities established, living creatures placed therein; and, finally, corresponding to the enumeration of cities at the beginning of the story:

"Nippur was established, E-Kur[1] was built,
Uruk was made, E-Anna[2] was erected,
Eridu was made, E-Sagila built."

The tablet on which this second story is recounted turns out to be an incantation text. Accordingly, after the story is finished, the writer passes on to a prayer and to instructions for the ritual in connec tion with the recital of the sacred formulas.

In the same way we find in other texts forming prayers or incantations references to the great con test against Tiamat, to the creation of mankind, and to early conditions existing on the globe. So, in one of these texts[3] the enormous size of the dragon

---

[1] "The mountain house"—the name of Enlil's sanctuary in Nippur.

[2] "The heavenly house"—the name of the goddess Nana's sanctuary in Uruk.

[3] King, ib., II, pp. 116-127.

is dwelt upon as covering about three hundred miles in length and six miles in breadth, his mouth meas uring six cubits and his ears(?) fourteen cubits. The variations in current tradition are illustrated in this account of the dragon by making the one who despatches it not Marduk but a god Tishpak; and, strangely enough, the dragon is represented as appear ing after mankind had been created and cities had been founded.   This touch is of importance as fur nishing a further proof for the thesis that all the versions of creation current among the Babylonians and Assyrians are merely poetic representations of the contest between winter and spring.   There is no real creation of the world in the correct sense of the term, but only a conquest of the waters at one time covering everything, driving them back, as it were, so as to afford a place for the dry land.

In the same way the gods, or at least the same group of gods, are regarded as having been in exist ence even at the beginning of things.   The only real act of creation is that involved in putting man on earth in order to serve the gods—and in connection with man, other forms of animal life; while verdure and plants are represented as springing up natu rally after the dry land had appeared.   Perhaps even animal life was placed here for the sake of man, just as the vegetation that sprung up on the earth is assumed to exist because it is necessary for man's subsistence.   Without pressing this point too far, emphasis should, however, be laid on the limited scope of creation in the Babylonian-Assyrian stories.

The main point of view is not to indicate the source or the successive stages in the work of creation, but to ascribe to the one god or the other the glory of having conquered the storms and rains of the win try seasons, symbolised by a great monster who is surrounded by a host of lesser monsters. In other words, the glory of some local deity is the leading thought in all these versions, and for our purposes it matters little whether the divine hero is Enlil, Ea, Marduk, Tishpak, or the goddess Aruru. The nature-myth predominates.

A still older form of the nature-myth has recently been discovered by Doctor Arno Poebel[1] in the col lections of the University of Pennsylvania. In con tradistinction to the main version, which is in Bab ylonian, this new text is written like the second version in Sumerian, but without an accompanying translation—an indication of its great antiquity. Coming from the temple archives at Nippur, it is natural to find a part in the work of creation as signed to Enlil; but associated with Enlil is his consort Ninkharsag,[2] besides Anu the god of Uruk, and a deity, Enki, or Ea, the water-god of Eridu. The association of Anu, Enlil and Enki clearly points to a combination of this Nippur version with older Uruk and Eridu versions. The Sumerian priests of Nippur evidently received their account of Creation from still older centres, of whose history

[1] "Historical, Grammatical, and Religious Texts Chiefly from Nippur," Text No. 1 in vol. VI of the new series of the 'Babylonian Publications of the Museum of Archæology of the University of Pennsylvania' (Philadelphia, 1913).　　　　　[2] Also called Nintu.

we know as yet practically nothing, but transferred the role of creator to their favourite, Enlil. In this version we are told:

"After Anu, Enlil, Enki and Ninkharsag had created the black-headed people,

.   .   .   .

The animals, the four-legged ones they artfully created.

.   .   .   .

Then he established the sublime commandments and precepts.
He founded . . . cities on clean spots.
Their names were called and they were allotted to . . .
[As the first] of the cities he assigned the city of Eridu to the leader Nudimmud
Secondly, he assigned the city of Bad-nagar-dish . . .
Thirdly, he assigned the city of Larak to Pabil-kharsag
Fourthly, he assigned the city of Sippar to the warrior Shamash
Fifthly, he assigned the city of Shuruppak to the god of Shuruppak."

The order in which the great cities of the Euphrates Valley arose naturally differs in the different versions, but it is interesting to note that in this new version also Eridu is assigned the first place, a valuable indication of the oldest source to which probably all the Babylonian creation stories are to be traced.

The story then passes over to an account of a deluge from which Ziugiddu, a king and priest (of Shuruppak[?]), is saved. The Creation myth thus serves in this version as an introduction to the description of the Deluge.[1] In its complete

[1] Doctor Poebel is of the opinion that the tablet in question forms one of a series which began with a full account of the creation of the

form the tablet (or a preceding one of the series) no doubt contained an account of the conflict be tween Enlil and the dragon which, we have seen, is the invariable feature of Babylonian creation stories, symbolising the change of seasons from winter to spring.

It is, in fact, because of the strong hold acquired by this ancient tradition of the world coming into existence in the spring as a result of the conquest of winter, that Babylonia and Assyria were pre vented from reaching out to a more impressive view of the creation of the world, one that would be marked by an attempt to trace the various steps in an evolutionary process.

To sum up then, the various Babylonian creation stories remain on the level of nature-myths. They contain a variety of interesting pictures as well as thoughts and suggestions which indicate the attempt to rise superior to the myth, but an attempt that is, on the whole, weak and completely fails. There is little if anything of a spiritual character in these tales. The gods impress one as majestic and grand, but with decided limitations of character due to the materialistic form in which they are conceived. Even man, though viewed as a special creation of

world after the conquest of the dragon by Enlil, then took up the nar rative of the great Deluge and passed on in another tablet to a list of kings from the time of the Deluge onward. If this view be correct, we would have in this continuous narrative a parallel to the biblical com pilation of narratives of Creation and of the Deluge with chronological lists sandwiched in (Gen. chap. 5). The high figures assigned in Genesis to the lives of the antediluvian patriarchs are again paralleled by the extraordinary lengths assigned to the reign of the earliest Baby lonian rulers in the tablet published by Poebel (ib., Nos. 2-4, of vol. VI).

one god or the other, whichever happened to be at the head of the pantheon in the centre in which the version arose, is not endowed with any spiritual powers. True, the blood of the god was given to man, but this gift merely reflects the current view that life comes from the gods and that there is a link uniting man with the higher powers. Man exists for the sake of the gods. Mankind is created to provide worshippers for the gods and to build temples in their honour. That is the characteristic last word of the Babylonian-Assyrian view of man's place in nature.

IV

Turning now to the story of Creation as recounted in the first two chapters of Genesis, we note, in the first place, that, as among the Babylonians, there were several versions current. Two of these, differing considerably from one another in matters of detail, are preserved in the first two chapters of Genesis.[1] In addition, we have scattered references, in poetical books like Job, in some of the Psalms, in poetical passages embodied in the orations of the Hebrew Prophets, and in the apocalyptic literature[2] which indicate the existence of a considerable amount of what may be called popular tradition in regard to the creation of the world, and which, it is quite possible, likewise existed in a definite literary

[1] See the analysis in Skinner's or Gunkel's Commentary on Genesis.
[2] Collected and discussed in Gunkel's *Schopfung und Chaos*, pp. 29–111 (Gottingen, 1895).

form. Since, however, it is evident from internal evidence that the collection known as the Old Testa ment represents only a portion of the literature produced by the Hebrews in pre-exilic and post-exilic days, there is a strong presumption in favour of the view that the two versions of the Creation preserved for us by no means exhaust the literary material once current among the Hebrews in regard to the ever-fascinating subject of Beginnings.

The second version, beginning with the fourth verse of chapter 2 and extending to the end of the chapter, is the briefer of the two and, evidently in the form preserved, assumes the existence of chap ter 1, the compiler contenting himself with intro ducing in the second chapter only such features as are not covered in the first. It begins with the state ment: "These are the generations of Heaven and Earth as they were created," to which there is added as an explanatory comment: "On the day that Yah-weh Elohim made Earth and Heaven." The second part of this verse is apparently attached in order to prepare us for what follows, which is entirely devoted to an account of what happened on earth —the springing up of verdure, vegetation, and the creation of man. Nothing whatever is said about the heavens—presumably for the reason already suggested that in the first version this has been covered, and we may therefore conclude that the second version was in this respect identical with the first. All that we learn therefore from the second version is that the earth, the special creation of which is not indicated, is a desolate waste because not fertilised by rain and because man was not there to cultivate the ground. The point of view, it will be observed, is distinctly agricultural; and this is borne out by the continuation of the story which tells how moisture arose from the earth and soaked or watered the ground and how God created man through dust from the soil and blew into his nostrils the breath of life. The earth thus becomes the mother of mankind, and the source of all life and vegetation. The earth having been watered, Yahweh Elohim plants a garden to the east of Eden —which appears to be used here for a district in southern Babylonia—and there he places man orig inally for the purpose of enjoying the fruits of the trees planted by God Himself and without any ef fort on man's behalf. But in verse 15 we come across a somewhat different tradition, according to which man was placed in the Garden of Eden "to cultivate it and to guard it," suggesting a com parison with the account of the creation of man as given by Berosus,[1] and according to which man is placed here because the earth was barren, there being none to cultivate it. From the same ground from which man is taken Yahweh Elohim creates the animals of the field, and the birds of heaven. It is noticeable that there is no reference in this version to animal life in the waters. The version in fact seems to glide rapidly over the whole work of creation in order to reach the main point of the

---

[1] See above, p. 85.

compiler, which is to set forth his theory of the posi
tion of man in nature, and the reason for the condi
tions of life which he finds, on the whole, to be hard
and harsh. On the one hand, man is the lord of
creation, as in the first version, and this is symbol
ised by the privilege accorded to him of giving names
to all the animals. There seems to have been still
present in the mind of this compiler the old notion
that the name was an essential part of the being.
He did not go so far as to assume that the one who
gave the name was also the creator, but, at least,
in supplying the name, he completed Creation itself
by the addition of an essential factor. But why,
this compiler asks himself, is it that man whose
superiority over the rest of creation is thus acknowl
edged, is himself a hard-working slave, compelled
to drudge in order to maintain life—that gift of
God, given to him by the Creator Himself? Our
compiler is a philosopher who ponders over the
problems of existence and whose conclusions are so
gloomy in character that he may with some justice
be called the father of pessimism. There is, to be
sure, a somewhat brighter touch in his account of
the creation of woman. He represents man as being
lonely and finding no worthy associate among the
animals. In the Babylonian epoch of Gilgamesh [1]
there is an interesting account of primitive man ac
tually living with the animals, and it may well
be that the compiler of the second version had a

[1] Tablet I, 86–91 according to Ungnad-Gressmann's edition of *Das Gilgamesch-Epos*. (Gottingen, 1911).

faint recollection of such a tradition.[1] He has, however, an exalted view of the superior position occupied by man in nature; hence he introduces the woman for the purpose of securing an associate worthy of man, but the associate alas! helps to bring about man's fall from divine favour.

Interested as the compiler is in all origins, he at taches to the account of the creation of woman the explanation for the marriage tie which binds man and woman to such an extent as to prompt him even to give up parental ties in order to establish a household of his own in association with the woman of his choice. The pessimistic note is unmistak ably struck in the third chapter in the remarkable story of the temptation and fall. In addition to the original purport of the story to explain the pres ence of death in the world,[2] it furnishes for our compiler the medium for explaining why man, orig inally placed on earth by a beneficent Deity who provided everything for him, is now forced to work in the sweat of his brow throughout his life until, exhausted with toil, he lies down to eternal rest in the ground whence he was taken. Work, according to this writer, is the curse put upon man through disobedience, while the woman's fate is painted in even gloomier colours. She will be under the con trol of her husband, at the mercy of his pleasure and his passion, and be obliged to endure the throes and

---

[1] See an article by the writer on "Adam and Eve in Babylonian Lit erature," in the *American Journal of Semitic Languages*, vol. XV, pp. 193–214.

[2] See above, p. 53.

pains of childbirth. Work and suffering are to be the fate of mankind. This gloomy and pessimistic outlook is continued in the succeeding chapters, par ticularly in the account of the Deluge, which is brought on through the growing wickedness of man kind; and even when, after the Deluge, God prom ises not to bring on another catastrophe, the reason assigned for the resolve is that it is not worth while to curse the entire earth for the sake of man, since "the inclination of his heart is towards evil."[1] God repents having made man, and therefore encompasses his destruction. The righteous is saved and a new race created, but without any hope of permanent improvement.

It will be evident from this brief survey that this second version of Creation has few points in com mon with any of the Babylonian versions discussed. Not only is there no chaos at the beginning of things and no conflict between the lower and higher order, but there is a total absence of any element that might be called mythical. The version, so far as preserved, is a very sober and rather prosaic record of the way in which vegetation arose, why man was created, how the beasts were created and named; and in all this the main purpose of the writer is evidently philosophical and religious, with the story itself merely as a framework. The point of view is of a remarkably advanced type, and it is fair to presume that this account represents the science of the day rather than the remnants of popular tradi-

[1] Gen. 8 : 21.

tion. Even the touch which might suggest a more primitive form of thought, according to which man is formed out of the dust of the earth and the breath of life breathed into his nostrils, is primitive only in so far as it assumes the material substance of man to be the same as that found in the earth; and yet the endeavour to trace back all things in and on the earth to the earth itself takes us into a realm of thought considerably removed from naïve and primitive speculation.

The case is quite different when we come to con sider the version of Creation in the first chapter of Genesis and extending through the third verse of the second chapter. This account, according to the modern analysis, forms part of a large compilation conveniently known as the Priestly Code, in which in a framework of history and law things are traced back to their beginnings. In its present form the account in the Priestly Code must be later than the second version, and yet in a comparison of the two the second stands on a higher plane of thought and has also a decidedly more rationalistic tinge. The purpose of the compiler or compilers of the Priestly Code in beginning the history of Israel with the crea tion of the world was twofold. In the first place, it was prompted by the natural desire to trace his tory back as far as possible, and, secondly, to show the workings of the great Power of the universe from the beginning of time, indicating through incidental references the special concern of this divine Power for the fate of the Hebrews as the chosen people.

In the second version there is no trace of this na
tionalistic view but the Priestly Code, having as its
starting-point the special place assigned to the peo
ple of Yahweh in the universe, the origin of the Sab
bath as a distinctly Hebrew institution is attached
to the work of creation. God Himself institutes the
seventh day as a day of rest, and the compiler does
not shrink from the anthropomorphic implication
in representing the Creator of the universe as rest
ing from his labours precisely as a man might. He
is concerned with the justification of the central
institution of Judaism.

It may seem strange at first sight, therefore, that
this narrative should be the one which contains many
points of resemblance to the main type of the Baby
lonian creation stories. One would have supposed
that a compiler so saturated with the monotheistic
Jewish spirit would have taken care to remove from
his account of Creation all traces that seemed to
be non-Jewish in character. That he did not see
fit to do so may be taken as a proof of the popu
larity assumed by the tradition embodied in the
first chapter, and also as an indication that the
compiler himself could not, or did not wish to cut
himself loose from popular traditions, but on the
contrary desired to use them in illustration of his
conception of divine government. The story of
Creation, in other words, becomes in the mind of
this compiler a kind of parable, told not so much
because it furnishes an account of the successive
creative acts, but because it illustrates the manner

in which all manifestations of the universe, includ
ing life in its various forms, go back to the one
cause—the 'Word' of Elohim. This emphasis in
the case of each creative act upon the power of the
'Word,' which when uttered brings about the Crea
tion itself, is the key-note to the chapter. Bearing
this in mind, let us proceed to a closer analysis with
a view of ascertaining exactly wherein the resem
blance to Babylonian Creation myths lies.

At the very beginning of this account we have
perhaps the most striking evidence of the ultimate
identity of the Hebrew and Babylonian Creation
traditions, for in the statement that the earth was
Tohu and Bohu ("void and waste") and that dark
ness was over the face of the deep (Tehom), we
have the Hebrew counterpart to the Babylonian de
scription of primeval chaos. At the same time the
description furnishes the evidence for the thesis that
in the biblical account the mythical element has
been reduced to the utmost possible minimum.
This is indicated by the use of the terms Tohu and
Bohu in place of personifications like Apsu and
Mummu, and more particularly in the entirely im
personal use of the term "Tehom" in the sense of
"watery deep," as against the personification of the
primeval waters as Tiamat, and this despite the
fact that the Hebrew version still uses the very
same term, "Tehom," as the Babylonian.[1]

---

[1] On the identity of Tehom and Tiamat, which is an amplified form of
tamtu, "sea," see Skinner's *Genesis*, p. 16, note 2; or Driver's *Genesis*, p.
28.

There are traces elsewhere in the Old Testa
ment that Tehom was once personified, though the
personification became, in the advanced Hebrew
thought, merely a poetical metaphor. In the beauti
ful twenty-eighth chapter of Job, where man's search
for wisdom is so impressively described, we read:
"But wisdom,—where may she be found, and where
is the place of understanding? Man does not know
her way and she is not found in the land of the
living; Tehom says, 'She is not in me,' and the
sea says, 'Not with me.'" Further on we read:
"Abaddon[1] and death say, 'We have heard a rumor
about her: God understands her way and He knows
her place.'" Elsewhere, as in the 104th Psalm as
well as in the various references to Rahab and the
Leviathan and the dragon, particularly in Isaiah
and Job,[2] we have the further proof that the He
brews were well acquainted with the nature-myth
in its more primitive form, for such figures as Rahab
and Leviathan pictured as huge serpents are merely
the reflections, in the form of poetical metaphors, of
the original personification of primeval chaos as a
period in which monstrous beings were in control.

V

It is worth while to consider some of these refer
ences to the nature-myth which will furnish the
point for the thesis here maintained that in the

---

[1] "Destruction," a name for the nether world, where the dead are hud·
dled together. See chapter IV.

[2] See Gunkel, *Schopfung und Chaos*, pp. 29–111.

Priestly Code the mythical element was intention
ally suppressed or, as it may also be put, the crea
tion of the world by a spiritual Being, universal in
scope and acting by the power of His word, being
incompatible with the representation of Creation as
a mere change in seasons pictured as a conflict against
a monster—the symbol of primeval chaos and law
lessness—the natural result would be to retain only
that modicum of the old nature-myth essential to
the account of the order of Creation. The pictures,
however, drawn of primeval monsters in poetical
passages in various parts of the Old Testament, and
the frequency with which these pictures are intro
duced, show not only that the Hebrews knew of
these nature-myths, but that the one symbolising the
change from the rainy to the dry season—applicable
to Palestine as well as to the Euphrates Valley,
though not in the same degree—had sunk so deep
into the popular mind as to leave its traces in the
literature of the postexilic period down across the
threshold of our era. When Job, in one of his
descriptions[1] of the divine Power which lay so
heavily on him in his unbearable sufferings, ex
claims:

> "By His power he has quieted the sea,
> With his intelligence shattered Rahab.
> The bolts of heaven are in terror before Him;[2]
> His hand has crushed the winding[3] serpent,"

[1] Job 26: 12–13.
[2] So the Greek rendering of this line, the Hebrew text of which is
corrupt.
[3] On this translation, see Gunkel, *Schopfung und Chaos*, p. 47.

there can be no doubt that the philosophical poet
has in mind the picture of a Tiamat, a great mon
strous serpent, suggested, as we have seen, by the
billows of the agitated sea. Rahab represents one
of the names of this monster and the parallelism
with "sea" leaves no doubt as to the character of
the personification. The lines imply a conflict with
Rahab in which God is triumphant. By His power
He subdues the monster, just as Marduk vanquishes
Tiamat; and we have a further reminder of the
Babylonian myth in the reference to the bolts of
heaven which, it will be recalled, Marduk attaches
to the gates established at either side of the heav
enly expanse, and at which he places watchmen as
guards. In another speech of Job,[1] portraying the
irresistible force of God's anger, the "helpers of
Rahab" are described as "bent" under the divine
wrath, a definite indication that among the Hebrews,
as among the Babylonians, Rahab-Tiamat was rep
resented as having an army of monsters to assist
her, and which Marduk captures after he has over
come Tiamat. Even more explicit is a passage in
a late chapter of the postexilic portion of Isaiah[2]
in the reference to Rahab as a being that belongs
to primeval days, to the very beginning of time.
Calling upon the people to place their trust in Yahweh as the supreme vanquisher of all foes, however
numerous and strong, the Prophet calls upon God
Himself to manifest His power as at the time when
He overcame Rahab.

[1] Job 9 : 13.   [2] Isa. 51 : 9.

"Awake, awake! gird on strength, O arm of Yahweh!
  Awake as in the days of Beginning,[1] the generations of distant
    times!
  Art not thou the one who didst shatter Rahab, crushing the
    dragon?"

The picture here forms a complete analogy to the
Babylonian myth—even to the conception of Rahab
as a dragon. Similarly in Psalm 89 : 11, in a de
scription of Yahweh's power in quieting the billows
of the angry sea, the same reference to the con
quest of Rahab is introduced as a metaphor; and
it is only a further and natural step in poetical
imagery to apply Rahab to Egypt as is done in
Psalm 87 : 4 and Isa. 30 : 7,[2] for Egypt, like Baby
lon with which it is placed in juxtaposition in the
former passage, is a huge monster in comparison
with the small and puny Israel, but Yahweh—so
poet and Prophet assume—will stand up against
Egypt, just as He quelled the uprising of Rahab in
primeval days. In the course of time the term
loses its original force of a proper name, as Tehom
lost it, and Rahab becomes a poetical synonym for
wickedness, violence, and hostility to Yahweh's
kingdom of justice and order. It is so used in
Psalm 40 : 5, which is to be rendered as follows:

"Happy the man who makes Yahweh his trust,
  And turns not to the Rahabs[3] and to lying rebels."

[1] So the literal translation of Hebrew phrase.
[2] The ordinary rendering of the close of this verse is senseless. By a
very simple procedure, Gunkel (p. 39) obtains the reading "the silenced
Rahab," i. e., the monster who has been overcome and made harmless.
[3] The plural form is used—a further indication of the disassociation
from its original personification.

Corresponding to the various names for the mon
sters associated with primeval chaos that we en
counter in the Babylonian myth of Creation—
Tiamat, Ummu-khubur, Kingu, besides Apsu and
Mummu—due, as has been suggested, to the com
bination of various versions to form the great Marduk epic—we have in Hebrew poetry, by the side
of Rahab, other designations conveying the same
picture. Prominent among these is Leviathan, oc
curring likewise in Psalms, in a prophetical utter
ance embodied in Isaiah, but which belongs to
the postexilic period,[1] and more particularly in
Job.

The 74th Psalm reveals its origin in the Maccabean period—perhaps just before the uprising—in
so unmistakable a manner that scholars are prac
tically agreed in assigning it to about 165 B. C.
It is, therefore, of special significance to find in so
late a production a poetical metaphor introduced
which would be unintelligible without the assump
tion that the imagery is based on a pure nature-
myth, and evidently the same myth that underlies
the references to Rahab—a conflict in primeval
days between Yahweh and a huge monster. After
describing the desolation wrought by the enemy—
the Greek supremacy—the defilement of the sanc
tuary, the burning of synagogues throughout the
land, and lamenting the absence of prophets and
of signs indicative of any relief, the psalmist ap
peals to God:[2]

---

[1] Chapter 27. See Duhm's *Iesaias*, p. 165.   [2] Verses 12–17.

"Thou, O Yahweh, art my king from of old,
Working salvation in the midst of the earth.
Thou hast divided the sea with thy arm,
Thou has broken the heads of the dragons in the waters.
Thou hast crushed the heads of Leviathan,
Gavest him as food for[1] . . .
Thou hast split fountain and brook,
Thou hast dried up the streams of primeval time.
Thine is the day, aye thine is the night.
Thou hast fixed the moon and sun,
Thou hast set all the bounds of the earth.
Summer and winter thou hast formed."

The entire description is evidently a reminiscence of the work of creation, though the poet avails himself of his licence in deviating somewhat from the conventional order set forth in the first chapter of Genesis. The creation of day and night, the work of the second day, is followed in a logical sequence by the reference to the creation of moon and sun,[2]—the work of the fourth day. This in turn leads to an allusion to the limits set to the dry land which forms part of the work of the third day. The reference to the two seasons resulting from the establishment of order and law in the universe re veals the substratum of myth in the description, for it will be recalled that the Creation epic is based on the change from the wintry and rainy to the dry and warm season. We are therefore justified

[1] The text is corrupt. The ordinary rendering, "for the people of the wilderness," is without sense.

[2] The precedence of moon over sun reminds us of the order in Baby lonian-Assyrian texts, where under the influence of astrological notions the moon-god, Sin, is invariably placed before Shamash, the sun-god. See Jastrow, *Religion Babyloniens und Assyriens*, II, p. 457. Poetic usage follows archaic traditions.

in interpreting verses 13–14 as a reminiscence of
the very first work of creation—the conquest of
the great monster and of her numerous brood. The
dragons in the waters represent the army of Tiamat, while Leviathan—here described as a many-
headed Hydra—is clearly synonymous with Tiamat
herself. Poetic licence leads the poet to introduce
in verse 15 the description of Yahweh's power in
causing springs to gush forth, brooks alternately to
stream with water and to be dried up.[1] Isaiah uses
the old nature-myth in apocalyptic fashion[2] to fore
tell the coming destruction of the enemies of Israel.
Leviathan, like Rahab,[3] becomes a symbol of a pow
erful nation—Egypt, Babylon or Assyria, as the
case may be. The myth is introduced as a mere
metaphor, and the Prophet, having in mind three
powerful enemies, has no scruples in suggesting three
monsters instead of one.

"On that day Yahweh will visit with his sword the cruel, the
mighty and the powerful,[4]—Leviathan, the winding[5] serpent, and
Leviathan, the twisted serpent, and he shall kill the dragon in the
sea."

The winding and the twisted serpent and the dragon
in the sea are identical—variant descriptions of the
great monster Tiamat.

[1] The reference might also be to "the fountains of the deep" (*tehom*)
which, when they are "split open" (Gen. 7 : 11), cause the destructive
Deluge.
[2] I follow Gunkel's interpretation (*Schopfung und Chaos*, pp. 45 *seq.*)
[3] Above, pp. 109 *seq.*
[4] Corresponding to these three terms we have three serpents—two
Leviathans and a dragon.
[5] The same attribute as above, p. 108.

We must turn, however, to the magnificent for
tieth and forty-first chapters of Job to learn the
extent to which poetic fancy went among the He
brews in picturing the primeval monster whom
Yahweh alone was able to subdue. To illustrate
the weakness of man in contrast with the Deity, and
therefore the folly of man to question God's ways,[1]
the poet asks:[2]

> "Canst thou draw Leviathan out with a hook?
> And with a cord fasten his tongue?
> Canst thou put a hook in his nose?
> Or bore his jaw with a ring?
> Will he make supplication to thee?
> Or speak soft words to thee?
> Will he make a covenant with thee?
> So that thou takest him for a servant forever?
> Wilt thou play with him as with a bird?
> Or tie him like a dove for a child?[3]
>
> .   .   .   .   .   .
>
> Canst thou fill his skin with spears?
> Or his head with fish spears?
> Just lay thy hand upon him and thou wilt not think
>   of a battle (with him) again!"

Yahweh alone can deal with Leviathan. He can
overcome him—catch him as one hooks a fish, use
him as a toy,[4] as one plays with a pet bird. All
this is poetic fancy, but the nature-myth runs
through the lines and is manifest in the reference

[1] The chapter belongs to the supplementary portion of the book of
Job.
[2] Chapter 40 : 25–32; in the English version, chapter 41 : 1–8.
[3] I follow Gunkel's (p. 50, note 2) ingenious and simple emendation
of the text.
[4] Cf. Psalm 104 : 26, "Leviathan whom thou hast formed as a play·
thing"—so the correct rendering.

to Leviathan's appeal for mercy to the powerful Yahweh who has captured him, as Marduk caught Tiamat and made her subservient to his wishes. The further description of the monster, strong of fangs (41 : 6), raising himself up to a great height (41 : 17), to whom iron is as straw (41 : 19), sug gests in various ways the description of the brood of monsters who constitute the army of Tiamat, though touches are added, such as the flames issu ing from his mouth (41 : 12–13), which appear to be original creations of the Hebrew poet who allows his fancy free flight. In the description of the huge monster Behemoth in chapter 40, though the poet probably has in mind the hippopotamus, there are allusions which suggest an association with Levia than; and it may be that Behemoth is also a des ignation for the primeval dragon, symbolising the chaos at the beginning of time. The huge size of both Leviathan and Behemoth reminds one of the description of the dragon in one of the Babylonian versions above discussed.[1] Be this as it may, enough evidence has been brought forward to show that up to a late period the Hebrews were perfectly famil iar with the old nature-myth of the conflict with the monster Tiamat, or whatever name we choose to apply to it; and it is also a justifiable conclusion that what has become a metaphor in Hebrew poetry was once popularly regarded as an actual occurrence, to account for the existence of law and order in the world in place of primeval chaos and lawlessness.

[1] Above, pp. 93 *seq.*

VI

Coming back now after this somewhat long di
gression to the first chapter in Genesis, we find that
here even the metaphor has disappeared as incom
patible with an account of Creation by a purely
spiritual Power, whose word alone suffices to bring
about the desired result. No conflict is required.
Indeed, the suggestion of a conflict would mark a
limitation to the supreme majesty of the divine com
mand. Hence the addition to the description of
primeval chaos, in the second verse of the first chap
ter, of the words "and the spirit of Elohim brooded
over the face of the waters," which dispose briefly
but effectively of the entire conception of any con
flict at the beginning of time. In place of the con
flict we have the picture of the divine afflatus hov
ering over the watery mass. We need not stop in
an attempt to specify the picture that the compiler
had in mind. The vagueness is inherent, the evi
dent aim being to remove all traces of any material
istic conceptions of divine Power. The limitations
of human language are particularly apparent when
we endeavour to describe the beginning of things,
but it is difficult to imagine a more profound and
at the same time a more sublime description of such
a beginning than is suggested in the simple phrase,
"The spirit of Elohim brooded over the face of the
waters." Throughout the chapter, in accordance
with this high plane of spiritualised religious thought,

the source of all creation is concentrated in the di vine command. The Deity in the Hebrew story is not an artificer who by a process of work gradually brings things into being; He is one whose word im mediately produces the result. *Fiat lux!* God said —"Light be, and light was."

In this creation of light as the result of the first utterance of God we may, I think, see a direct pro test against the Babylonian version which makes some particular personification of nature—the water-god, Ea; the storm-god, Enlil; or, in the latest ver sion, Marduk, the sun-god—the creator of everything. The sun being recognised throughout antiquity as the source of light, Marduk himself is the light. The Hebrew poet, reflecting the view of the Proph ets to whom God is the supreme spiritual power rising above the universe, makes the light a part of His Creation. *Fiat lux* represents the protest against the assumption that a power which itself represents the light can be the source of being. There is One superior even to the light by whom light must be first created. We find a trace again of earlier conceptions, recalling the description of Marduk's making a covering out of one side of Tia-mat stretched across the heavens to prevent the upper waters from flowing out, in the biblical de scription of an expanse (*rekia*) to separate the waters below from the stars above. The expanse, which evidently is still conceived as a material substance, is called "heaven." Similarly, we have another direct trace of the common origin of the Hebrew and Babylonian traditions in the conception that the gathering of the waters below the heavens to one place reveals the dry land. The earth is there fore assumed as in existence, merely submerged through the waters abounding everywhere. When, therefore, we read, "Elohim said, Let the waters under the heaven be gathered to one place so that the dry land may appear, and it was so," we must admit the parallelism with one of the versions of the Babylonian stories, in which it will be recalled the gathering of the waters into a channel results in the appearance of terra firma.[1]

The vegetation of the earth follows in the biblical account as a natural consequence of the gathering of the waters. The thought is here, as I have al ready indicated, on a higher plane than that which we find in the second chapter according to which the earth existed in a barren state until it was soaked through moisture and until man came to cultivate it.

In the account of the creation of the great bodies in the heavens, the sun and moon, and to which a later commentator added the stars, we have a most suggestive parallel with Marduk's regulation of the movements of the heavenly bodies after his victory over Tiamat, and of which we have encountered a reminiscence in a description of the conflict with the Leviathan.[2] As in the Babylonian account, the pur pose of the lights in the heavens is to regulate time and seasons, or, in other words, to furnish a basis

[1] Above, p. 89.   [2] Above, pp. 113 seq.

for the calendar. But whereas in the Babylonian version we find the moon placed in supreme con trol, time being calculated according to its phases, in the biblical version emphasis is laid upon the two lights, the greater one for the control of day, and the lesser one for the control of night. The cir cumstance that Marduk was in reality a personi fication of the sun necessarily hampered the Baby lonian priests in their endeavour to explain the existence of movements in the heavens. Under the sway of astral theology the moon, planets, and stars constituted the main occupants of the heavens, and, as a matter of fact, in the astrological texts of the Babylonian and Assyrian priests the moon and planets play a very much more important part than the sun, which is invariably, in any enumera tion, placed after the moon.[1] The Hebrew com pilers, freed from the shackles of astral conceptions of the universe, and assuming at the head of the uni verse a spiritual power superior to the sun and to the light of which the sun is regarded as a symbol, placed sun and moon precisely in the same cate gory. It may be that in the term "as signs" (verse 14), in connection with sun and moon, there is a trace of the observance of the heavenly bodies to obtain "omens," which would point to the influ- ence of the astral theology of Babylonia and As syria, but through the addition of "and for seasons, days and years" the calendrical purpose served by

---

[1] See Jastrow, *Religion Babyloniens und Assyriens*, II, p. 457. See a trace of the same order in Hebrew poetry; above, p. 112, note 2.

the sun and moon is emphasised—perhaps with in
tent to remove the possible implication of astrology
in the use of the two heavenly bodies as "signs."

The question has often been asked, Is there not a
strange inconsistency in the biblical story in assum
ing the creation of light at the very beginning of
time as the work of the first day, whereas the sun
is not called into being until the fourth day?   The
question, it seems to me, is an idle one and misses
the point of the biblical poem.   No doubt the com
pilers of Genesis knew as well as we do that the illu
mination of the earth is due to the sun; common ex
perience would have been sufficient to have made this
self-evident.   In describing the work of the fourth
day, the aim is rather to specify the position ac
corded to the sun in the regulation of material phe
nomena.   Standing under the influence of the popular tradition, which assumed the purpose of the
heavenly bodies to be the regulation of the calen
dar, the paragraphs about the moon are retained,
but consistent with the higher conception which
makes both sun and moon the products of the one
Power presiding over the universe, the older form of
the tradition is essentially modified.

The creation of animals follows, and it is inter
esting to note the order in creation: first, the life
in the waters and then the birds flying over the
earth across the expanse of the heavens.   There are
further specifications regarding these two classes of
animals, but the creation of land animals is not
mentioned until the work of the sixth day.   It is

doubtful whether in the mind of the compiler any special significance was attached to this division in the creation of animals or whether he laid any stress on the order—water animals, air animals, and land animals. So far no parallel to this order has been encountered in any of the Babylonian and Assyrian versions, though it is, of course, possible that one may yet be found. The order follows perhaps a logical sequence. Since water and the atmosphere above the waters are supposed to be in existence earlier than the land, the animals of the water and of the air are mentioned first. It is, how ever, of importance to note that among the life that swarms in the waters, "the great dragons" are sin gled out for special mention. The word used for dragons[1] is identical with the term occurring in the poetical allusions to the nature-myth of the con flict between Yahweh and the great primeval mon ster, pictured as a dragon and accompanied by an army of dragons.[2] The introduction of the term is hardly accidental, and I have no hesitation in recog nising in the specific mention of the "great dragons" as the creation of Yahweh, a further protest against the nature-myth which assumed the great dragons, including their leader Tiamat or Rahab or Levia than, as pre-existent. This is again, therefore, a deliberate effort to expunge the mythical element which we have seen to be one of the characteristic aims of the Creation version in the Priestly Code.

[1] *Tannīnīm*, plural of *tannīn*.   [2] Above, p. 109.

VII

So far, then, we have encountered plenty of traces of the existence among the Hebrews of the same nature-myth as is revealed in the various Baby lonian versions to account for the creation of the world, but with the unmistakable tendency in the biblical versions to remove the mythical aspects and to minimise this element of myth when it can not be entirely eliminated. The wide departure from Babylonian traditions is, however, particularly apparent in the spirit of the transformed Hebrew tradition which changes the Creator from a van quisher of hostile forces, and from an artificer after the fashion of a human workman, into a spiritual Power, acting by His 'Word' alone. The Word brings about light, the Word causes the dry land to appear and clothes the fields with verdure, the Word brings forth trees and plants, and fills water, air and land with living beings. This 'Word of Yahweh' is frequently introduced in the Prophets and Psalms to describe not merely the power but the very essence of the Deity, conceived as a uni versal Being and pictured as a spiritual force. To be sure, in Babylonian and Assyrian hymns the 'word' of Enlil, of Marduk, of Ea, of Shamash, and so through the list of the chief gods of the pan theon, also plays a prominent part. Compositions bewailing some great catastrophe that has overtaken the land describe the power residing in the word

of a god, which causes heaven and earth to tremble
and spreads terror on all sides:

> "The word that causes the heavens on high to tremble,
> The word that makes the earth below to quake,
> The word that brings destruction to the Anunnaki,[1]
> His word is beyond diviner and seer,
> His word is a tempest without a rival." [2]

The conception, however, remains on a material
istic basis, and when applied to other than storm-
gods whose 'word' is the thunder, it is the actual
strength and power of the god that is meant. We
have a trace of this conception of the word in po
etical metaphors occurring in Psalms such as the
twenty-ninth:

> "The voice of Yahweh is upon the waters,
> The God of glory thundereth.
>
> .   .   .   .   .   .
>
> The voice of Yahweh is full of power,
> The voice of Yahweh is full of might.
>
> .   .   .   .   .   .
>
> The voice of Yahweh hews flames of fire,
> The voice of Yahweh shakes the wilderness,"

but the higher point of view, marking the departure
from the Babylonian conception, finds an expression
in the scene of Elijah on the mount[3] where a strong
wind, a violent earthquake and fire passed before
the Prophet. Yahweh was not in the storm, or in
the earthquake, or in the fire, but manifested Him-

---

[1] Above, p. 91, note 1.
[2] See many other illustrations in Jastrow, *Religion Babyloniens und
Assyriens*, II, pp. 26 *seq.*, and Zimmern in *Der Alte Orient*, XIII, 1 pp.
21–27.
[3] I Kings 19 : 11–12.

self in the "still, small voice"—a decided contrast, therefore, to the "voice of Yahweh" in the Psalm from which we have quoted. The "thin, small voice" illustrates the endeavour to spiritualise the power of Yahweh, an endeavour that finds its full expression in the Word of the Deity as conceived by the Prophets, and of which the Word that creates the light, the heavenly bodies and the earth and all there is in it, is a direct reflection. The 'Word' of God in the development of Hebrew religious thought becomes more than a mere phrase or a metaphor; it shows a tendency to become *personified*, as though it had an independent being, though at the same time always identical with the divine Power Himself. When in the famous eighth chapter of the book of Proverbs, celebrating the power of wisdom, Wisdom is similarly personified (verse 23):

> "Yahweh acquired me [*i. e.*, Wisdom] at the beginning of his way, before his works of primeval days.
> I was set up from the very beginning of the earth when there were no deeps,[1]
> I was produced when there were no fountains,[2]
> I was in honor[3] before the mountains were settled,
> Before the hills I was produced,
> Before yet he had made the earth.
> When he established the heavens, I was there,
> When he fixed a circle around the face of the deep.[4]

. . . .

[1] *Tehomot*, the plural of *tehom*, originally the personification of the deep, as we have seen.

[2] The fountains of the deep which feed the streams and rivers. See the illustration, Fig. 1, in Schiaparelli's *Astronomy in the Old Testament*.

[3] Conjectural emendation of the Hebrew text, suggested by the parallelism.

[4] *Tehom*, as above.

When he gave a bound to the sea,
Beyond which its waters were not to pass;
When he appointed the foundations of the earth,
I was by him constantly,
His daily delight,
Rejoicing before him at all times,"

it is clear that wisdom is here used almost as a syno
nym for the divine 'Word,' which naturally is the
'word' of Wisdom. The description given of Crea
tion may be regarded as a poetical paraphrase of
the account of Creation in Genesis. It is based on
this account, and Wisdom thus associated with every
phase of the work of creation, existing even before
primeval chaos, is the spirit of God Himself "brood
ing over the waters," as well as the divine 'Word'
through which everything is created. The three
terms, God, Word, and Wisdom, are almost iden
tical. Word and Wisdom become theological con
cepts, endeavours to picture the workings of a Power
conceived entirely as a spiritual force. This per
sonification of wisdom as the companion of God in
the work of creation, the medium through which
the Divine transforms His desires into actions, is re
flected in the twenty-eighth chapter of Job[1] to
which a reference has already been made. After
describing the hopeless search of man for wisdom
—not to be found in the sea nor in the depths nor

[1] Above, p. 107. The chapter has no connection with the book of Job,
and is only loosely related to the problem with which the book deals.
It is an independent composition, a fragment perhaps of a larger dis
quisition on wisdom, closely allied to the eighth and ninth chapters of
Proverbs. We must, however, be grateful to the editor who inserted
the chapter on Job, and thus preserved for us one of the gems of ancient
Hebrew literature.

in the hidden recesses of the mountains to which man penetrates in search of gold and precious stones —the poet in a sublime height of rapture exclaims:

> "When he fixed a bound to the rain,
>   And a path for the flash of the thunder,
>   Then he saw and celebrated her.
>   He established and searched her out,
>   And said to man:
> 'Behold the fear of the Lord is Wisdom[1]
>   Removing from evil—Understanding.'"

Concomitant, therefore, with the minimising of myth in the development of Hebrew views of Creation, we have the process which leads to the personifica tion of the 'Word' of God—more specifically pic tured as 'Wisdom'—as the associate of the Deity in the work of creation. The further growth of this personification of the Word or of divine Wis dom leads to the famous doctrine of the *Logos* or 'Word' as set forth in the writings of Philo of Al exandria and which finds its reflection in the open ing words of the Gospel of John that so succinctly and admirably sum up the entire process of thought involved:

"In the beginning was the Word and the Word was with God and the Word was God."

A comparison with the chapter from Proverbs, from which we have quoted, shows the identity of the 'Word' and 'Wisdom,' for Wisdom (like the

---

[1] Evidently a paraphrase of Prov. 9 : 10:
"The fear of the Lord is the beginning of wisdom,
And the knowledge of the Holy—understanding."

'Word') was in the beginning; she was "with God" and, as we have seen, was not to be distin guished from God. God, Word, and Wisdom are three in one. We thus have, under the influence of the higher conception of divine government of the universe as voiced in the utterances of the Hebrew Prophets, the transformation of the 'Word' of power and strength—such as the 'word' of the Babylonian and Assyrian gods is, and as the 'Word' of Yahweh at an earlier stage of the Hebrew religion was—to the 'Word' of wisdom, the 'Word' that is 'Wisdom'; and along with this transformation the personification of the Word, suggested in the Genesis account of Creation and receiving its theo logical formula in John's definition of the *Logos.*

The minimising of myth—practically to the ex tent of a complete elimination—and the enthrone ment of the divine command, leading by a natural process to the personification of the 'Word' of God, are the two features in the account of the five days of Creation that suffice to show the wide and complete departure of Hebrew traditions from their Babylonian counterparts; and it will, I think, be admitted that the departure is of more significance than the fact of the common possession of a nature-myth with which both Hebrews and Babylonians started out and which is still apparent in the ac count in Genesis despite its complete transforma tion.

VIII

It is in the work of the sixth day, however, that the biblical narrative rises to its greatest height, in its account of the creation of man endowed from the very beginning with the spirit of the divine Creator. A greater contrast between the statement in the impressive Hebrew narrative of the creation of man in the image of God, as against the Baby lonian view of man's being created for the sake of the gods, to provide temples and worshippers for them, can hardly be imagined. The difference be tween the two points of view represents the wide gap between the materialistic conception of the gods as powers of nature, who by virtue of their power exercise control and who in return demand homage and tribute just as an earthly ruler does, as the means of securing favour and grace, and on the other hand the conception of a Power expressed in spiritual terms who is the ultimate source of all life and who gives to man his special place in nature by imbuing him with an element directly taken from the divine source of all life.

In the somewhat modified form given by Berosus of the creation of both man and animals through the mixture of the earth with the blood of the god Bel,[1] who had asked one of the gods to cut off his

---

[1] *I. e.*, as will be recalled, originally the god Enlil, of Nippur, whose traits are transferred to Marduk, who becomes the "Bel," or "lord," of the Babylonian pantheon.

head, there is, to be sure—as has been pointed out[1] —a suggestion of the thought that human life, as also animal life, contains the same essence as that attributed to the gods, but the suggestion stops with the very primitive notions associated with blood as the source of life. The Babylonians were unable to conceive of life, as manifested in man and in animals, without blood, and accordingly this con ception of blood as the essence of life was trans ferred to the gods.

In the second biblical version there is still a trace of the earlier materialism in the manner in which Yahweh Elohim is represented as taking the dust of the ground and breathing the breath of life into the nostrils, in consequence of which man became "a living soul." It is hardly open to question that in the narrative of the first chapter of Genesis all traces of any materialistic aspect have been *inten tionally* removed, or, as we ought rather to put it, the religious thought reflected in this chapter has advanced to such a point as instinctively to revolt against the merest suggestion of the divine Power of the universe working after the manner of man, just as the entire narrative endeavours to avoid any suggestion of an anthropomorphic conception of the Deity. It was not necessary for the com piler to specify or even to make perfectly clear to himself what he meant by the phrase "in the image of God," any more than it was necessary or perhaps possible definitely to indicate the thought

[1] Above, p. 85.

in mind in describing the spirit of Elohim as "brood
ing over the face of the waters." What he wishes
to bring out is the special position occupied by man
in the world and to account for man's wonderful
power in making nature subservient to him, in suc
cessfully combating the hostile elements of nature,
in rearing great civilisations—to account for his
achievements in art and literature, in government
and in thought. The aim of the compiler was to
explain all this through the infusion of the divine
spirit into man at the time of the creation of the
first human pair. 'The image of God" was chosen
as the most appropriate phrase to express the idea
that there was reflected in man the spirit of the
divine, just as the "Word" of God, or "Wisdom,"
came to be chosen as the term to convey a picture
of divine action.

To sum up, therefore: the biblical narratives of
Creation in both versions that have come down to
us reflect the advanced stage to which Hebrew
thought was brought through the rise of ethical
monotheism, and represent in consequence a wide
departure from Babylonian traditions, which even
in their most developed and latest form remain on
the level of nature-myths and are clogged through
the materialistic view taken of the powers of the
gods. The points of resemblance between the He
brew and the Babylonian traditions of Creation in
dicate that Hebrew thought at one time occupied the
same level as that on which Babylonian civilisation,
even at its climax, continued to stand. Accept-

ing these points of resemblance as indications that Hebrew and Babylonian traditions revert to a com mon source, and that through the direct contact between the two peoples at an early period even the shape taken by the tradition in Babylonia in fluenced in a considerable measure the Hebrew forms of the narrative, we are, it seems to me, by virtue of this admission, in a far better position to esti mate at its real and full value the sublime height to which particularly the biblical version in the first chapter of Genesis rises. To treat this version in cold, prosaic fashion as a quasi-scientific story of evolution is to close our eyes to its beauty as a poetic production and to the depths of religious and ethical thought which it reveals. I have no sympathy with the efforts to force the order of Creation in the biblical narrative into accord with the results and dicta of modern science. Such at tempts necessarily involve forcing the phraseology of the Hebrew original and reading views into the text for which there is no warrant; and even then the attempt fails. In my opinion, it is an injustice to the aim and spirit of the narrative to look at it from the point of view of modern science. It is a religious document, an ethical parable; and science is *not* religion. In its proper setting, the biblical narrative conveys a picture of a spiritual Power pre siding over the government of the universe—one that for poetic impressiveness and depth of religious thought maintains its unique place. We must look upon the narrative as an expression of the peculiar type of monotheism, saturated with ethical ideals, which resulted from the teachings of the Prophets. Our thought should be directed to the picture of the one great Power bringing the universe into being by His Word and placing in nature, as the crown ing point of Creation, man imbued with a portion of the same divine spirit. Viewed in this light, such questions as are sometimes raised as to the signifi cance of the six days of Creation appear trivial, and the attempt to convert the six days into periods trite. We ought to recognise once for all that the creation of the world in six days, or even six periods, rests on views that are not compatible with modern geology and biology, which start from entirely dif ferent points of view. The six days have no more real significance than the seven tablets which com prise the main Babylonian version of Creation. By adding to the six days the seventh as the day of rest, we obtain a complete correspondence in num bers between the Hebrew and the Babylonian nar rative, and we have plenty of evidence to show that Hebrews and Babylonians shared the view which gave to the number seven a sacred signifi cance.[1] It is, however, of importance to note that, in place of a seventh day corresponding to the sev enth tablet in the main Babylonian version, we have attached to the biblical narrative, as its symbol of the sacredness of the number seven, the institution of a day of rest, to be celebrated every seventh day,

---

[1] See Hehn, *Siebenzahl und Sabbat*, for many illustrations among both peoples.

and which constitutes one of the chief contributions of the Hebrews to the religious treasury of mankind. In the opening verses of the second chapter of Genesis this institution is directly carried back to the example set by the Deity in sanctifying the seventh day as one set apart from the balance of the week. The manifest purpose in thus attaching the Sabbath to the work of creation is to justify the importance that it acquired in the religious life of the Hebrews, more particularly in the postexilic period.

The significance of the Sabbath itself, and the reason why it rose to such importance, together with the consideration of a possible relationship to a corresponding Babylonian institution, will form the subject of our next chapter.

CHAPTER III

THE HEBREW AND THE BABYLONIAN SABBATH

I

AMONG the problems directly created through the discovery of the cuneiform records of Babylon and Assyria, one of the most important, and at the same time one of the most intricate, is the question whether the Babylonians had an institution that may be compared to the Sabbath of the Hebrews, which up to within a short time ago was regarded as an absolutely unique contribution of the He brews to the religious thought and the religious insti tutions of mankind. The problem began with the discovery of an equation in a cuneiform text[1] fur nishing in parallel columns synonyms or explana tions of certain terms as follows:

$$\hat{u}m \; n\hat{u}kh \; libbi = shabattum,$$

which, literally translated, would be

"Day of rest of the heart" = shabattum.

At first sight, this would seem to indicate beyond any possibility of doubt that the Babylonians rec-

[1] II Rawlinson, Pl. 32, Nr 1, 16 = *Cuneiform Texts from Babylonian Tablets, etc., in the British Museum*, Part XVIII, Pl. 23, 17 (K. 4397).

ognised a day of rest, and that they called this
day by a term which certainly suggested the He
brew Sabbath.   There was, to be sure, an element
of doubt as to the observance of a "day of rest"
in Babylonia or Assyria, owing to the fact that the
term shabattum, or Sabbath, had not been found
in any literary or religious text, but only on a tab
let of a purely lexicographical character, and that
numerous business documents of all periods showed
that at no time was the seventh day singled out
as one on which the ordinary activities of life were
interrupted.   Yet the force of this objection was
weakened by the consideration that the lexico
graphical tablet contained other terms, such as *um
bubbuli*, a designation for the end of the month;
um nubatti, explained as "a day of distress" which
had been found in religious and other texts, so that
it was a fair inference to assume that the term sha
battum belonged to the religious nomenclature of the
language.   In addition to this passage in the lexi
cographical tablet, a cuneiform text had also been
published,[1] from which it appeared that the seventh,
fourteenth, twenty-first, and twenty-eighth days of
the month had a peculiar significance.   To be sure,
the tablet showed that the nineteenth day had the
same character, and, furthermore, that certain pre
cautions against eating food cooked over a fire,
against riding in a chariot, against putting on fes
tive garments, and the like, were prescribed *merely*
for the king.   Little importance was at first at-

_____
[1] IV Rawlinson, 2d ed., Pl. 32–33.

tached to this limitation by scholars,[1] who were naturally carried away with astonishment upon finding even a partial parallel to the Hebrew Sab bath. It was assumed that, while in the text in question the special significance of the five days was limited to a particular month, namely, to one in tercalated after the sixth month, the restrictions would hold good for the same days in the other months of the year, the general designation of such days being in Babylonian terminology *umu limnu*, that is, "evil day" or "unlucky day."

Scientific research is full of illustrations of the danger of judging from appearances only. The comparison between the Babylonian shabattum and the Hebrew Sabbath turned out to be a most significant instance. As more religious texts from the great royal library of Nineveh were published, it was found that the term "day of rest of the heart" was of frequent occurrence and, curiously enough, appeared, not in connection with a day of cessation of labour, but in appeals to an angered deity to whom a penitent worshipper who had felt the severity of the divine wrath poured out his grief and voiced his hope for a return of divine grace. This hope was commonly expressed by the phrase "May thy heart be at rest; may thy liver be assuaged," heart and liver being the two organs in which, as we know, the Babylonians and Assyrians, and, indeed, the Hebrews and other ancient peo-

---

[1] See the first thorough discussion of the question by Lotz, *Quæstiones de Historia Sabbati* (Leipzig, 1883).

ples, at one time placed the seat of the intellect and
the seat of life, respectively.[1] It followed that the
"rest of the heart" meant the pacification of the
mind or spirit and that the "quieting of the liver"
was to all practical purposes a synonym; or, if any
actual differentiation between the two phrases was
intended, the resting of the heart would indicate
the change of a mental disposition from a disturbed
to a quiet, and therefore to a favourable state, and
the pacification of the liver to a calming of the emo
tions.   In this way the supposition that the Baby
lonians had a day of rest appeared to be completely
shattered.   The day of rest of the heart was sim
ply a technical term for a day of pacification, that
is to say, one on which it was hoped that the an
gered deity would cease from manifesting his dis
pleasure.

There remained, however, the term *shabattum*,
which certainly suggested a connection with the
Hebrew Sabbath.   In fact, the identity of the two
terms could hardly be denied, though there was a
slight variation of a grammatical nature, which need
not detain us here.   Suffice it to call attention to
the fact that we have in Hebrew, besides the term
shabbath, another term—*shabbathon*, which corre
sponds more closely to the Babylonian shabattum.
Shabbathon is ordinarily regarded as an intensive
form of the word for Sabbath, indicating a Sabbath
of special significance, but I venture to think that

---

[1] See the writer's article on "The Liver as the Seat of the Soul," in
Studies in the History of Religions Presented to C. H. Toy, pp. 143–168
(New York, 1912).

it is merely an adjectival formation having the force of "sabbatical" or "Sabbath-like." We shall have occasion to come back to this point later on. For a long time scholars continued to be puzzled by the Babylonian term, and the camps were divided be tween those who still clung to the thesis that the existence of the term pointed to a Sabbath insti tution among the Babylonians, and those who either proposed a different reading of the signs, such as shapattum,[1] or who believed that the resemblance was merely accidental.

Another lexicographical tablet published about nine years ago by Mr. T. G. Pinches[2] furnished a satisfactory solution to the difficulty. In a list giving the specific names attached to certain days of the month, such as the first, ninth, tenth, etc., it was found that the fifteenth day of the month was designated by this very term shabattum. The conclusion was obvious that among the Babylo nians, the term corresponding to Sabbath simply meant the period of full moon. From other sources

[1] Many of the cuneiform characters have this double value, either with a hard or a middle sound of the palatals, labials, or dentals, as e. g., uk or ug, pal or bal, ta or da, etc.

[2] Proc. Soc. Bibl. Archæology, 1904, pp. 51–56. Various days of the month were entered in this list with their special names, e. g., the ninth day as tilti; the tenth day as esherti; the nineteenth day as ibbu, "clear"; the twenty-fifth as arkhu Til(la), etc. We find also designations, as um bubbuli for the day of the disappearance of the moon at the end of the month; shulum for "unlucky day"; rimku and takiltu for "purification" days; isinnu, "festival"; akitu, "New Year's Day"; eshsheshu and um arkhi for the day of the new-moon. The purpose of the list, prepared as an exercise for the pupils of the temple school, evidently was to group together the technical terms connected with ritualistic and ceremonial observances for special days of the month—a kind of commentary to a religious calendar.

we knew that the underlying verb, *shabâtu*, was a synonym of *gamaru*, meaning "to complete." Shabattum was, therefore, a designation of the time when the moon reached its full or complete size, or, to put it more scientifically, when moon and sun were in opposition, and the full outlines of the moon were illuminated by the sun's rays. It was obviously the day marking the middle of the month that was described as an *um nukh libbi*. Now what significance had Babylonians and Assyrians attached to the period of full moon that made the middle of the month a day of pacification of divine anger? The answer to this question is furnished by the astrological literature of Babylonia and Assyria, which forms a large section of the tablets of the royal library of Nineveh. The serious study of these astrological texts did not begin until a few years ago, and at the present time forms one of the most active branches of Assyriology.[1]

It turns out that the Babylonians and Assyrians had three chief forms of divination, or, as we may put it, the priests developed three elaborate methods of determining what the gods, to whom all events were ascribed, had in mind and were proposing to carry out. The first and probably the oldest of these forms was divination through the inspection of the liver of a sacrificial animal, based on the theory that the liver was the seat of the

---

[1] See the survey of this literature in the author's *Religion Babyloniens und Assyriens*, II, pp. 415–457, and copious translations of astrological reports, and from the collections of astrological omens (moon, sun, the five planets and stars, and constellations), *ib.*, pp. 457–748.

soul, that is, of the mind and of the emotions com
bined, and that in the case of an animal devoted
to a deity and accepted by the latter, the liver of
the animal in question became, as it were, identical
with the liver or soul of the god, so that the care
ful inspection of the liver furnished a tangible means
of noting the disposition of the god. Strange and
even absurd as such a notion may appear to us,
the system not only continued its strong hold upon
the people of the Euphrates for thousands of years,
but passed on to other nations, to the Etruscans,
to the Greeks, and to the Romans, perhaps also
to Eastern nations, and survives among primitive
peoples to the present time.[1] Even Plato, the great
philosopher, was not prepared to throw this method
of divination aside entirely, and in describing it he
makes use of a metaphor which admirably describes
the fundamental principle of the system. In a pas
sage in one of his dialogues[2] he speaks of the liver
of the sacrificial animal as a mirror in which the
image of the gods is reflected. According to pecul
iar signs observed in the liver, the state and size
of the lobes, the formation of the gall-bladder and
the gall-ducts, the surface traces of which are par
ticularly striking in the case of the liver of a freshly
slaughtered sheep which was the common animal
of sacrifice in Babylon and Assyria, certain conclu
sions were drawn as to coming events, based on the

[1] See the author's paper on "The Liver as the Seat of the Soul,"
above referred to, p. 137, and also copious translations of liver-omens in
Jastrow, *Religion Babyloniens und Assyriens*, II, pp. 227–411, and pp.
214–219 for the spread of hepatoscopy to other nations.
[2] Timæus, § 71.

two chief principles of divination: (1) association of ideas, and (2) observation of events that actually followed shortly after the inspection of a liver for purposes of divination.

A second form of divination, more scientific in character and which was likewise developed into an elaborate system, consisted in observing the move ments of the heavens; while a third system was based upon observing peculiarities and signs in the young of animals and in infants, at the time of birth. In regard to this third system, it is sufficient for our purpose here to indicate that the underlying theory was a natural importance attached to de viations from the normal in the case of animals and infants, any unusual phenomenon portending by a natural association of ideas some unusual event that was being planned by the gods. The moment of birth was selected as significant because of the mys tery attaching to the appearance—so strange and so striking—of a young life issuing from another life.[1]

Of these three methods of divination, the second, through the observation of the movements of the heavenly bodies, is the most impressive,[2] and there

[1] For a full discussion of this third system, traces of its spread to other nations, and the part it played in giving rise to the belief in monsters, sent, as the name indicates, as "signs" to give warning of portending disaster, see the writer's monograph, *Babylonian-Assyrian Birth-Omens* (*Religionsgeschichtliche Versuche und Vorarbeiten*, ed. Dietrich und Wunsch, vol. XIV, No. 5). Copious specimens of Babylonian-Assyrian birth-omens, both official reports and extracts from the omen collec tions of the priests, will be found also in Jastrow, *Religion Babyloniens und Assyriens*, II, pp. 837–931.

[2] See, further, the chapter on "Astrology," in the author's *Aspects of Belief and Practice in Babylonia and Assyria*, pp. 207–264 (New York, 1911).

are good reasons why astrology should still retain
its hold among so many people, even among the
intelligent classes at the present time. The direct
influence of the sun and moon on human affairs
and on conditions existing on our planet were as ob
vious to ancient peoples as they are to us. An ag
ricultural community is dependent primarily upon
the sun. The phenomenon of vegetation through
the sun's rays, after the storms and rains of the
winter season have passed, is sufficiently mysteri
ous to have led to sun-worship everywhere through
out antiquity. To a people living in an earlier
stage of culture than that represented by tilling the
soil, the movements of the moon were of great im
portance. Its regular phases formed a means of
calculating time. Nomads living in southern climes
are guided in their wanderings, which during the
great portion of the year take place at night rather
than in the daytime, by the moon. As civilisation
advanced and observation became more exact, it
was noted that other bodies in the heavens change
their position in the course of the year. It was
natural, therefore, in addition to personifying the
sun and moon as gods, to regard the planets or
wandering stars likewise as deities; and if the planets
were gods there was no reason why all the other
stars should not also be looked upon as divine beings.
Naturally, a step of this kind was not taken until
the Babylonians had passed far beyond the primi
tive stage of culture; and we find, as a matter of
fact, that in its higher stages animism, by which

is meant the personification of the powers of na
ture, led the Babylonian and Assyrian priests to
place the entire sphere of divine activity in the
heavens.   In other words, there developed in the
course of time in the Euphrates Valley what may
be called an astral theology, which not only recog
nised the heavens as the seat of the activity of the
gods and goddesses, but which coloured the entire
religious thought and impressed itself on the cult.
Deities that were originally personifications of nat
ural powers which had nothing to do with the stars
were identified with heavenly bodies.   So, for ex
ample, the leading goddess of Babylonia, appear
ing under various names, chief of which were Nana
and Ishtar, and who was essentially a goddess of
vegetation, symbolising the power of the earth, was
identified with the planet Venus.   The god Marduk, the head of the Babylonian pantheon, origi
nally the personification of the sun, was identified
with the planet Jupiter, merely because Jupiter was
the most prominent of the planets and because the
sun itself had become associated with another god,
Shamash—a term which became generic for the sun
in general.   With the sun, moon, planets, stars, and
constellations thus identified as gods and goddesses,
a rational basis for astrology was obtained.   Ninib,
the old solar deity of Nippur who continued to hold
a rank next to Marduk, was associated with Saturn,
only some degrees less prominent in the heavens
than Jupiter.   Nebo, as the son of Marduk, was,
in consequence of this association, identified with

the smallest of the planets, Mercury; and Nergal, the sun-god of midsummer, bringing pestilence and death in its wake, was identified with the "un lucky" planet Mars. It will thus appear that three of the planets were originally sun deities, and no doubt this original character of Marduk, Ninib, and Nergal had something to do with their being pro jected on the heavens—smaller suns as it were by the side of the sun-god *par excellence*, Shamash.[1] By a further association of ideas, the movements of the heavens were explained as the activity of the gods preparing the events on earth. Hence the great importance of observing this heavenly activ ity as an absolutely certain means of finding out a little beforehand what was going to happen. Baby lonian-Assyrian astrology thus rested on a sup posed correspondence between heaven and earth, and by virtue of this basis was given a quasi-scien tific character which removed it from the sphere of pure caprice or of mere idle fancy. Astrology when it made its appearance reflected the science of the day and not, like hepatoscopy (*i. e.*, liver divination), the popular beliefs. This relatively higher character of divination through the heav enly bodies must be taken into account in explain ing the coalition of astrology and astronomy through the Middle Ages, and its persistence even to the present day, though it has now become a popular superstition without even quasi-scientific warrant.

[1] Saturn, in fact, is frequently designated in astrological texts as "the star of Shamash"—its satellite, so to speak. See Jastrow, *Aspects of Belief*, etc., p. 223.

The night-time being the period when the activ
ity of the gods in heaven could be observed, the
moon became by a natural process the most impor
tant factor in astrology, indicated by the fact that
in the enumeration of the gods, the moon-god, called
Sin, invariably takes precedence over the sun-god,
Shamash.

II

We need not stop here to discuss the details of
the astrological system unfolded by the Babylonian
priests, and which passing to the Greeks formed
the basis for mediæval astrology, as well as for such
phases of it as still survive to the present time.
Suffice it to say that here also the same funda
mental principles that hold good for other systems of
divination may be observed: the association of ideas
in connection with certain phenomena and the ob
servation of events that actually followed upon cer
tain combinations of heavenly bodies, or upon pe
culiar phenomena noticed in the moon or in one of
the planets. Now, in the observation of the moon
there were three periods to which special signifi
cance was attached: (a) the appearance of the new
moon or conjunction of moon and sun, (b) the op
position of the sun and moon, or full moon, and (c)
the disappearance of the moon for a few days at
the end of the month. These three periods marked
the transition from one stage to another, and it is
an observation to be noted in the case of religions
and religious rites everywhere, that periods of trans-

ition were imbued with special significance. So the transition in nature from winter to spring, from summer to winter, was a period fraught with special significance. It is not an accident, but a direct re sult of this importance attached to times of transi tion, that the chief festivals of all religions are coin cident with the time of transition of one season to another. In this way we have as the midwinter festival, the Saturnalia of the Romans, the Han- nukah festival of the Jews, the Yule-tide of the Teutons, and the Christmas week—all falling at the time of the winter solstice. Spring, summer, and harvest festivals are likewise coincident with holy days in practically all religions, though by a more or less arbitrary connection of the nature fes tivals with real or traditional events in the history of a people or in the life of the founders of the great historical religions—Judaism, Buddhism, Zo- roastrianism, Islamism, and Christianity—the origi nal character of these festivals becomes partially obscured through this superimposed layer. By the same process the "transition" periods in the life of the individual—birth, puberty, marriage, and death —become the occasion for official or unofficial ob servances and ceremonies[1] that have their modern representatives in baptism (or in some other rite of initiation such as circumcision), confirmation, the marriage ceremony, and the funeral rites of Judaism, Christianity, and Islamism.

---

[1] See Van Gennep, *Rites de Passage* (Paris, 1909), for copious illustra· tions of these customs among all peoples.

Periods of transition are naturally associated also with a certain element of uncertainty. Such a pe riod marked the end, as it were, of one era and the beginning of a new one. The coming of something new turns men's thought to the future—unknown and mysterious. One could never be certain what the future had in store, and there is in festivals celebrated at periods of transition an undercurrent of anxiety and uncertainty, often disguised under an artificial jollification, partly with the view of throwing off more sombre thoughts, and partly in the hope that the joy might become a symbol of what the future had in store.[1] In the case of the moon, it was natural that this element of uncer tainty would have a special force at the end of the month, when the moon entirely disappears. Myths represented this disappearance of the moon as the capture of the moon by hostile powers. The mo ment of reappearance could not be calculated by a people devoid of exact science, and when the re appearance was delayed, a feeling of terror ensued lest the moon might not be released. Great was the rejoicing when at last the thin edge of the new moon was seen—a rejoicing all the deeper if by some chance the heavens were obscured through clouds on the night of the expected reappearance, and the element of uncertainty thus increased. To this day travellers in the interior of Arabia tell us

[1] So the popular custom of masquerading in the fall (All Saints'), or in the spring (Purim among the Jews), both indulged in at transition periods, are survivals of the endeavour to deceive the evil spirits that are supposed to be particularly active and malevolent at these seasons.

of the joy, the shouting and dancing and clapping of hands with which the new moon is received by the nomadic Arabian tribes.[1] In the Jewish church, likewise, the appearance of the new moon is still observed as a solemn ceremony, accompanied by a special benediction on the reappearance of the orb of night.[2] The young moon increases in power every night, and the growth was naturally associated with increase, with prosperity, and with the favour able disposition of the gods until the full propor tions are reached, marked by an almost immediate transition to a period of waning strength and power. The middle of the month thus became a time only second in significance to the anxious days at the end of the month. The astrological texts and the official reports of the court astrologers are full of references to the exact time when the moon be comes full.[3] If this happened at the normal pe riod, the fourteenth or fifteenth day of the month, the portent was regarded as favourable. But if, through the lack of the exact method of calcula tion, the moon appeared to be full on the thirteenth or twelfth day, that is, too early, or if, as the ex pression in the omen texts reads, "the moon was de layed," and the opposition did not occur until the sixteenth day, the event was full of ominous signif icance. The time, therefore, when the moon had completed its growth was indeed a moment when

[1] See, e. g., Doughty, *Arabia Deserta*, I, p. 366; II, p. 305.
[2] Dembitz, *Jewish Service in Synagogue and Home*, p. 152.
[3] See the examples in Jastrow, *Religion Babyloniens und Assyriens*, II. pp. 466–482.

pacification of the deity was essential to the wel
fare of the people. In this sense the Babylonian
shabattum was "a day of rest of the heart," a day
when the gods were particularly implored to show
themselves merciful and favourable. The descrip
tion or explanation of the term shabattum, with
which we started out, thus characterises the day as
one which had "pacification" as its central theme,
and which expressed the hope that "rest of the
heart" of the gods might be its outcome. We can
well understand that special ceremonies were pre
scribed for the middle of the month, which empha
sised the hope that the opposition would appear
at the right time. If it came too early or too late,
there was all the more reason why the gods, thus
manifesting in an unmistakable manner their dis
pleasure, should be appealed to, that their heart
might be at rest and their liver assuaged—the
constant refrain in pacification hymns recited at a
time when from a national catastrophe, or from
some other disastrous occurrence, the conclusion was
drawn that some god had been offended, or that the
gods in general were angry. Attempts would then
naturally be made to pacify them.

Now it must be frankly admitted that up to the
present time we have not found any direct refer
ence to pacification ceremonies at the time of the
full-moon, but the significance attached in astrolog
ical texts to the period of opposition justifies us in
assuming that such ceremonies actually existed, and
it is significant that in the text to which I referred

at the beginning of this chapter, the fourteenth day appears among the days marked as evil or unlucky. The same is the case in another text at our dis posal, in which the lucky and unlucky days for the whole year are noted.[1] In all cases the middle of the month appears as unlucky or uncertain, because marking a period of transition. This phenomenon of lucky and unlucky days is common to other religions of antiquity, such as the Egyptian and the Roman,[2] where likewise we have elaborate lists indicating days that are favourable and days that are unfavourable, and I need only remind you of the fact that in the Roman calendar the ides (*i. e.,* the middle) of every month was an inauspicious occasion. "Beware the ides of March," says the soothsayer to Julius Cæsar. The historical annals of Assyrian rulers are likewise full of references to favourable and unfavourable days. If a corner stone was to be laid, or an important expedition planned, or any undertaking to be inaugurated, the kings tell us that through the *barû*-priests, as the diviners were called,[3] a favourable day for the en terprise was selected. Naturally, the middle of the month, or the shabattum, was not the only period marked as unfavourable. The second phase of the moon, or the seventh day, when the moon

---

[1] *V.* Rawlinson, Pl. 48–49.

[2] See, for the Egyptians, Wiedemann, *Religion of the Ancient Egyptians,* pp. 262 *seq.;* for the Romans, Wissowa, *Religion und Kultus der Romer,* pp. 365–376.

[3] *Bâru* means "seer," but in the sense of looking at something, "in specting" a liver, observing a phenomenon in the heavens, or noting a birth sign as a means of forecasting the future.

was half full, and the fourth phase, or the twenty-first day, the time of the last quarter, also marked transitions though not specially noted in the as trologers' reports.   In this way we can account for the fact that in the calendar for the intercalated sixth month[1] the first, seventh, fourteenth, and twenty-eighth days were all marked as *ume limnuti*, or "evil days," on which the king as the represent ative of the gods, and therefore closer to them, had to observe certain restrictions in order not to arouse their anger, and through ceremonies at the end of the day to insure their pacification.   This special position occupied by the kings is well known to us from customs found throughout antiquity. Mr. J. G. Frazer, in his admirable work on "The Early History of Kingship," furnishes numerous in stances of this divine or semi-divine character of the kings that hedges them in, because on the equable relations between the king and the gods the welfare of the entire community depended. Everywhere throughout antiquity the kings are therefore obliged to exercise special precautions so as not to arouse the displeasure or anger of the gods.   Taboos of all kinds were prescribed, some perpetual, to be observed at all times, others tem porary, limited to specific or to regular occasions. It was to the king that the gods stood in a pecul iar relation, as, on the other hand, the welfare of the individual, according to the ancient view, was closely bound up in that of the community.   The

---

[1] See above, p. 135.

omens and portents in the divination texts of Baby
lonia and Assyria therefore bear upon public wel
fare, on crops, on famine, on pestilence, on war,
victory, and defeat. A significant event happen
ing to an individual was supposed to be a sign of
importance for the whole community sent by the
gods as a warning to all, and not merely to the
individual to whom it happened. To be sure, there
was also room in the Babylonian religion for the
special needs and hopes of the individual, but in
general it may be said that the gods were supposed
to concern themselves with the people as a whole.
If an exception is made for the king and the mem
bers of the royal family, it was due to the peculiar
position held by the rulers in their official, rather
than in their individual, capacity.

Our investigation up to this point would seem
to show therefore that the Babylonians and As
syrians had a shabattum or Sabbath, which marked
the middle of the month as a period of impending
change from the full power of the moon to the be
ginning of the decrease, and which, as a period of
transition, was fraught with special significance, with
an element of uncertainty and dread, because the
moon was approaching the period of decline and
ultimate disappearance. It may be said that from
this point of view the entire second half of the
month should have been regarded as an anxious
period, during which it was particularly impor
tant to do nothing that might rouse the displeasure
of the gods; and this may well have been the case,

but the more specific time of transition had a spe
cial import. If the transition passed without any
unfavourable sign, there was a feeling of compara
tive reassurance that all would be well.

Furthermore, we may conclude that the restrict
ive rites ordained for the king at the middle of the
month are to be viewed as precautions. If he is
not to ride in his chariot, it is not because the four
teenth day was a day of rest from labour, but be
cause it was dangerous to show himself in public
on that day; and if he is not to eat meat cooked
by the fire, it is because the fire as a sacred element
should not be handled indiscriminately at a time
when it might become an element of danger to the
entire community. Similarly, if he is not to put
on festive garments or to proceed on an expedition
(as the text tells us), it is again because the day
was not a favourable one for a display of joy or
of power. The Babylonians and Assyrians felt
deeply that unless the gods co-operated no human
undertaking could be successful. With this result
we must rest content until further texts throw addi
tional light upon the Babylonian Sabbath.

III

Has this Babylonian shabattum any bearing on the
Sabbath institution of the Hebrews? To this ques
tion I believe an affirmative answer must be given,
although it will be found that here, also, the special
line of development of religious thought among the

Hebrews led to entirely original points of view, so that, despite certain elements of the Hebrew Sab bath which may be associated with the Babylonian shabattum, the Hebrew Sabbath is an expression of religious ideas and of a conception of divine gov ernment utterly distinct from that which we find in the religion of Babylonia and Assyria. Even those who are not disposed to accept any relation ship whatsoever between the Babylonian shabat tum and the Hebrew Sabbath must admit that the occurrence of a term in Babylonia that forms a practical equivalent to the designation of the He brew institution calls for an explanation, for the supposition of an accidental coincidence may be dismissed without further argument.

We have seen that the Babylonian shabattum stands in direct relation to the significance attached to the phases of the moon in astrology. In view of this, it is not without import that in the biblical books new-moon and Sabbath are frequently asso ciated with each other. When the child of the Shu-nammite woman[1] is taken sick the wife calls upon the husband to let her have one of the young men and one of the asses, in order that she may run to the "man of God." Her husband in astonishment answers: "Wherefore wilt thou go to him to-day? It is neither new-moon or sabbath"—a distinct implication of a close association between these two periods on which it must have been customary to consult "men of God," that is, diviners through

[1] II Kings 4 : 23.

whom an oracle might be secured or an answer to some question obtained.

In the prophetical books, likewise, we find new-moon and Sabbath closely associated. Isaiah,[1] in denouncing the bringing of offerings by those who regarded worship as giving them the privilege of doing shameful deeds, declares: "Bring no more vain oblations,—incense is an abomination unto me. New-moon and sabbath, calling an assembly—go, I cannot bear iniquity with solemn convocation." The Prophet Amos[2] in describing the greed of the people for gain represents them as saying: "When may the new moon be gone, that we may sell grain, and the sabbath, that we may open wheat?"

In addition we have at least one passage in one of the Pentateuchal Codes which appears to con tain as a survival the use of the word Sabbath as a designation for the middle of the month, precisely therefore as the Babylonian shabattum. In the twenty-third chapter of Leviticus, forming part of what is known as the Holiness Code, among the reg ulations for the so-called Feast of Weeks (*shebu'ôth*), it is stated that this feast begins on the fiftieth day after the beginning of the Passover festival. Now the Passover festival falls on the fifteenth day of Nisan, that is, the first month. When therefore it is said (vs. 15): "And you shall count from the morrow after the *sabbath* . . . seven complete sab-

---

[1] Isa. 1 : 13; *cf.* also 66 : 23.

[2] Amos 8 : 5. See also Hosea 2 : 13, and Ezek. 46 : 2. In the latter passage the ordinance reads that the inner eastern gate shall be open on the Sabbath and on the day of new-moon, but otherwise is to be closed.

baths shall there be," the simplest explanation for this passage, which has occasioned considerable diffi culty to commentators, is that the fifteenth day, or the middle of the month, is here actually desig nated by the term "sabbath." I cannot stop to consider this interesting passage in detail,[1] but it may be proper to point out that all the Penta- teuchal Codes show traces of considerable editing, and that every series of regulations can be analysed into older and later component parts. In the very passage in question the expression "the morrow after the Sabbath" belongs to an older stratum than the addition "seven sabbaths shalt thou complete," where the word Sabbath is clearly used in the very general sense of "week." In this transition in mean ing from the use of a term designating the middle of the month to the designation of a week of seven days[2] there lies, however, the whole history of the Hebrew institution. We are fortunately in a po sition to follow this history, at least along its main lines, though naturally when we try to reconstruct it from its beginnings we cannot expect to find more

---

[1] See the details in an article by the writer, "The Morrow After the Sabbath," in the *American Journal of Semitic Languages*, vol. XXIX, No. 3.

[2] We thus have no less than four distinct uses of the term *sabbath* in Hebrew: (1) the sacred occasion celebrated every seventh day, (2) "week," (3) middle of the month, (4) a designation of certain festival days as "Sabbath," namely, the first day of the harvest festival, i. e., the fifteenth day of the seventh month—a survival of the original appli cation of Sabbath to the full-moon, and by extension to the eighth day of the festival because celebrated in like manner as the first day (Lev. 23 : 39). It should be noted that the latter part of verse 39 in which "sabbath" is applied to the two festival days in question represents an addition to the verse.

than some traces of the time when ideas were asso
ciated with the Sabbath day of a totally different
character from those which mark the developed
institution.

Up to the present, then, we have encountered
among the Hebrews indications of a close associa
tion between the new-moon and the Sabbath, and
in the second place a survival, though a faint one,
of the application of the term to the middle of the
month, or, if that be not granted, at least an appli
cation different in character from the ordinary con
notation of the term. Proceeding a step further,
it can be shown that among the Hebrews, as among
the Babylonians (and, as we have seen, among prim
itive peoples of antiquity in general), transition pe
riods were fraught with religious significance. It
is surely no accident that the spring festival of the
Pentateuchal Codes, having originally an agricultural
character as marking the ripening of the wheat,[1]
and to which an historical import—the traditional
Exodus from Egypt—was attached, was celebrated,

---

[1] This is the *massoth*, or festival of "unleavened bread," *i. e.*, eating the
cakes made from the new crop of wheat—unleavened in nomadic fashion.
The Pesach, or Paschal festival, marked by the eating of a young lamb,
had nothing to do with the *massoth*, except for the fact that the spring
time is also the period when the lambs are born. In order to give to the
spring festival a Jewish significance, the "unleavened bread" was ex
plained as due to the haste with which the people were obliged to leave
Egypt without having the time to leaven the dough. Furthermore, by a
play on the word *pesach*, which means to "leap over," the term was ex
plained as a reminiscence of the special protection vouchsafed the He
brews on the night when the first-born in every Egyptian house was
stricken and the demon of disease "leaped over" (Ex. 12 : 13 and 23)
the houses of the Hebrews, frightened off by the sight of the blood of
the slaughtered lamb that had been sprinkled on the door-posts.

as we have just seen, at the middle of the month,
on the fifteenth day of the month—a shabattum
in the full Babylonian sense. The festival in the
fall, corresponding to the Passover in the spring
and celebrated at the time of the closing of the
harvest of the fruits, was likewise celebrated at
the middle of the month, on the fifteenth day of
Tishri, *i. e.*, the seventh month.[1] To this festival,
likewise, an historical significance was attached. It
was to serve as a reminder of the years of the wan
derings of the Hebrews in the wilderness. But it
is evident that the name of the festival, the Fes
tival of Booths,[2] is rather to be accounted for as
a survival of the perfectly natural custom of the
people actually to dwell in the fields during the
harvest days.

Now, harvest-times cannot be definitely fixed for
any specific day. The spring festival marking the
beginning of the ripening of the early wheat cannot
be narrowed down to a fixed day. A certain leeway
must be allowed according to the more or less fa
vourable weather conditions, and the same is the
case with the harvest festival in the fall. The se
lection of the fifteenth day is evidently directly as
sociated with the significance attached to the middle
of the month rather than based upon observation
that on this day the early and the late harvest ac
tually begins. The period of seven days prescribed
for both the Passover and the Festival of Booths
must, similarly, be directly connected with the third

---

[1] Lev. 23 : 34.   [2] In Hebrew, *Sukkoth.*

phase of the moon, the week of anxiety and uncer
tainty during which the moon is gradually waning
until the last quarter is reached. If this explanation
be adopted, we are further justified in concluding
that this period of the middle of the month had a
significance among the Hebrews, quite independent
of the particular association with the agricultural
conditions prevailing in the first and seventh months
of the year. We may go a step further. One of
the most solemn festivals in the Hebrew calendar,
which has retained this character even up to the pres
ent time among observant Jews, is the celebration
of the New Year on the first day of the seventh
month. It is generally assumed by scholars that
this festival was not actually instituted until after
the period of the exile, but there is every reason to
suppose that the day had a religious import of some
kind before the reconstruction of the Hebrew com
monwealth. The very fact that, as we know, the
Hebrews adopted the Babylonian calendar under
the influence of conditions existing in the exilic pe
riod, and that in this calendar the year begins in
the spring and not in the fall, is a proof of the
antiquity of the celebration of the first day of the
seventh month as one of special import. It may
well be that originally this day was celebrated as
the beginning of the late harvest month so that
there would be a direct association again between
the new-moon and the full-moon periods. We must
not, however, press this point too far, and for the
purpose of our argument it is sufficient to recog-

nise that the new-moon's day of this particular
month became a most solemn occasion. It may be
well to bear in mind also that the Hebrews, like
the Babylonians, waited anxiously each month for
the appearance of the first edge of the new-moon.
In the Talmudic treatise of Sanhedrin[1] we are told
in detail how each month the court sat in Jerusalem
waiting for messengers to announce that from some
eminence they had actually seen the new-moon with
their own eyes, and it was only upon the assurance
thus given by two eye-witnesses that the beginning
of the month was officially announced. Such a
survival from a period when time was calculated
through direct observation is a most important wit
ness of the significance at one time attached to the
appearance of the new-moon and which, incrusted in
tradition, survived far into the period when among
the Jews, as among other nations, astronomy had
reached a point which made it superfluous to wait
for eye-witnesses in order to ascertain the actual
beginning of the month. Up to the present time
in the orthodox Jewish ritual the new-moon is cel
ebrated as a half-holiday, and there is included in
the prayer-book a special prayer which is to be said
in salutation of the new-moon, and with the face
directed towards the orb of night.

The patient sufferer Job, in declaring his inno
cence and enumerating the things that he did not
do, says that he did not salute the moon "by throw
ing a kiss at it," [2] in allusion, evidently, to a cere-

[1] Talmud Babli, Sanhedrin, fol. 102; Rosh ha-Shana, II, 7.
[2] Job 31 : 27.

mony of greeting that must have been so common as to be at once understood despite the rather brief manner in which it is referred to. There is another Jewish festival, though of late origin, which is like wise celebrated in the middle of the month, the one known as Purim. We cannot stop to consider in detail this interesting festival, celebrated on the fourteenth day of Adar (the twelfth month), and which is described in the late biblical book of Esther.[1] Let me content myself by pointing out that preced ing the festival of the fifteenth, there is a fast pre scribed for the day before—a distinct indication again of the anxiety associated with the middle of the month, followed by a period of rejoicing that the crisis marked by the beginning of the waning

---

[1] See Professor Paul Haupt's paper on Purim in the *Beiträge zur Assyrio- logie*, vol. VI, No. 2, filled with a wealth of learning and marked by illumi nating discussions of mooted points, though I cannot agree with all of Haupt's deductions. Briefly put, Purim, as its foreign name indicates, is in reality a Persian spring festival, marked by ceremonies symbolical of the reappearance of the sun of spring-tide, which was adopted by the Jews, just as they adopted under Roman influences the midwinter festival of the Romans. To give the foreign festivals a Jewish colouring, events —real or traditional—were attached to them; the midwinter festival was made commemorative of the victory of the Maccabees in the year 160 B. C., while, to account for Purim, an elaborate story was told, in part based on actual events, how the Jews were saved from a dire de struction planned by a prime minister of the Persian king through the intervention of one of their own people, Mordecai. In commemoration of this escape the festival was instituted, while the fast was explained as an ordinance prescribed in anticipation of the destruction and in the hope of securing divine succour, which did not fail to come. The chief characters in the book of Esther—Mordecai and Esther—are purely ficti tious, the names being adaptations of the Babylonian deities, Marduk and Ishtar (regarded as the consort of the chief god), and some of the episodes in which these personages are introduced were suggested by a Babylonian nature-myth symbolising the triumph of Marduk as the spring-god in association with Ishtar as the goddess of vegetation, over the storms of the winter season—pictured as an evil counsellor planning havoc and destruction.

of the moon had been successfully passed without
any serious consequence.

Enough evidence, I believe, has now been brought
forward to show that transition periods, and more
particularly the first and the middle of the month,
had a special significance for the Hebrews, quite as
much as for the Babylonians. We should therefore
be prepared to find also some traces of the ideas
associated with lucky and with unlucky days. To
begin with the former, we have at least one inter
esting reference to a lucky day. In the first Book
of Samuel, chapter 25, in connection with the story
of David's relations to Nabal, David is represented
as sending his young men to Nabal, who was rich
in flocks, and with insolent assurance asking for a
present, because he and his young men allowed the
shepherds of Nabal to shear the sheep without
pouncing upon them. In sending his message,
David says (vs. 8): "Let the young men find favour
in thine eyes, for we have come on a good day
(*yom tob*)." From a mere allusion of this char
acter it might be hazardous to draw large infer
ences, but when we find that this expression, "good
day," is the one still in current use in the Jewish
church for every holiday or festival, it will be ad
mitted that the explanation of the term must be
sought in the significance of the particular day as
a good or lucky one.

As for unlucky days we may point to a custom,
still holding good in orthodox Judaism, according to
which marriages are not to be celebrated during the

seven weeks intervening between the Passover and the Festival of Weeks, with the exception of the thirty-third day. The name given to this thirty-third day, *lag beomer*,[1] that is, the thirty-third day of the "waving" period, shows that it is con nected with the counting of the seven weeks from the middle of the first month, when the first sheaf of wheat is "waved" as an offering to insure the happy completion of the spring harvest.[2] This whole period of seven weeks was looked upon as a time of uncertainty, when it was particularly im portant to exercise great precaution so as not to of fend the agricultural gods or spirits who preside over vegetation. In Frazer's *Golden Bough*[3] those who are interested can find numerous illustrations of the importance of propitiatory ceremonies to make the field spirits favourably disposed, more particularly during the ripening period. The prohibition of marriage during this period is merely a survival of other restrictions that must have been enforced during these weeks.[4]

[1] See the article under "Omer," in the *Jewish Encyclopedia*, for a brief account.

[2] See Lev. 23 : 11.

[3] Third ed., Part V, "Spirit of the Corn and of the Wild," especially chapters II, III, and V.

[4] There is always associated with marriage, both among primitive peo ples and in the advanced civilisations of antiquity, a feeling of fear lest the jealousy of evilly disposed demons be aroused to mar the joy of the occasion. Hence arise all sorts of precautions to avoid this hostility, in cluding the custom among the Greeks of the bridal pair exchanging clothes on the wedding-night, the bride masquerading as the husband and the husband as the bride in order to deceive or to confuse the evil demons. See Gruppe, *Griechische Mythologie und Religionsgeschichte*, p. 903, note 3.

IV

We are now prepared to take up the question whether in connection with the Sabbath institution we can actually find traces among the Hebrews of a Sabbath day regarded as an inauspicious or, let us say, as an austere occasion. To answer this question we must consider briefly the history of the institution itself. In a former chapter[1] I referred to the fact that the enactment of the Sabbath is directly attached, in the Priestly Code, to the work of creation. That circumstance is, as a matter of course, significant only as a proof of the sanctity that the Sabbath had in postexilic days acquired when the Priestly Code received its present form. In order to emphasise the sacred character of the day it is carried back to the beginning of time, and stamped as an institution to mark the termination of the divine work of creation. God Himself is repre sented as setting the example of rest on the seventh day. Certainly no higher authority could be given for the observance of the seventh day as a day of rest and cessation from all labours. Such is evi- dently the thought running in the mind of the compilers of the Priestly Code. In accord with this view we find in one version of the Decalogue (Ex. 20 : 11) the Sabbath specifically set down as an institution to commemorate the completion of the creation of the world. In this Decalogue, how-

[1] Above, pp. 132 *seq.*

ever, it is generally recognised that the original
form of the ordinance in regard to the Sabbath
read simply, "Remember the Sabbath day to keep
it holy," and that the succeeding verses represent
later additions, specifying the character of the sev
enth day as a day of cessation from all work, indi
cating in detail the inclusion in the ordinance of
all the members of the family, the household, the
cattle, and even the stranger within the gates.   As
for the reason assigned for the institution of the
seventh day, it is not without significance that in
the other Decalogue in Deut. 5 there is no refer
ence to creation.   The emphasis in this version
is likewise laid upon cessation from labour, with
the same specification of those who are to be in
cluded in the ordinance, with the addition, how
ever, of further details such as "thine ox, thine
ass," which incidentally furnish the proof that both
in Exodus and Deuteronomy the original law has
been amplified by later layers.[1]   In Deuteronomy,

---

[1] Such layers superimposed upon the original form of a law are char
acteristic of all the codes to be distinguished in the Pentateuch.   They
represent comments and decisions, explaining and illustrating the appli
cation of the laws.   The process which thus led to the steady amplifica
tion of the original ordinances is of the same order as we encounter in
the great compilation of Rabbinical Judaism known as the Talmud,
where a sharp division is made between two sections, (a) the "Mishnah"
furnishing the laws, and (b) the "Gemarah" giving the discussions and
decisions of the Rabbis upon each law.   Thus in the case of the Sabbath
law of the Decalogue, the question would naturally be asked, What is
meant by "keeping it holy"?   To this the reply is "cessation from all
labour."   Further questions would then be put, Does this include all
members of the family?   Answer—Yes.   How about the household out
side of the immediate family of the master of the house?   Yes, the house
hold, too, must rest from all labours.   The cattle also?   Yes.   Should it
include even a stranger, that is, one who does not belong to the tribe or

moreover, a further emphasis appears to be laid upon the inclusion of all the servants in the house hold. "Thy man servant, and thy maid servant," shall rest, and in connection with this the people are asked to remember that they were servants in the land of the Egyptians. The Sabbath thus be comes an institution in commemoration of the time of bondage and servitude in the traditional history of the people. Now the very existence of varying reasons for the origin of the Sabbath justifies us in instituting an independent investigation. I do not deny, as a matter of course, the significance of the view expressed in the Priestly Code that the idea of rest is sanctified by the Almighty Himself. That is a very exalted view, to be looked upon as the flowering of the Hebrew religion, an impressive ex pression of the spiritualistic content of the faith upon which the Prophets had stamped their relig ious ideals. But while paying our tribute to the religious value of the doctrine, we must neverthe less keep ourselves free in an historical investigation for other and possibly more accurate points of view. The emphasis laid in both Decalogues upon cessa tion from labour, and the inclusion in this ordinance of the members of the household and of the domes tic animals, forms a more definite point of departure for determining the real character of the Sabbath

community? Again the priests decided in the affirmative. For an il lustration of the complicated process resulting from this embodiment of the "Gemarah" with the "Mishnah" in the biblical laws, see an article by the writer, "An Analysis of Leviticus, Chaps. 13 and 14" (the so-called leprosy legislation), in the *Jewish Quarterly Review* (new series), vol. IV, No. 3.

from the moment when it became a distinctly Hebrew institution. Throughout the Pentateuchal Codes the conditions of life assumed are those pre vailing in agricultural communities. The laws are such as apply to agricultural communities prima rily. The ideal life implied in these codes is that of the head of a large household, the possessor of lands cultivated by himself and his servants, and from the produce of which he sustains himself and his family. Commerce is recognised but looked upon askance.[1] The simple life of the country is given the prefer ence over the display and luxury associated with cities. When labour is spoken of in these codes it is labour in the fields that is meant. The Sabbath thus becomes, in the mind of the compilers of the Pentateuchal Codes, a distinctly agricultural insti tution. As such it may be traced back to pre-exilic days, though we have plenty of evidence that the day was not observed in the earlier periods of He brew history with that strictness that characterised it in later times. The fundamental view for the pre-exilic period is well expressed in a phrase used in connection with the Sabbath "that one may

---

[1] This is illustrated by the prohibition against taking interest (Ex. 22 : 24) on loans—a primary condition of commercial activity, since commerce cannot be carried on without credit, and credit involves inter est. The ordinary translation of "usury" (i. e., excessive interest) for the Hebrew term used is incorrect. Ordinary interest is meant. To be sure, the law in its original form is limited to the fellow Hebrew ("to my people," as Ex. 22 : 24 puts it; and a subsequent comment or decision adds (Deut. 23 : 21), "You may take interest from the stranger," but this is a concession to later conditions when commercial activity had sup plemented the earlier agricultural stage. The anti-commercial spirit of the original legislation crops out in other passages.

refresh himself." [1] Evidently the original purpose was not to make the day one of hardship by re fraining from every form of physical exertion, but a day of recreation, a day when one could interrupt the labours of the week and gather fresh strength for the coming week. In other words, the Sabbath was a humane institution. But the evidences of laxity in the observance may also be regarded as a proof that this kind of a Sabbath remained to a large extent an ideal. We may question, in fact, whether in an agricultural community a *strict* ob servance of a cessation from all labour every sev enth day was feasible. During a part of the year work in the fields is of such importance that a day lost may prove a very serious disadvantage. We must not, however, press this point too far, and it may be granted that in a general way it became customary among the Hebrews to inter rupt the ordinary vocation during one day in the week.

Now, by the side of this humane purpose we find traces in other portions of the Codes of a more aus tere significance given to the Sabbath. When we are told, for example, that the people were forbid den to leave their houses on the Sabbath day,[2] not to kindle any fires,[3] and therefore not to eat any thing cooked on a fire,[4] it may, of course, be argued that such restrictions represent the endeavours of the postexilic period to project the strict regula tions back into early days. Such an argument

---

[1] Ex. 23 : 12.   [2] Ex. 16 : 29.   [3] Ex. 35 : 3.   [4] Ex. 16 : 23.

seems to me, however, to be forced, and if one reads the passages carefully in which these restrictions are specified, one gains the impression that they repre sent a genuine tradition and point to a survival of earlier ideas associated with the Sabbath. I am in clined to lay particular stress upon the reference to a prohibition of the use of fire, for the reason that fire among all nations was looked upon as a sacred element. There are abundant traces of this view in the Old Testament; witness the scene in the book of Exodus in which Yahweh Himself appears in the fire of the burning bush,[1] and the statement that the voice of Yahweh was heard out of the smoke and thunder and lightning of Mount Sinai.[2] Fire as a sacred element had to be used with precaution. The sons of Aaron suffer instant death because they brought a "strange fire" into the sanctuary,[3] a phrase which we would be at a loss to understand, unless it meant that the fire as a sacred element had not been kindled with the proper ceremonial.

If, therefore, the people are cautioned against using fire on a certain day, is it not a natural in ference that the day itself was unfavourable for such purposes? Again, it will certainly be admitted that the prohibition to leave one's house is hardly con sistent with an institution which interprets cessa tion from labour as a means of "refreshing oneself." Staying in the house all day would hardly be re garded as an essential condition to recreation. The precaution not to leave one's house is rather of the

---

[1] Ex. 3 : 4.   [2] Ex. 19 : 16–20.   [3] Lev. 10 : 1–2.

same order as the prohibition in the nineteenth
chapter of Exodus (vss. 12–13) in which the people
are cautioned not to approach the sacred mountain:
'Take heed to yourselves that you go not up into
the mount, or touch the border of it." In accordance
with this we are told that the people "removed and
stood afar off." If one is prohibited from actu
ally leaving one's dwelling, the natural inference is
that there is some danger lurking from which one
can protect one's self only by remaining within doors.
The incident of the wood-gatherer on the Sabbath
day (Num. 15 : 32–36), whose case is brought be
fore Moses, and who, by the decision of the latter,
is stoned, shows that the point of view is not cessa
tion from labour, in which case the statement that
"it was not clear what should be done to him"
(vs. 34) would be superfluous, but rather the danger
of the act on an inauspicious day. The point which
I wish to emphasise is that in such incidental refer
ences we may recognise the traces of an earlier
point of view associated with particular days, or
with a particular period when special precautions
had to be exercised so as not to arouse the wrath
of the deity by some act however innocent in itself.
Now, the Babylonian shabattum, as a day of paci
fication, was an occasion of this kind, and it is just
here where the connection may be recognised be
tween the Babylonian and the Hebrew Sabbath.

Another point of contact of the same general char
acter is the observance of the Sabbath every sev
enth day. The number seven plays a great role

among the Semites,[1] and may, no doubt, ultimately
be connected with the moon changing its phases
every seven days. It is because seven marks a pe
riod that the work of creation is described as being
accomplished in seven days, though we have seen
that, outside of this point of view, no special signifi
cance is to be attached to the enumeration of the
order of Creation in six divisions. But, on the
other hand, in the separation of the observance of
the Sabbath from the periods corresponding to the
four phases of the moon, which we have seen play
such a part in Babylonian and Assyrian astrology,
we have again an illustration of the wide departure
of the Hebrew religion from the course followed in
the development of religious thought and of relig
ious institutions among the Babylonians and As
syrians.   The Babylonian shabattum never changed
its character.   It remained for all times an *um nukh
libbi*—a day marking a transition in the monthly
course of the moon, on which special precautions
had to be observed, marked by rites intended to
appeal to the angered god or goddess in the hope
that it might become a "day of pacification," by
which was primarily meant the hope that the anx
ious transition period might take place at the nor
mal time.   This shabattum as an austere and som
bre occasion partakes more of a day of atonement,
such as is prescribed in the Priestly Code,[2] on which

[1] See Hehn, *Siebenzahl und Sabbat*, pp. 1–44, for illustrations among
Babylonians and Assyrians.

[2] Lev. 23 : 27–32.   This day of atonement, though not introduced till
the postexilic period as a distinctively Jewish festival, is based on an old

the people were ordered to castigate the flesh by abstaining from food and to implore the Deity for forgiveness of their sins,[1] that is, for a removal of the divine wrath. It is, perhaps not accidental that this Hebrew day of atonement, which, increasing in austerity, retains its severe and rather gloomy character to this day in the orthodox Jewish ritual, where it is designated as an "awful day" (*yom nora*)—a veritable *dies iræ*—should have been des ignated by a term *shabbathon*,[2] which forms a more complete parallel to the Babylonian shabattum than

institution, as the rite of sending a goat laden with the sins of the people into the wilderness (Lev. 16 : 10) sufficiently shows.

[1] Sin, according to the general Semitic point of view, manifests itself through some actual misfortune that has set in.

[2] Lev. 23 :32. The word *shabbathon* contains an old ending, *on*, which corresponds to the final *um* in *shabattum*. (The interchange from *m* to *n* is frequent in Semitic languages.) The ordinary translation of *shabbathon* by "sabbaths" is a mere guess, for the ending *on* does not designate a plural. To be sure, in the passage in question we find *shabbath* added to *shabbathon*, but I cannot help thinking that this is a sub sequent addition, or perhaps a gloss of some late editor, who, no longer understanding the original connotation of *shabbathon*, suggested an iden tification with *shabbath*. The gloss then crept into the text—as glosses in ancient manuscripts generally did—and we obtain the meaningless description of the 'day of atonement' as a *shabbath shabbathon*, which, as a makeshift, was interpreted as "sabbath of sabbaths," or as a "sabbath of rest," which is still more meaningless, since every Sabbath is a Sabbath of rest. The use of *shabbathon* by itself in verse 24 of the chapter for the first day of the seventh month, which, according to Ezekiel (45 : 20, following the reading of the Greek version), was a day of atonement, is a proof for the thesis here maintained. To be sure, the first, fifteenth, and twenty-second days of the seventh month, *i. e.*, the New Year's Day, the beginning, and end of the harvest festival, are also designated as *shabbathon* in this twenty-third chapter, which is composite in character; but these days are also of the nature of transition periods. The application of the term *shabbathon* to them points to the use that the term had acquired to designate an "austere" day, because of the association of this quality with the *shabattum* as the "full-moon" period. *Shabbathon* would thus have the force of a "sabbatical" day—a day having the character of a "Sabbath" in the original sense of a "transition" period.

the ordinary Hebrew expression *shabbath*. This He
brew *shabbathon* is thus a genuine counterpart to a
Babylonian *um nukh libbi*, whereas the Hebrew
Sabbath, steadily moving away from its earlier con
notation, assumed a totally different character, and
became one of the most significant contributions of
the Hebrews to the spiritual treasury of mankind.
Its separation from any association with the moon's
phases, to be celebrated every seventh day with
out reference to a lunar calendar, marked the com
plete departure from the character of the Babylo
nian shabattum. In no more effective way could
the new meaning that the day had acquired be em
phasised. With that separation from the moon's
phases the transition *motif* passed away to leave
only faint traces of the force it had once enjoyed
among the Hebrews in common with the Babylo
nians and Assyrians. The link uniting Hebrew and
Babylonian traditions was snapped, never to be
forged again.

To sum up, then, we have traces among the He
brews of lucky and unlucky days, of a significance
attached to periods of transition, of the importance
of the new-moon and of the full-moon, of the special
import connected with the number seven, of pre
cautions exercised on certain days which have left
their traces in some of the Sabbath regulations of
the Pentateuchal Codes. But, starting from this
common ground, the Hebrews developed an entirely
distinct institution which retained little except the
name in common with the Babylonian counterpart.

The Sabbath as a distinctively Hebrew rite starts
out as a humane institution with a view to secure for
the people recreation from the labours of the week,
and to offer an opportunity particularly for those in
a dependent position to "refresh themselves." This
Sabbath ordained for every seventh day without
reference to the phases of the moon, becomes an
entirely unique institution. The idea of resting
becomes a significant expression of the ethical view
of human life and of its relationship to the Divine
as implied in the utterances of the Hebrew Prophets.
The material conception of labour was given a spir
itual interpretation through the sanctification of
labour on the one hand, and the recognition, on the
other hand, of the obligations of the one who em
ploys labour. One day was to be set aside on which
all classes should be placed on a level of equality.
Even the animal subject entirely to the will of man
should enjoy a Sabbath. Nor should any distinc
tion be drawn between the citizen and the stranger.
All classes alike should have the benefit of a day
set apart from the other days of the week as sacred.

V

The question now arises at what period in
Hebrew history shall we place the line of demarca
tion leading by a further process to the distinc
tively Hebrew Sabbath? If, as I believe, the Deca
logue in its *original* form dates from the days of
Moses, the connotation of the day as "holy" marks

the first step.   It is not necessary, and perhaps not
justifiable, to assume that in the form given to the
fourth commandment by the traditional organiser
of the Hebrew tribes into a nation the Sabbath
was ordained as a day of rest.   To Moses, Yahweh
was still essentially the God of the Hebrews, the
old tribal deity who had become the special pro
tector of the new nation formed by the union of
the separate tribes, and who in return demanded
loyalty and obedience from his special charges; but
it is obviously with intent that the day is desig
nated in the Decalogue as "holy."   However much
more the term came to mean with the further de
velopment of the ethical ideals of the Prophets, it
certainly had when applied to a particular day at
all times a higher connotation than is involved in
designating a day as *limnu* or *tabu*, as "unlucky" or
"lucky."   The Babylonian shabattum was dreaded
as an "unlucky" day which it was hoped by ap
peals to an arbitrary deity to convert into a "lucky"
one.   The Yahweh of Moses, as the earlier Yahweh
of tribal days, could be angry, and, indeed, the Pentateuchal narratives of the times of Moses are full
of occasions when the national protector manifested
his displeasure; but he is not a deity whose humour
is dependent upon a particular season.   Yahweh
still manifests himself in thunder and lightning, and
in so far shows traces of His origin as a storm-god
dwelling on the top of the mountains whence the
storms come.   Even in late Psalms, where original
conceptions of Yahweh leave their traces in poet-

ical metaphors, Yahweh is represented as treading on the high mountains whose voice is heard in the thunder,[1] but Yahweh's anger is never aroused with out just cause. The advance in Moses' conception of a national deity over national or tribal gods of the groups closely allied to the Hebrews, like the Moabites whose national deity was Kemosh, or like the Ammonites whose special protector was called Milkom, consisted in representing Yahweh as ruling His people by laws of justice tinged with mercy. It is from this point of view that we must view the tradition which makes Moses the author of He brew legislation. Moses becomes in tradition a law-giver, and a portion of the Pentateuchal laws in their original form can indeed be traced back to his period [2] —because Yahweh rules according to law and not caprice. But a deity who thus mani fests himself, obedience to whom is set forth in

---

[1] See, e. g., Psalm 29—above p. 123.

[2] In saying this, let me not be misunderstood as assuming that we have these laws in their ancient form, or that Moses himself wrote down any laws or any portion of the Decalogue. For centuries laws, which after all represent merely established usage, must have been transmitted orally, as poetic utterances were so handed down from generation to genera tion. The Song of Deborah in Judges, chapter 5, bears all the earmarks of a contemporary production, and yet it could not have been written down for three or four centuries after the events that it celebrates. So in regard to those portions of the Pentateuchal Codes which are to be carried back to the Mosaic period merely because they fit in with con ditions that prevailed at the time, we must assume that they formed the basis of decisions, but that they were transmitted orally, and no doubt were subject to all kinds of minor modifications before being written down, and, even after they were committed to writing subject to constant amplifications, and to combination with later enactments. Moses is simply the great traditional figure that stands out at the beginning of Israel's national existence, just as the names of certain Prophets become typical for a later period.

statutes and ordinances based upon justice, is a holy
god—a god marked by attributes that separate him
from mere personifications of natural forces.   We
shall have occasion to see[1] that Babylonians as well
as Assyrians attributed ethical motives likewise to
some of their gods and goddesses, and that there
was indeed a striking development of the ethical con
ception of divine power among them, but that did
not hinder even gods like Shamash the sun-god,
who is primarily the god of justice in both Baby
lonia and Assyria, from being arbitrary in dispens
ing favours or in showing displeasure.   As we shall
have occasion to point out in further detail in a
subsequent chapter, the consciousness that the dei
ties were personifications of natural forces or of nat
ural phenomena never died out in Babylonia and
Assyria.   Despite the infusion of higher ideas into
the conception of Shamash, he remained the sun-
god—the personification of the great orb of light.
Yahweh, in becoming a "holy" god, was placed on
the highroad leading to the disassociation from the
personification of the storm as which he started out.
The process, however, must have been of gradual
and, on the whole, of slow growth for, as already
suggested, many passages in the Pentateuchal narra
tives, which bear all indications of having preserved
traditions in an early form (though not necessarily
in their original form), still reveal the conception
of Yahweh as a product of the animistic stage of
religion.   Another factor that led in the same di-

[1] Chapter V.

rection was the recognition of Yahweh as the only god of the people. The evidence is abundant that this was part of the work accomplished by Moses. The emphasis laid upon the unique relation of Yah weh to his people, though paralleled in a measure by the position of Kemosh among the Moabites, and of Milkom for the Ammonites, was yet peculiar in this respect, that Yahweh absolutely brooked no rival. Not even a consort was given to him, whereas the famous Moabite stone[1]—the most significant monument of Palestinian religious ideas prevailing in the ninth century B. C.—shows that Kemosh had a consort and was surrounded by a court of minor deities; and the same was, no doubt, the case among other Palestinian groups of tribes. The influence of the new teaching is to be seen when the Hebrews, dispossessing the Canaanitish settlers of Palestine proper, and adopting, with the transfer from the nomadic to the agricultural stage of life, the Baal cult of the Canaanites, convert Yahweh into a Canaanitish Baal.[2] The old storm-god takes on the traits of a solar deity presiding over agri culture, such as the local Baals everywhere were. It is against the rites connected with the Baal cult that leaders like Elijah and Elisha and the earlier Prophets protest as incompatible with Yahweh wor ship, but it is clear that the people as such were not only unconscious of any defection, but believed that they were doing honour to their national god

[1] See the article on the subject under "Moab," in Hastings's *Diction-ary of the Bible*, or in the *Encyclopædia Biblica*.
[2] See above, p. 29.

by giving him the attributes of Baal. With one deity gathering to himself the attributes of all other personifications of natural powers, the tendency in evitably sets in to disassociate Yahweh from any particular personification. A storm-god who is also a sun-god, who is a god presiding over fertility among men and animals, and who is furthermore a god of vegetation, who is a god of war, and who protects the boundaries of fields, who is a god of wisdom, giving laws to his people, and through whose oracles the future is divined—in short, a god who possesses all the qualities ordinarily distributed among the members of an extensive pantheon—is on the way to become the symbol of divine power in general, and is permanently removed from the conception of a mere personification of *some* phe nomenon of nature.

The transfer of the attributes of the Canaanitish Baals to Yahweh upon the conquest of Canaan by the Hebrews and their permanent advance to the agricultural stage of culture entails another conse quence that must have acted as a factor of no small import in leading, by a slow process of evolution, to a more spiritual conception of Yahweh. The tribal deity of the Hebrews or of some of the tribes that eventually formed part of the later confederation had his seat on the top of Mount Sinai. It mat ters little for our purposes whether Yahweh was originally the national deity of the Midianites,[1] and

---

[1] See Gressmann, *Mose und seine Zeit*, pp. 434 *seq.* This is also the view of Eduard Meyer, *Die Israeliten und ihre Nachbarstämme*, p. 67, and of Budde, *Religion of Israel to the Exile*, pp. 19 *seq.*

that some Hebrew tribes adopted him through their
affiliations with Midianites. The supposition has,
I believe, much in its favour; but, whatever our
attitude towards it may be, the important fact
about which there can be no dispute is that Mount
Sinai represents the original seat of Yahweh. Now,
already in the Song of Deborah,[1] the authentic
character of which as a contemporaneous document,
though not committed to writing for several centu
ries, at least, after the event that it celebrates, is
beyond dispute,[2] Yahweh is represented as coming
from Mount Seir in Edom, while at the same time his
seat on Mount Sinai is also referred to. What can
this mean except that Yahweh wanders with his
people from place to place? He comes from Sinai
to Mount Seir as he comes to Kadesh, where the
people settle for some time; and accordingly, when
the Hebrews came to Palestine proper, Yahweh's
central sanctuary is eventually placed on Mount
Zion, an ancient sacred centre with which Yah
weh originally had nothing to do.[3] The ark or box
containing some symbol of Yahweh's presence—
perhaps a sacred stone—is carried about from place
to place; and later tradition assumes that there
was also a portable sanctuary within which the box
was placed. The important feature in all these
traditions is that Yahweh actually leaves his origi
nal seat and makes his presence felt wherever his
people happen to be. This disassociation of a na
tional deity from any particular spot reaches its

[1] Judges 5 : 4-5.   [2] See above, p. 176, note 2.   [3] Above, p. 26.

climax in the identification of Yahweh with the
large number of local Baals of the Canaanites.
Each large centre as well as all the smaller ones
had a Baal, who was a local deity regarded as the
protector of the fields of the district.   With Yahweh
identified with every one of these local deities, the
conception of a deity confined to *one* locality neces
sarily disappears.   The Yahweh sanctuaries scat
tered throughout the country upon the complete
dispossession of the Canaanites through the He
brews, expressed more effectively than any mere for
mula could that Yahweh was not limited to any sin
gle locality, that he was no longer a local god, but
was to be found wherever his people had taken pos
session.   His jurisdiction was coextensive with the
geographical boundaries of Israel.   It was, indeed,
limited by these boundaries to such an extent that
David could complain that he had been driven out
of Yahweh's presence because forced by Saul to pass
over into the territory of the Philistines; but within
the political domain of Israel, Yahweh could be wor
shipped everywhere.   It thus turns out that the
assimilation of the Yahweh cult to the Baal cults
against which tradition makes Elijah and Elisha
voice their protest represents in reality an advance
in the conception of Yahweh, leading in the direc
tion of giving him a character different from both
national and local deities of other groups, inasmuch
as he is not localised in any particular centre.   From
this point of view, the later endeavour to centralise
the cult in the temple at Jerusalem, advocated by

the Deuteronomic Code and assumed by the later
ones, is really a step backward, inasmuch as it again
laid so strong an emphasis upon the presence of
Yahweh in *one* particular spot. Yet, for all that,
the instinct of Elijah and Elisha in opposing the
Baal rites was correct, for these rites were foreign
and their adoption by the Hebrews was due to the
popular belief that what past experience had shown
the Canaanites to be the proper method of secur
ing the favour of the local Baals and of the spirits
supposed to house in the fields must be continued
by the conquerors in order to insure for them also
the rich blessings of the soil. The rites, moreover,
involved symbols like the Asherah pole, the symbol
ical dedication of children by passing them through
the fire, and perhaps also child sacrifice before un
dertaking the building of a house or some other
enterprise, which were distasteful in the eyes of
purists, as well as foreign in origin; but in large
measure the delocalisation of Yahweh implied by
his leaving Mount Sinai to wander with his people,
and then to become identified with the local agri
cultural deities of the Canaanites, paved the way
for a more spiritual conception of Yahweh as a
deity not limited to any special place. The process
of thought involved does not *necessarily* lead to
monotheism, but it favours this issue, which was to
be brought about in due time.

A fourth feature of no less significance was the
emphasis laid upon imageless worship of Yahweh,
which we may likewise trace back to the days of

Moses, even though we find a symbol like that of the brazen serpent surviving to the days of Hezekiah.[1]   Appealing to the image of a serpent as a means of cure from serpent bites falls within the category of sympathetic magic,[2] of which there are many other traces among the Hebrews to a relatively late period; but the brazen serpent was, we may feel sure, never regarded as an image of Yahweh. The Books of Kings and the writings of the Prophets show us that, under the influence of the Canaanites and other groups in Palestine and surrounding dis tricts, the Hebrews had adopted the Asherah symbol[3] —a pole standing next to the altar—that images of Malik and of other deities were set up in and around Jerusalem;[4] but here, too, we may question whether the people, although they heaped upon Yahweh the attributes of all other gods, assumed that any of these symbols and images were pictures of Yahweh. At the most, we must conclude that Moses was not as successful in bringing about imageless worship as he was in imbuing the people with the view that Yahweh was the only god of the people, and that as such he concentrated within himself the powers and attributes of all others.   "Who is like unto thee, O Yahweh, among the gods?"[5]   Though perhaps slower in making itself felt, the influence of the doctrine, "Thou shalt not make any graven

[1] II Kings 18 : 4.

[2] See, for numerous illustrations of the various kinds of sympathetic magic, Frazer, *The Magic Art*, chapter 3 (London, 1911).

[3] Above, p. 31.   [4] See, *e. g.*, II Kings chapter 23.

[5] Ex. 15 : 11.

image,"[1] must nevertheless have worked as a leaven in raising the popular conception of Yahweh, and in leading them eventually to disassociate him from any specific personification of a natural force, in bringing about a spiritual conception of a divine protector which was to find its more complete ex pression in the utterances of the Prophets of the eighth and seventh centuries.

VI

We are not in a position to trace in detail the further development of the Sabbath institution from a shabattum to a day of recreation from the labours of the week, but for our purposes it is sufficient to recognise the line of demarcation signalled by the designation of the day as "holy." We may, per haps, go a step further and attribute to the period of Moses the institution of every seventh day as holy, though the original form of the text in both Decalogues merely specifies "the day of the Sab bath." Be that as it may be, the separation of the day from the phases of the moon would follow as a natural corollary from the conception of the day as "holy" —set aside by a god whose chief trait was likewise holiness.

The references that we have to the Sabbath in the Books of Kings would seem to indicate that up to the time of the exile the Sabbath had not yet

[1] Ex. 20 : 4; Deut. 5 : 8—so the original form of the commandment to which as usual a "Gemarah" in the form of decisions amplifying the "Mishnah" is attached.

assumed the character which we are accustomed to associate with it.   From passages above cited,[1] we must conclude, as pointed out, that there was still preserved in the mind of the people an association of the Sabbath with the new-moon.   The associa tion was due, no doubt, primarily to the force of tradition, and may have become a semiconscious one—a mere conventional usage; but a passage like II Kings 4 : 23, from the days of Jehoram the son of Ahab (c. 800 B. C.), indicating the custom of going to a "man of God," that is, to a diviner, on the Sabbath day, to secure an oracular answer to some question, is significant as a testimony that at the end of the ninth century the Sabbath had not yet acquired the character of a day of rest.   It had, however, become a "holy" day, albeit the popular idea of holiness still connected it with a favourable occasion for consulting the oracle.   On the other hand, assuming that the passage belongs to the au thentic portion of Amos, which I see no reason to question, Amos's complaint of the greed of the peo ple who cannot wait till the end of the Sabbath day in order to carry on barter and exchange,[2] and Jeremiah's vain appeal [3] to the people not to carry burdens into Jerusalem or out of Jerusalem, nor to do any work on the Sabbath day, shows that the Sabbath restriction against the ordinary pursuits of the week was already recognised, though the force of the argument is lessened somewhat by the juxta position in Amos of the Sabbath with the new-moon,

---

[1] See pp. 154 *seq.*   [2] Amos 8 : 5.   [3] Jer. 17 : 21–24.

for which a similar restraint must be assumed. The same applies to Isa. 1 : 13, where we again find this association with the new-moon, though the juxta position in the following verse of "new-moons and fixed festivals" is an indication that the phrase "new-moons and sabbaths" had become a purely conventional one, and can no longer be used to prove that in the actual cult the Sabbath was dependent upon the phases of the moon. Both passages—the one in Amos and the one in Isaiah—point to sacri fices as a prominent feature of the official observ ance of the Sabbath in the temple during the eighth century. All this leads us to the period of the Exile as the time when the Sabbath assumed its definite character as a sacred day of rest. The destruction of national independence, with its accompanying temporary extinction of national life, forms the crit ical juncture in the religious evolution of the He brews, leading definitely from Hebraism to Judaism. The period before the Exile may be designated as the preparation for Judaism, the Exile as Juda ism in the making, and the postexilic age as Judaism made and paving the way for Talmudical Judaism, on the one hand, and for Christianity on the other. It was during the Exile that the spirit manifested its fullest force which prompted writers imbued with the high ethical ideals and religious fervour of the Prophets to review the past history of the peo ple[1] from the point of view of relationship to a deity who was conceived as a spiritual Power of universal

---

[1] See above, pp. 45 *seq.*

scope, ruling by self-imposed laws of righteousness
and demanding obedience to ethical ideals as the
absolute condition of His favour and mercy.   The
popular myths and early traditions were interpreted
in the light of the teachings of the Prophets, as il
lustrations of the conception of a universal God en
throned in righteousness and holiness; and the legisla
tion likewise became saturated with the same spirit.
Not that the process was completed by the time of
the partial restoration of the Jewish state under the
benign Persian protectorate, for we must come down
at least a century further before the spirit created
by the Exile had spent its entire force to give way
to a new movement in which legalism gradually as
sumed stronger sway and threatened to check the
ethical idealism of the Prophets.   The so-called sec
ond Isaiah voices distinctly and unmistakably the
new spirit as applied to the Sabbath institution.
In a famous chapter[1] which attempts with impres
sive nicety to hold the balance between ceremonial
observance and the true religious spirit manifesting
itself in adherence to high ideals of conduct, he draws
a picture of the ideal Sabbath—the Sabbath de
manded by a deity conceived in terms of the purest
ethical monotheism.[2]   "If thou turn away thy foot
from the Sabbath (not) doing thy pleasure on my
holy day; and call the Sabbath a delight, the holy
of the Lord, honored; and shalt honor it by not
following thy wonted ways, nor finding thy own
pleasure, nor (merely) speaking words,[3] then wilt

[1] Chap. 58.   [2] Isa. 58 : 13-14.   [3] I. e., mere lip-service.

thou delight thyself in Yahweh; and I will cause
thee to ride upon the high places of the earth and
feed thee with the heritage of Jacob, thy father."
Here we have at last a Sabbath at once holy and hu
mane, a day set aside for higher spiritual purposes,
and marked by an interruption of the ordinary pur
suits of the week—a day not of restrictions but of
recreation, in which man is to "refresh himself,"
which should fill him with delight, bringing peace.
to his spirit and rest to his body. It is this Sab
bath that becomes the central institution of Juda
ism, and in this form it can only be accounted for
as the outcome and expression of the teachings of
the Prophets, superimposed on the older layer of
the "holy" day instituted by Moses. We search in
vain among the religions of antiquity for such a
day of rest and spiritual recreation. How far—how
infinitely far removed from the Babylonian shabattum or from the "lucky" and "unlucky" days that
play so important a role in all the religions of an
tiquity. It rises superior to the festivals that mark
transition periods in nature and which Judaism also
preserved, and stands far above the level of the
rites and customs set aside for transition epochs in
human life!

VII

The further development of the Hebrew Sabbath
presents two phases on which, in conclusion, we must
briefly touch. On the one hand, while the spiritual
conception of a day of rest was never lost sight of,

curiously enough the restrictive element connected with the older Sabbath, and of which we have found some traces in the Pentateuchal Codes,[1] is accentu ated as we approach the period when the religion of the Prophets develops into the elaborate regu lation of the minute details of life. For want of a better name we call this period that of Rabbinical or Talmudical Judaism because of the authority acquired by the Talmud, which is a vast compila tion of laws and of discussion on laws, and which represents the outcome of the activity of the Jew ish rabbis in the schools in Palestine and Babylonia, organised for the study of the laws of Judaism. It is an error to suppose that these rabbis, whose au thority was derived solely from the respect they en joyed as versed in the law, *imposed* the minute cere monies upon the people which are embodied in the Talmud. At first, no doubt, the strict observance of the Sabbath was felt as a hardship by the people, as is evident from Nehemiah's memoirs,[2] but when it had once become established, the sense of sacri fice gave way to a zeal to be as exact as possible. There seems to be no doubt that during the two centuries following upon Nehemiah, the tendency towards hedging themselves around with all kinds of restrictions developed among the people, and all that the rabbis did during the following centuries was to codify and regulate in a more precise form

[1] Above, p. 168.

[2] Neh. 13 : 15-22, speaks frankly of the difficulties he encountered in securing an observance of the Sabbath, which appears indeed at that time to have been one of the busy market days of the week.

ceremonies that in part represented ancient tradition and in part were regarded as logical consequences following upon certain premises. Restrictive regulations in regard to the Sabbath, based
upon incidental biblical references to the prohibi
tion to leave one's house or to kindle fire, led to a
strict observance of the letter, which finally had its
outcome in minutiæ that approached in their ex
treme the point of absurdity. It was found, as a
matter of fact, impossible to carry out in a literal
sense such a regulation as not to leave one's house,
which would actually prohibit one from walking in
the open air. By a species of casuistry it was as
sumed that two thousand paces might constitute the
limit of an average settlement, and one was there
fore permitted to walk this distance; but in order to
extend this limitation one might on the day before
the Sabbath place something—it might be a piece
of bread—at the end of two thousand paces, which
would make the limit a fictitious home, by means
of which subterfuge one could walk a distance of
four thousand paces. Another way of beating the
devil around the stump was to connect the separate
dwellings grouped around a common court—as was
customary in the Orient—by means of ropes unit
ing the spaces between the houses. Through this
device they would fictitiously constitute one dwell
ing. The prohibition of labour on the seventh day
was interpreted in the most literal sense, without
reference to its original import to interrupt the or
dinary pursuits for livelihood or for gain, and ex-

tended to carrying any burden whatsoever on the holy Sabbath. Advantage was once more taken of the phrase, "not to leave one's dwelling," to permit of the exception that *within* the house things might be carried, and in order to extend this concession again so as to enable you to carry a chair from your house to your neighbour's or even to carry your pocket handkerchief (which would come under the category of a "burden") outside of your house, the fictitious union of the houses of the court was once more resorted to. I have purposely introduced these illustrations to show the extreme to which the rabbis went in their desire faithfully to observe the letter of the prohibition against work on the seventh day, because such extremes bring out the contrast between what the Sabbath was intended to be in the minds of the later Prophets—a day of "refreshing oneself" and of spiritual recreation—and what it necessarily became through the unfortunate application of legal principles and deductions to what was intended to be interpreted in a humane and purely ethical spirit. For all this, although the Sabbath of Talmudical Judaism (like its natural successor many centuries afterwards, the Sabbath of English and American Puritanism) was inevitably to lead to the worship of the letter, yet we must be careful not to conclude from the elaborate discussions in the Talmud as to the precise manner in which detailed observances had to be carried out, that the spiritual influence of the Sabbath was lost upon its pious observers. While it must be admitted that the Sabbath as observed particularly by the Pharisees in the days of Jesus justified the taunt involved in the protest that "the Sabbath was made for man, not man for the Sabbath," yet such was the devotion of the people to what is ordinarily spoken of as "the yoke of the law,"[1] and of which the strict Sabbath observance is merely one of many illustrations, that the followers of Rabbinical Juda ism took the yoke willingly and cheerfully upon themselves; and during the Middle Ages, which for the Jews extended up to a much later period than for the rest of the civilised world, it was the attach ment to the law, even to the letter of the law, that proved an element of power and of spiritual strength. It is sufficient to point to Heine's charming poem[2] on the Sabbath to prove that even he, cynically in clined as he was, and moving far away from any attachment to the faith in which he was reared, felt and realised the religious power of the Sab bath institution which could, as by the touch of a magic wand, transform the cowed beggar of the week to a prince in dignity and majesty. The influence of the Hebrew Sabbath upon the religious world outside of the pale of Judaism is too obvious to require demonstration. While the "day of assem bly," as the Friday of each week is called in Islam- ism, does not partake primarily of the character of a day of rest, yet the institution was unquestion-

[1] See C. G. Montefiore's judicious remarks on this theme in his *Religion of the Ancient Hebrews*, pp. 503 *seq.*

[2] See Heine's *Sammtliche Werke*, ed. Elster, I, p. 433, entitled "Prin- zessin Sabbat."

ably suggested by the example of Judaism to Mo
hammed, who aimed to make the day one of spiri
tual recreation in the sense in which the Hebrew
Prophets understood it. Christianity, after waver
ing for some time,[1] settled upon "the Lord's Day"
—the day of the traditional resurrection—as the
day of rest, but the spirit of the day is identical
with that of the Hebrew Sabbath, and in the course
of its development it became subject to a similar
tendency, as already intimated, to exalt the letter
over the law. Even at the present time the same
struggle is going on within the Christian and the
Jewish churches between the observance of the spirit
and the adherence to the letter in connection with
the time-honoured institution.

The net result of our survey of a comparison be
tween the Babylonian shabattum and the Hebrew
Sabbath has been to furnish another illustration of
the main thought that I am endeavouring in this
investigation to bring out, to wit, how it came about
that Babylonians and Hebrews, starting out with
so much in common, should have ended by having
so little in common, and this despite a steady stream
of influence from the great civilisation unfolded in
the Euphrates Valley that affected the Hebrews
during the formative period when they were work
ing out their formulæ of religious faith and prac
tice. The Babylonian shabattum, like the Baby
lonian Creation myths, remained attached to the

---

[1] The early Christians observed the seventh day as an occasion of
solemn assembly and prayer.

forces of nature of which it was a symbol and an expression. The Hebrew Sabbath, cutting loose from its original connection with the phases of the moon, became a symbol of man's superior dignity, a reminder, by introducing a break in his regular worldly occupations, of his double nature—a com bination of the finite body with an infusion of a portion of the spirit of the Infinite Himself. Such an institution has in its developed form nothing but the name and the starting-point in common with the Babylonian counterpart. The Hebrew Sabbath by sanctifying a day set apart from the rest of the week sanctifies labour. It gives to labour a dignity that places it far above the merely material neces sity or the desire for material gain, and thus directs man to the path along which he is to proceed to reach his destined goal.

The historical view of the Hebrew Sabbath which I have tried to set before you, the spirit of which, we have seen, was transferred to the day that Chris tianity set aside as a day of rest, so far from tak ing away any of its significance enhances its char acter by enabling us to see the gradual infusion of the ideals and aspirations of the Prophets into old traditions and time-honoured observances. To em- phasise this position I cannot do better than quote from an admirable passage in one of your distin guished president's volumes:[1]

"So customs, forms of observance and worship

[1] Henry C. King (president of Oberlin College), *Reconstruction in Theology*, p. 159.

which Israel shared with other Semites are not forth
with under revelation set aside; they are retained
but regulated, purified, given new motives and teach
ings and so put on a different religious basis.   God
begins where the people are"—a happy phrase, in
deed, to describe the process that we can follow in
the unfolding of Hebrew traditions and of which
we shall have another illustration in a consideration
of Hebrew and Babylonian views of life after death.

CHAPTER IV

THE HEBREW AND BABYLONIAN VIEWS OF LIFE
AFTER DEATH

I

In approaching the subject of the views held by
the Hebrews and Babylonians regarding life after
death, we must take as our point of departure the
fact that the belief in the continuation of conscious
ness in some form after death comes naturally to
man at an early stage of his mental development.
In fact, the thought of a complete annihilation of
consciousness seems to be beyond the grasp of prim
itive man, just as it is beyond the intellectual reach
of a child who cannot imagine that life should
ever come to an absolute stop. Death is, of course,
recognised by people even in a primitive stage of
culture, but it is viewed as something that was in
troduced at some given time either by an accidental
circumstance, or through the influence of evil powers
hostile to man. Among all savages stories abound[1]

---

[1] See Frazer, *Belief in Immortality*, I, chapters II and III, in which the
savage conception of death is admirably set forth with a wealth of illus
tration of the myths about death, of which Frazer recognises several
distinct types. Frazer calls attention to the curious parallel between
savage conceptions of death and the modern biological view which claims
that death is not a physical but an economic necessity. See below, p.
199, note, for another curious parallel between primitive and modern
points of view.

of the way in which death came into the life of man. We have seen[1] that in the biblical story of the fall of man the purpose to account for death is likewise involved. The point in all these stories is that life as such is not *necessarily* terminated by death, which represents a stage of belief only a few degrees re moved from the impossibility of conceiving of a total extinction of life. But even death, as thus explained, does not in the mind of primitive man mean a loss of consciousness, which in some form or other is assumed to survive after life has left the body. The doubt on this subject does not set in until a much more advanced stage of thought. We have only the faintest indications of such a doubt in Babylonian literature, and as for the Hebrews a sceptical attitude towards the continuance of life after death does not set in until a very late period and possibly reflects the influence of Greek thought.

We find both Babylonians and Hebrews starting out with a general conception of some subterra nean cave or hollow in which all the dead without distinction are gathered. The name given to this place in Babylonian is Aralu, and it corresponds in every particular to the early Hebrew conception of "Sheol." The etymology of Aralu escapes us, but in all probability it merely connotes a large compartment or cave. Not without significance is the fact that the cave is located deep in the earth, for such a view points distinctly to burial as the first method of disposing of the dead among Sem-

---

[1] Above, pp. 53 *seq.*

ites; and in passing it may be remarked that we have no reason for believing, though the asser tion is often made, that the Sumerians, representing the non-Semitic stratum in Babylonian civilisation, burnt their dead.

The place where the dead are gathered forms, therefore, the secondary consideration, being due to the accident or circumstance of burial. The primary idea is that of a continuation of conscious ness somewhere and in some form after the spirit of life has fled. People in an early stage of thought are not given to much speculation regarding the na ture of this continued existence. They accept it, as already intimated, because they cannot conceive the contrary. But we find only weak attempts at picturing life after death in any definite form. Prim itive logic leads to the supposition that the dead are weak, unable to do much or indeed anything for themselves, and in general they are supposed to lie in Aralu in a state of languishing inactivity. To be sure, there is also another side to the picture, for primitive logic is marred—as is sometimes ad vanced logic—by a certain degree of vagueness and inconsistency. Life was naturally conceived as an active force, and the personification of this vital force leads to assigning to it a material shape. A force or power without shape represents again an idea beyond the intellectual grasp of primitive man, and accordingly, to give a single example, the strug gle of man against disease was pictured as a con test with some malevolent spirit which had entered

the body to battle with the spirit or power of life.
A cure meant success in driving or exorcising the
evil demon out of the body,[1] while death was the
triumph of the malicious spirit, which had suc
ceeded in taking the place of the spirit of life and
in driving the latter out of the body. In this way
there arose the idea of the disembodied spirit which
was supposed for a time at least to be hovering near
the body, trying in hopeless fashion to return to
its temporary abiding-place and becoming a source
of danger to the living because without control.
We have, therefore, in connection with the dead,
two ideas which it is difficult, from the modern
point of view to reconcile with one another: the
belief, on the one hand, that while consciousness
survives, the dead are weak and inactive, and, on
the other hand, that the spirit of life because dis
associated from the body is moving about some
where and constitutes an element of danger to the
living. No doubt the natural terror aroused by
death is responsible, in part at least, for this fear
of the dead. But however we may account for it,
in trying to make clear to ourselves the views held
by Babylonians and Hebrews at a certain stage of

[1] Medicinal remedies were at this stage of belief ill smelling drugs in
tended by their odour to force the demon to flee, much as we use pungent
liquids to drive away mosquitoes. The medicaments were reinforced
by incantation formulæ which likewise were supposed to have the power
of driving off the demon. This earliest phase of medicine, which looked
upon disease as due to invisible spirits, curiously enough suggests the
latest phase of medical research which assumes disease to be due, in so
many instances, to invisible germs that have planted themselves in the
body. Modern medicine is, likewise, largely an endeavour to cure the
disease by driving out the germ. (See above, p. 196, note.)

their development, we must bear in mind these two
aspects, the one leading to natural sympathy for
the helpless dead and to care for them with that
love which they inspire while living, the other to
devices for the purpose of protecting the living from
the spirits of the dead. Dreams in which the dead
appear to come back helped to maintain the belief
of an association of the spirit of life with the de
ceased. Nor did the fact that the spirit was not
ordinarily visible prevent this belief from retaining
its hold upon people, for it was a characteristic
trait of all spirits, whether malicious demons of
death or good demons that protect the living from
all manner of accidents and impending catastro
phes, to be under ordinary circumstances invisible,
or to have the power of making themselves invisible.

Of ancestor-worship, or, what amounts to the same
thing, of worship of the dead, we find scarcely any
traces in Babylonian or Assyrian literature, but that,
no doubt, is due to the comparatively late date of
the literary productions in which religious ideas are
introduced. The hymns and prayers, and even the
incantations and divination texts of Babylonia and
Assyria, reflect the stage of belief concomitant with
a fully developed pantheon, and, moreover, a pan
theon in which the chief gods who were originally
personifications of natural powers were identified
with heavenly bodies, with the planets and stars,
that led, as we have seen, to an elaborate astral-
theological system.[1] A trace, however, of ancestor-

[1] See above, p. 143.

worship is to be seen in the deification of kings, which we encounter at various periods in Babylo nian and Assyrian history, and in the faint dividing-line separating heroes of the past, like Gilgamesh, the chief figure of the Babylonian epic, from the gods. Gilgamesh, described as two-thirds divine and one-third human, is thus at once a deified an cestor and a divine power associated more partic ularly with the sun. At the root of this identifi cation of the spirit of the departed person with divine power of a higher or lower order lies the idea that life has various, aye, innumerable mani festations, but is in essence everywhere the same. Life in man, life in nature, the life in the trees, in the rivers, and even life in the invisible spirits, whether beneficent or malicious, was not differen tiated except in its manifestations. Life was power, and therefore the transition of the power mani festing itself in an individual to a manifestation of an invisible character after the individual had lost his power was looked upon as perfectly natural.

Here, again, we must be warned against seeking consistency in the application of the fundamental idea leading to deification of the dead. Analogy forms the chief element in early logic, but this an alogy does not go further than drawing distinctions between various degrees of the various manifesta tions of the power associated with life. The growth of a priestly organisation proceeding hand in hand with attempts at systematising the popular beliefs leads to a differentiation between higher powers, who become the gods of the organised pantheon, and the lower powers, who constitute the demons —beneficent or malevolent,—while the spirits of the dead occupy a place half-way between the powers of a higher and a lower order, with the tendency, however, that as the higher powers become limited to the chief figures in the pantheon, the spirits of the departed fall to a lower level and are chiefly asso ciated with the malevolent demons from which the living must seek protection. In the case of the Babylonian and Assyrian religion analogy results also in providing a special pantheon for the dead, corresponding to the sharp distinction naturally drawn between the dead and the living. The gods who represented the personification of the powers of nature prior to the stage when these powers were identified with astral phenomena are of importance to the living because the living stand in need of them. Happiness, prosperity, success in this world cannot be achieved without the assistance of the gods from whom in a very literal sense all blessings were supposed to flow. Prayers and sacrifices and divination rites, as well as incantation formulæ, were all means of making the gods favourably disposed towards human undertakings, or they served at least as aids towards ascertaining their disposition at any particular juncture. The dead in Aralu do not praise the gods because there is nothing that the gods can do for them. They are not, indeed, beyond human needs, for the argument from an alogy leads to the belief that the dead require food and drink, but they were beyond needs that could be supplied by the gods, whose concern was exclusively with the living. On the other hand, in addition to food and drink which had to be supplied to them by the living, they required protection against the malicious demons who hovered in the lower world as they infested the upper world, and for this purpose the dead were placed under the supervision and control of a special series of gods who were associated with the great cavern that lay in the earth. In this respect the Babylonian religion did not differ from what we find among the Greeks, who likewise had two classes of deities— deities for the living, the gods gathered together on Mount Olympus, and the gods housed in the lower world, the so-called chthonic deities. But while these chthonic deities were originally identified with serpents and other animals that dwelt underground, among both Greeks and Babylonians they became the counterparts of the gods who ruled the surface of the earth and to whom the living stood in close relations.

By a natural association of ideas the ruler of Aralu was pictured as a goddess. The force of analogy that led to picturing the power of vegetation, the life-giving power of the earth, as a great mother, gracious and merciful and full of love and sympathy, brought about as a counterpart a wicked stepmother, known as Ereshkigal ("Ruler of the Great Place"), who acted as a prison keeper whose function it was to keep the dead safely in Aralu and to prevent any possible escape to the upper world. In time a somewhat more lenient aspect was given to this grim goddess, who also saw to it that the dead were left undisturbed in their resting-place; but this modification of an earlier conception did not go very far, and, on the whole, Ereshkigal retained her character as gloomy, ill-tempered, easily aroused to anger—in short, a stern guardian of the lower world.

II

There is a curious story[1] among the Babylonian myths of the way in which Ereshkigal was forced to submit to the rule of a male consort, the god Nergal. It is related that on one occasion the gods assembled together for a feast. Ereshkigal, though invited, declined to come, and sent her messenger, Namtar, the demon or god of pestilence, to present her excuses. Namtar was received with due con sideration by the gods, with the exception of the grim warrior among the gods, the god of disease and death, Nergal, who refused to stand up when Nam tar entered the assembly. The messenger reports this insult to his mistress, whose fury is described as beyond all bounds. Nergal, however, undis mayed, makes his way to the nether world and de mands admission to an interview with Ereshkigal. "Let him enter," says the goddess to the gatekeeper,

---

[1] See the English translation by the writer, in his *Religion of Babylonia and Assyria*, pp. 584 *seq.*, and a more recent German translation by Ungnad, in Gressmann's *Altorientalische Texte und Bilder*, pp. 69-70.

Namtar, "so that I may kill him." Nergal and Ereshkigal meet in a deadly encounter, which is described in most vivid terms. Ereshkigal shrieks and fumes, but Nergal clutches her hair and drags her forcibly from her throne, and is about to chop off her head when the goddess yields and appeals to Nergal. "Be my consort," she says to him, "and I will be your wife. The control of the lower world I will place in thy hands, and to thee I will give the tablet of wisdom. Thou shalt be the master and I the mistress." It is hardly to be expected that the union begun in such a manner could have been a particularly cheerful one, certainly not for the dead, who were now under the control of two masters vying with each other in grimness and severity.

The purpose of the myth is manifestly to account for the existence of the double tradition, an older one which pictured the goddess as the ruler of the nether world, and a later one which made Nergal, originally the sun-god, associated more particularly with the sun of midsummer that brings suffering and pestilence in its wake, a natural symbol of the grim power that carried the living to Aralu.

The differentiation between good and evil spirits led, in the course of time, to an association of the demons of disease and misfortunes of all kinds with Nergal and Ereshkigal. These demons, whose very names suggest the terror that they inspired, were known by such epithets as "Burning Fire," "The One Who Lies in Wait," "Wasting Disease," "Distress," and the like. They became the court gathered around Nergal and his queen, and served more particularly as keepers of the seven gates which shut in the gathering-place of the dead, and as messengers sent upon the earth to do the bidding of the divine Power. The views thus developed by the Babylo nians and transmitted to the Assyrians regarding Aralu and the fate of the dead became gloomier and more depressing as time went on. Far better, one might suppose, would it be for the dead to be deprived of all consciousness rather than endure the tortures of eternal inactivity and comparative neglect in a great prison from which there was no possible escape. The sad condition of the dead is well portrayed in another Babylonian myth well known, no doubt, to many of you, and which I need therefore only sketch in rapid outline.[1]

The goddess Ishtar, the great mother-goddess who brings about vegetation on earth, the loving mother of mankind, who provides for the perpe tuity of the human race, is represented as paying a visit to Aralu. The poem begins by a description of "The Land of No Return," as it is called, to which Ishtar, here introduced as the daughter of the moon-god Sin, directs her steps. The land is de scribed as "a dwelling of darkness," known as Ir- kallu, a great palace which one enters but from which one never comes out. The way leading to it is a road from which no traveller returns. The in habitants of the great dark palace sit in dense dark-

---

[1] Frequently translated, *e. g.*, by the writer, in the *Religion of Babylonia and Assyria*, pp. 565–573, recently by Ungnad, in Gressmann's *Altorien- talische Texte und Bilder*, pp. 65–69.

ness, never seeing a glimmer of light, "with earth as their nourishment, and clay as their food." They are pictured as clothed with wings like birds. Ishtar upon entering this region seems to take on some of the characteristics of Ereshkigal, for in threatening language she demands admission of the gate keeper. "Open the gate, that I may step in. If thou openest not the gate nor permittest me to step in, I will smash the door, break the lock, destroy the threshold, remove the gates and carry the dead back to eat and to live, till the dead are more numerous than the living."

The gatekeeper yields, and Ishtar passes from one gate to the other. At each gate the goddess is obliged to give up some ornament or part of her raiment—her tiara, her earrings, her necklace, the ornaments upon her breast, the girdle around her loins, the spangles around her feet, and, finally, the cloth around her body, until, when the seventh gate is passed, she enters naked into the presence of Ereshkigal. The latter makes Ishtar a prisoner in her palace, who is thus forced to share the fate of the dead.

The story itself is a simple nature-myth such as we find among many peoples, symbolising the gradual decay of nature as the winter season approaches. The months of storm and rain, when desolation appears to hold sway, is the time when Ishtar is kept as a prisoner by her grim sister. Accordingly, we are told in this poem itself that after Ishtar had passed down to "The Land of No Return" all fertility ceased— "The bull does not mount the cow, the ass bends not over the she-ass, man does not bend over his wife." [1] The gods put on mourning robes and lament the disappearance of Ishtar. Shamash weeps and appeals to the moon-god Sin. Ea, the god of humanity, takes pity on the state of affairs and creates a being whose name, Asushu-namir, signifying "His Exit is Brilliant," clearly reveals his nature. Asushu-namir is sent to "The Land of No Return" to open the seven gates and to secure the release of Ishtar. Ereshkigal is represented as full of fury at the demand to give up her prisoner, but she is forced to yield. She gives the order to sprinkle Ishtar with the water of life and to take her away. Ishtar passes through the seven gates, at each of which the ornament which has been taken from her is returned, until, when she steps into the light and the sunshine, she reappears in all her splendour and glory. The season of desolation is followed by the release of the earth from the ban laid upon it. With the coming of spring nature revives and becomes increasingly beautiful, until, with the approach of summer, she recovers her full power. The story, however, in its application to the human prisoners of Aralu, emphasises the sad conclusion that for them there is no return. The goddess may be released, but the dead are condemned to an eternal sojourn in the land of darkness.

---

[1] A reference, perhaps, to the existence of a pairing season among mankind as among animals, for which Westermarck, *The History of Human Marriage*, chapter II, finds other evidence.

III

With such views of the great gathering-place of the dead, variously designated in the religious lit erature as a great city or a great palace, the thought of death was naturally bound up with sad reflec tions and inspired terror, a terror that was com municated even to the great heroes of the distant past, whom tradition had closely associated with the gods themselves. I have several times referred to a hero, Gilgamesh, whose exploits are woven into an elaborate tale, covering twelve tablets, that has been properly designated as the national epic of the Babylonians. The story is of a composite character, into which a large number of incidents have been introduced which originally had nothing to do with the hero,[1] who, so far as we can ascertain from the material at our disposal, was a ruler and conqueror who came from Elam, to the east of the Euphrates Valley, and who established his rule in Uruk as a centre. As happens everywhere with the growth of legend, twining itself around a real or a fictitious character, the attributes and achievements of minor heroes are attached to the popular idol. Gilga mesh is thus brought into direct association with a figure, Engidu, who embodies probably a tradition of the first man and of the early condition of man on earth.[2] He is represented as seeking out the

[1] See the analysis in the author's *Religion of Babylonia and Assyria*, chapter XXIII, or in Gressmann-Ungnad, *Das Gilgameschepos*, pp. 82 *seq.*

[2] See an article by the writer, "Adam and Eve in Babylonian Litera ture," in the *American Journal of Semitic Languages*, vol. XV, pp. 193-214.

hero of the great Deluge who alone escaped from a general destruction of mankind, merely so as to offer an opportunity to introduce the story of the great catastrophe which had lingered in the minds of men. Through this same process of assimila tion Gilgamesh also becomes the medium for trans mitting the solutions of the theologians and priests in regard to the mysteries of the universe. The Gilgamesh epic in this way comes to reflect the religious thought of Babylonia and Assyria as well as the old myths and the faint historical traditions of the past. Through one of the incidents in the epic we obtain a further view of the conceptions associated with Aralu, as well as the more advanced thought in regard to life and the position of man in nature.

Engidu, the friend and companion of Gilgamesh, perishes through the wiles of the goddess Ishtar. Gilgamesh does not know whither his friend has gone. The story intimates that death is a mys tery which mortal man is hopelessly trying to solve. The hero himself is smitten with disease, and is afraid that the same fate which overtook Engidu will seize him. In this episode the nature-myth, symbolising the change from the summer to the win ter season, is woven around the character of the hero god to whom, as affiliated with the sun-god, the same story of decline of power can be applied as to the goddess Ishtar.

In a pathetic manner Gilgamesh is represented as wandering from place to place in search of some means of escaping the fate in store for him. His disease increases and his strength is waning. He comes to the maiden Sabitu, who dwells at the seashore, and asks her how he can find immortal life. The maiden urges him to give up the search. "Why dost thou wander from place to place? The life which thou seekest thou wilt not find. When the gods created man they fixed death for mankind. Life they kept in their own hands."

Here is the gist of the Babylonian teachings in regard to the fate of the living. The last word of the theology of the priests strikes the sad note that man must give up the search for immortality. Life is under the control of the gods. At their pleasure they send the spirit of life to man, and when they will it the spirit departs, never to enter the body again. The ethical lesson drawn from this belief is embodied in the further advice given by Sabitu to Gilgamesh to enjoy himself as long as life lasts, to eat, drink, and be merry, to live with the wife of his bosom, and to keep his head anointed with oil and his garments pure. We will have occasion to take up this advice in the next chapter. Here I wish to point out the import of the teaching that death cannot be avoided. We are long past the primitive thought that death was introduced at a particular juncture in the career of humanity; it is a necessity, a dire law of nature decreed by the gods themselves. This episode of Gilgamesh is re corded in the last and twelfth tablet of the epic, a position which indicates that it represents a supplement to the story and belongs therefore to a later period of literary composition. Herein its impor tance lies, that we have embodied in the most im portant literary product of Babylonia and Assyria, as the final summary of the exploits of a great hero, the thought that he, too, like every other mortal, must face death and wend his way to the eternal prison-house. But Gilgamesh desires at least to know the condition of the dead. He feels that it will be a comfort to him and enable him to meet death with resignation if, at least, he knows what is in store for him, in what form consciousness after the spirit of life has fled will survive. He appeals from one god to another for this information, but the gods decline to give the answer to his quest. Finally he comes to Ea, the friend and protector of mankind, who, taking pity on Gilgamesh, orders Nergal to permit the spirit of Engidu to rise up from a hole in the ground.[1] Engidu appears, and as Gilgamesh recognises his friend he is filled with hope.

"Tell me, dear friend, tell me the law of the earth which thou hast experienced, tell me." But the sad answer comes back: "I cannot tell thee, my friend, I cannot tell thee. If I were to tell thee the law of the earth which I have experienced, you would sit down and weep the whole day."

The moral lies on the surface. Man must not think too much of death. He must avoid speculat-

---

[1] The scene forms a close parallel to the rising up of the spirit of Sam uel before Saul at the behest of the sorceress of Endor, described in I Sam. 28 : 7–19.

ing on the fate in store for him and turn his thoughts
to this world rather than to the next. Gilgamesh,
however, persists and implores his friend, even at
the risk that certain knowledge of the fate in store
will cause him to weep the whole day, to be told
the truth. Accordingly, Engidu tells him that those
who die on the field of battle and are carefully bur
ied "drink clear water." Such a one is reunited
with his father and mother and wife; but "he whose
corpse is thrown on the field, his spirit finds no rest
in the earth, and he is obliged to subsist on food
thrown into the street." The picture drawn at the
close of the epic of Gilgamesh is incomplete—dis
appointingly so. But what may be gathered is
that one's fate in Aralu is alleviated somewhat
in case one has met death in a good cause. The
answer indicates likewise the stress laid upon the
proper disposal of the dead, and which included
providing them with food and drink—a duty that
devolved upon the living. The Babylonians them
selves must have realised that this provision for the
dead was soon neglected by the survivors. The
succeeding generation, or at most the second genera
tion, thought of offering food and drink to those
who had gone before, but what did the present gen
eration know or care for those who had lain in the
ground for centuries? And so the great epic ends
in striking a note of intense sadness, if not of de
spair.

IV

It is not surprising, however, to find that the Babylonians were not satisfied with the rather hope less outlook depicted at the close of the Gilgamesh epic. The problem of what happens to man after death occupied men's thought, despite the advice given to the hero not to inquire about it. It is a question that will not be suppressed. And so we find in another part of the Gilgamesh epic the hero in search of a remote ancestor, who appears to have secured immortal life. This ancestor turns out to be no other than Utnapishtim, the hero of the Deluge, who escaped destruction at a time when all others around him perished. I cannot stop here[1] to enter into a detailed account of the interest ing Babylonian tale which originally had nothing to do with the Gilgamesh epic. It represents an ancient tradition of some particularly severe inunda tion that had taken place in the district of which Shuruppak was the centre. The Babylonian Deluge is merely the ordinary nature-myth suggested by the stormy and rainy season, which at the present time as in ancient days inundated a considerable portion of the Euphrates Valley. It was only through the perfection of an elaborate system of canals and the proper care of these canals that an annual deluge was prevented and the development of Babylonian civilisation made possible. Nor was

[1] See the Appendix for further details.

there in the original story any indication of the moral that the virtuous man is saved while sinners perished, or that Utnapishtim had been singled out by his exemplary conduct for immortality. He was saved because he was wise enough to understand a mysterious warning sent by Ea, the friend and bene factor of mankind.

Having understood the warning, Ea tells him to build a ship, into which he takes the members of his family, his possessions, his household, including cattle and flocks, and is thus saved from destruc tion. This story, as a popular one, is taken up by the compilers of the Gilgamesh epic, and, in order to bring about the connection with Gilgamesh and Utnapishtim, the former is described, in his search for health and his longing to escape death, as hear ing of the strange fate that befell Utnapishtim. The conclusion that Utnapishtim is immortal and still living in the days of Gilgamesh appears to be a later folk-lore addition to the original story, su perinduced no doubt, in part, by the belief that one who had been so singularly favoured by the gods must have stood in a closer relation to them than other mortals. Be that as it may, the point of the story which interests us here is the closing episode. Gilgamesh, after a perilous journey, comes to Utnapishtim and asks him to tell him how he came to be placed among the assembly of the gods and secured immortal life. He listens in amaze ment to the story that Utnapishtim relates, which is designated as a hidden history—a kind of mystery. A trace of an older view, according to which Utnapishtim had suffered the fate of all humanity, is to be seen in a description given of Utnapishtim lying on his back and resting. It is clear from this that he does not share the life of the gods, but the fate of an ordinary mortal, retaining consciousness after death, but condemned to a sad inactivity. The close of the story is therefore to be regarded likewise as a subsequent addition made at a time when Utnapishtim became identified with the gods, and added with the view of attaching to the story a doctrine regarding the possibility of securing im mortal life.

The waters had subsided, and Enlil, the god of the upper atmosphere and of the storms, who was more directly responsible for the Deluge, had be come reconciled to the special grace accorded by Ea to Utnapishtim. Ea, as the friend of humanity, pleads with Enlil not to bring on another deluge; to diminish mankind, if need be, through lions, through hunger, or through pestilence. This ap peal evidently represents again a later addition to the original tale, embodying reflections on the dreadful catastrophe by some one who voiced in this way the hope that mankind would be spared another such catastrophe. The answer of Ea to the question of Enlil, "Who has escaped? No one was to have remained alive," is given very briefly by Ea in these words: "I showed a very wise man a dream, through which he learned the secret of the gods." Ea is then represented as stepping on a ship, placing Utnapishtim and his wife before him, touching their foreheads and blessing them. "Here tofore Utnapishtim was an ordinary man. Now Utnapishtim shall be a god as we are. Utnapish tim shall dwell in the distance, at the confluence of the streams. Then they took me and placed me to a distance, at the confluence of the streams."

I have no hesitation in suggesting that the refer ence in this phrase to Utnapishtim's position as an ordinary man, and that henceforth he and his wife were to be like gods is a later insertion, indicated as such by the addition of the wife, who is not men tioned in the succeeding lines, where the dwelling of Utnapishtim is described as situated "at the con fluence of the streams." But the addition of the closing lines is, nevertheless, significant as pointing to an endeavour to furnish a more hopeful outlook to man in contemplating the fate in store for him after death. The thought of these closing lines is clearly intended to point the way to the possibility of man rising after death to a higher state. The spirit of life in man was regarded as of the same character as the life about him in nature; but, since all life was of one kind, man shared this spirit also with the gods who were pictured as human in their motives and actions. The dominance and achieve ments of man separate him sharply from the rest of creation. What more natural than that the thought should arise that man, in whom there was an element which united him to the gods, should also share the attribute of immortality with the

gods, since he possessed in common with the latter
a power and wisdom not given to the rest of crea
tion, and which seemed to indicate that he was
specially picked out for divine favour?

It was reflections of this character that led to
the singling out of exceptional individuals, such as
rulers and heroes, to be placed on a par with the
gods. The deification of kings and heroes is unin
telligible except on the assumption that the spirit
of life in man is regarded as the same in substance
with that which the gods enjoy. If, then, certain
individuals were favoured through securing immor
tal life, where could they be placed except with the
gods? There was no escape from the conclusion
that such individuals were admitted to the assem
bly of the gods. The hope was thus at least held
out to mankind that through special favour some
may escape the ordinary fate. The reference to
the dwelling of Utnapishtim "in the distance at
the confluence of the streams" is exceedingly in
teresting. We may properly assume that the
streams meant are the Euphrates and Tigris, and
perhaps other rivers known to the Babylonians.
The confluence is the great ocean, which, for the
Babylonians, began with the Persian Gulf. Is the
distant place, therefore, to which Gilgamesh was
destined, a counterpart of the Greek idea of the
Island of the Blest, the first faint beginnings of a
Paradise reserved for those who had secured divine
favour? It is not impossible that such is the case,
though it may be added that beyond this vague

indication no other evidence exists. The mere vagueness, however, of the description is suggest ive. The story is intended to voice a hope, but nothing more. The narrator feels that he is in the presence of a mystery. Utnapishtim explicitly states that the story which he is about to tell to Gilgamesh is mysterious, and Ea emphasises that through a dream "a wise one among men learned the secret of the gods." The distant place at the confluence of the streams is also a mystery—per haps the greatest of all in the mind of the com piler—and for this reason he desists from any further description. We are, however, I think, justified in concluding from this reference to some special place reserved for such favoured ones as Utnapishtim that among the Babylonians, at least, the beginnings of a revulsion against the primitive materialistic view of life after death had set in. Whether this reaction went any further than is implied in the closing words of the Deluge episode we cannot say. It is not impossible that further material may be found pointing to a development, at least for some distance, along the line of a distinction in the fate of the dead according to the pleasure of the gods —a differentiation carried somewhat further than in the Gilgamesh epic, and which may have led to the assumption of two places where those who have completed their earthly careers were trans ferred—a kind of Paradise for those who had secured divine favour, by the side of Aralu for the great masses. There are allusions in some of the hymns and penitential prayers to the power of Marduk and other gods in restoring the dead to life, and though this probably means nothing more than bringing those on the brink of the grave back to health and to the enjoyment of life, still the epithet itself is significant as an indication of the power assigned to the great gods who hold life and death in their hands.

It is, however, exceedingly unlikely that the doctrine of a differentiation in the fate of man developed up to the point of a general belief in immortality in any real sense of the term as more than mere consciousness after death, or even up to a deeper conception of immortality itself. The materialistic aspect of Babylonian and Assyrian civilisation, taken as a whole, prevented the fuller development of an ethical and spiritual factor in the growth of religious thought. Without this factor the religion of a people soon reaches its definite limitations. The relationship between gods and men becomes a give-and-take arrangement, limited moreover to the experiences of this world. To be sure, as conditions of life become more complex and more refined, some ethical considerations are also taken up into the religion. The gods are represented as being favourable to those who are good, but the definition of good remains largely materialistic, inasmuch as no sharp distinction is drawn between a good act from pure motives and one dictated by selfish considerations, or between a sin falling within the category of a moral transgression and one which merely means the disregard of some religious rite demanded by the gods and imposed upon the people by priestly regulations. This lim itation in the unfolding of the ethical and spiri tual factor, which we shall consider more fully in the next chapter, proved a barrier against the higher development of views regarding man's fate after death, as it also checked the rise of a system of ethics freed from materialistic or purely practical implications. It is the introduction of this ethical element in the earlier views held by the Hebrews in common with the Babylonians regarding life after death that led to the profound change involved in passing from the view of Sheol, as indicated in the older portions of the Old Testament, to the sharp distinction between the fate of the good and the fate of the wicked, leading in turn to a contrast be tween heaven and hell, and culminating on the spiri tual side in the doctrine of the immortality of the soul and of an ultimate resurrection.

V

We need not stop to furnish the proof that the early conception of Sheol among the Hebrews dif fered in no essential particular from that which we have indicated among the Babylonians, for it lies on the surface in almost all the books of the Old Testament. And let me remind you once more that the Assyrian and Babylonian view is practi cally identical with that which we know was commonly held in a certain stage of culture by people in various parts of the world—practically every where. There is one gathering-place for all—gen erally situated somewhere in the earth—and it is merely in details of a secondary character that the descriptions of the kind of life awaiting those who have closed their earthly career differ.[1] There is no need, therefore, for assuming that the Hebrews obtained their early views from the Babylonians, or vice versa. The existence of a term shu'alu in Baby lonian, which certainly suggests the Hebrew Sheol, and which is one of the designations for the grave, is the one point of direct contact, but it should be added, although I believe in the identification of the two terms, that the reading of the Babylonian signs is not absolutely certain. The point is not of any great importance, because, as indicated, there is nothing particularly distinctive, either in the He brew or Babylonian early views, that separates the conception from what is found elsewhere. Sheol is the general gathering-place of the dead, precisely as is Aralu. It is sufficient to point to the pa thetic lament of Jacob that he will "go in sorrow to Sheol."[2] It is not Sheol that he dreads, but the frame of mind in which he will encounter death. The current belief, apparently, was that those who leave this world in sorrow retain that disposition in the grave. The familiar biblical phrase of "being

---

[1] See the descriptions gathered with marvellous skill and patience from all peoples, primitive and advanced, in Frazer's *Belief in Immortality*, now the standard work on the subject (2 vols., London, 1913).

[2] Gen. 37 : 35.

gathered to one's fathers" is a synonym for death, and refers merely to family burial. It is not, as is sometimes claimed, inconsistent with the view of a single gathering-place in a deep hole underneath the earth. The general conception regarding Sheol is also illustrated in the various poetical epithets given to it, such as "the Pit," "Destruction," "the Land of Forgetfulness," "the Place of Silence," and so forth. One of these names, "Refaim," marks the dead as being weak. Sheol represents the con trast to life and everything connected with life. As so effectively expressed in the book of Job (10 : 22): "It is a land of darkness, of dense darkness, where even light is dark." There the dead lie huddled together, conscious but inactive. The striking pic ture in the fourteenth chapter of Isaiah, of the dead rulers of the earth with their crowns on their heads, greeting the mighty Babylonian king, "Art thou also become weak as we are? Art thou become like unto us, thy pomp brought down to the grave?" is familiar to us all. There is an interesting touch in a passage in Ezekiel [1] which implies that dishonour in this life clings to those in the nether world. As among the Babylonians, we find that proper burial and affectionate care of the dead were essential to the condition of comparative quiet. No doubt the Hebrews also, like the Babylonians, were at one time prompted to this care for the dead by the consideration that in this way the living would be protected against mischief at the hands of the de parted spirits.

[1] 32 : 27.

It is in the Psalms that we obtain the first defi
nite glimpse of a more hopeful view. To be sure, we
still find in many of the Psalms the view that those
in Sheol cannot praise God, that all relations between
the dead and the Deity are cut off.[1] But in other
productions which must be placed at a later period
we find such remarkable utterances as: "My flesh
also shall dwell in safety, for Thou wilt not leave my
soul to Sheol; neither wilt Thou suffer Thy holy
one to see corruption" (Psalm 16 : 9-10); and,
"God will redeem my soul from the power of
Sheol, for He shall receive me" (Psalm 49 : 15).
Vague as such indications are—they may be multi
plied many times—they are sufficiently definite to
justify the conclusion that the belief in a differen
tiation of the fate of the dead had taken a strong
hold on popular belief, to speak roughly, within a
century or two before the exilic period.

The significance, however, of the passages in the
Psalms furnishing the hopeful outlook is that they
occur in connection with a distinction between the
good and the wicked. So we note that in the first
passage quoted, the assurance of the psalmist that
God will not leave his soul in Sheol, is based upon
his trust in God. "I will bless the Lord who has
given me counsel." "I have set the Lord always be
fore me. Because He is at my right hand I shall not
be moved." "The righteous shall inherit the land,
and dwell therein forever." "Mark the perfect man,

[1] E. g., Psalm 6 : 5: "In death there is no remembrance of thee; in
the grave, who shall give thee thanks?" or Psalm 88, which strikes this
same note, only more forcibly.

and behold the upright, for the latter end of that man is peace." "The latter end of the wicked shall be cut off, but the salvation of the righteous is of Yahweh." It is the righteous who need not stand in fear of death. Their souls will be redeemed from Sheol.

The key-note therefore for the brighter outlook is religious, the same note which is struck so forcibly in the utterances of the Prophets, and which becomes the dominant note in the reconstruction of the religious life after the Exile. It has been remarked that there is too strong a tendency among critical students in the Old Testament to make of the period of the Exile the sharp dividing-line between earlier religious conceptions and more advanced ones. There is a certain truth in this criticism, and it is, I believe, decidedly erroneous to assume that higher views held in reference to the relationship between man and the Deity, entailing superior views of sin and atonement and of life after death, belong necessarily to the postexilic period. There must have been a long antecedent development before we reach such a position as is taken in many of the Psalms. The pre-exilic Prophets furnish the proof of such a proposition, and we have seen that we are justified in regarding Moses as a precursor in the movement which culminates in ethical monotheism. But the critics are right, I believe, in maintaining that the full realisation of what the Prophets meant did not come until the great lesson of the Exile had sunk deep into the minds and hearts of the people. The significance of that lesson lay in the realisation that failure was a condition to ultimate success, that national humiliation was essential in order to bring about spiritual triumph, that Yahweh's compara tive indifference to the fate of His own people was the means by which there was impressed upon the people the spiritual conception of divine govern ment, faintly outlined by Moses and then unmis takably voiced by the Prophets in their endeavour to show that Yahweh was not like other gods cir cumscribed in his interests, and ready to overlook faulty conduct and low ideals if only external hom age were rendered to him by those who regarded themselves as his favourites. The trust of the psalmist in divine justice and righteousness finds its highest expression in such utterances as "I walk through the valley of deep darkness, I will fear no evil," [1] which could only have been reached by such a profound national experience as that which marks the destruction of the southern Hebrew kingdom, following within about a century and a half upon that of the northern kingdom.

VI

It was not so much the political changes involved in the catastrophe, though these were profound, as the reflex of the downfall of Jerusalem in the spirit of the people that makes the Exile a sharp point of division in the religious attitude of the people at large. Here, through an illustration the force of

[1] Psalm 23 : 4.

which was tremendous, the lesson of the Prophets was impressed upon the people that Yahweh demanded loyalty to ethical ideals, and not, like other gods of the nations, a mere observance of ritualistic ordinances. It is no wonder that the people declined to give serious heed to the threats of an Amos, an Isaiah, or a Jeremiah. Why should they be held up as sinners? In comparing themselves to other nations, the Hebrews of pre-exilic days did not find that they had sunk deeper into the mire of materialism, or were more indifferent to the precepts of religion than other nations. They certainly were not as cruel and rapacious as their enemies, the Assyrian and Babylonian conquerors. They were not any worse, surely, than the Phœnicians, or the Moabites, or Ammonites. The argument had force and could not be gainsaid. Prophet and people were speaking a different language. Both used the same term Yahweh as the designation of the God to be worshipped, but the Yahweh of the Prophets had moved far away from the conception of a merely national protector. All the Prophets were deeply stirred by the inadequacy of the prevailing cult, survivals of primitive Semitic customs, or borrowed largely from the practices of the Canaanites as a means of bringing about a spiritual communion between the worshipper and his deity. The thought that Yahweh demanded clean hands, pure thoughts, righteous conduct, rather than sacrifices and the observance of new-moons, Sabbaths, and festivals, was a revolutionary one.

The impending catastrophe of a complete submis
sion of the people to foreign conquerors was fore
seen by the Prophets, and indeed was so evident
that no one with clear vision could help foreseeing
it. But while the masses thought that through still
more zealous devotion to the conventional cult Yahweh might be induced to ward off the coming dis
aster to the state, the Prophets were preparing the
people to understand the lesson of the unavoidable
downfall. It was because of the influence exerted
by these Prophets that the ethical element in the
conception of divine government of the universe re
acted on the entire religious thought, and to a large
extent also on the religious life of the Hebrews dur
ing the so-called Exile, and more particularly in postexilic days. The entire past history of the people
was viewed in a different light when the new cri
terion introduced by the Prophets was applied to
the review of this history. The simple conditions
in the patriarchal times loomed up as the ideal in
contrast with later periods marked by the change
to city life and by the concomitant extension of
commerce, of worldly interests, of political expan
sion, and other factors that accompanied what was
undoubtedly an advance in culture. The tradi
tional figures of Abraham, Isaac, and Jacob became
the types of the true worshippers of Yahweh, and
though some of the tales told of these ancestors,
particularly those associated with Jacob, retained
many incidents inconsistent with the ideals of the
Prophets, on the whole the popular stories were re-

cast in such a way as to bring out the main thought that Yahweh demanded a pure disposition rather than an external show of devotion through offerings or through the observance of sacred days. The older laws are interspersed with ethical reflections added during this period, and which were intended to bring out as the main purpose of ceremonial observance the resolve of the people to regulate their lives ac cording to the standards of righteousness and jus tice which Yahweh had imposed upon his chosen people. The upshot of all this was to extend the differentiation between good and bad conduct be yond the confines of this life. Such was the force of the doctrine of the Prophets that righteousness alone exalteth a people and that only those who walk in straight paths can obtain divine favour, that it came to be looked upon as inconceivable that the same fate should be measured out to good and bad alike. On the other hand, the reconciliation of such a doctrine with existing facts was a difficult task. If Yahweh was the just ruler whose sway was not limited to one particular people, why was it that power counted for so much in this world—power of arms, power of position, power of wealth?

The only solution for this dilemma was the assump tion of retribution for the sins of nations at a dis tant time when righteousness shall prevail through out the world, and for individuals in the better fate in store for those who suffer because of their at tachment to ethical ideals in this world. The He brews, sobered and humiliated by the loss of national

independence, began the work of rebuilding the na
tional life on a religious and not on a political basis.
Resigned by force of circumstance to being politi
cally dependent upon a foreign power, the Hebrews
developed a religious commonwealth which aimed
to avoid a conflict with the powers that be. This
endeavour was aided by the wise and generous pol
icy, inaugurated by Cyrus, of allowing the people as
much liberty under Persian rule as was consistent
with a recognition of the political supremacy of the
Persian government over Palestine.

The result was the transformation of the Hebrews
into a religious community, though naturally cen
turies elapsed before the national ambitions which
actuated a considerable portion of the people were
entirely moved into the background. Indeed, from
a certain point of view, these national ambitions
never entirely died out, but the application of the
new doctrine of retribution had the result of re
moving the time for the fulfilment of national am
bitions to a remote period in the future, which de
prived them of a large part of their political force.
Yahweh would restore his people even to their po
litical strength in due time, but this time would not
come till the kingdom of divine righteousness was
formally established in all parts of the world. Then,
but only then, were Israel's sufferings as a nation
to cease, and retribution to be afforded for the hu
miliation and for the loss of national power endured
by the people.

We are less concerned, however, with this phase

of religious development than with the effect of the new doctrine of retribution on the individual. The older view regarding life after death left little place for individual claims. According to this view all the living were to be gathered into one place, and, even if a distinction was to be made, it was not done according to the life led by the individual on earth. But with the application of the divine pre cepts of justice and righteousness to the individual as well as to the people as a whole, a new hope was held out for those who suffered in this world be cause of their fidelity to higher standards of con duct. An analogy was drawn between the people regarded as a unit and the virtues of the individual. The sufferings of the pious and righteous were merely a picture of what Israel itself was obliged to endure. The Messianic hope and the retribution promised for the individual in the future world were thus closely bound up with each other, representing two phases of the same thought. The literature of the centuries succeeding the exilic period down to the beginning of Christianity, and even for some dis tance beyond the appearance of this new force, is taken up with these two ideas of Messianic hope and of the retribution of the individual. Israel would receive the reward for its sufferings in the distant future when the rule of righteousness would be established throughout the world, and the pious and God-fearing individual who suffered poverty, humiliation, and apparent failure in his earthly ca reer would find his compensation, after his earthly career had closed, for clinging to the law of God. That later, beyond the grave, the pious would find the reward for observing the law was eloquently described in the beautiful nineteenth Psalm, which voices the postexilic point of view:

> "The law of Yahweh is perfect, refreshing the soul;
> The ordinances of Yahweh are sure, making wise the simple;
> The precepts of Yahweh are right, rejoicing the heart;
> The command of Yahweh is pure, enlightening the eyes."

Here you have a perfect expression of the concep tion of divine precepts that illustrates the wide gap between the popular view in former days, which identified the laws of Yahweh with ceremonial reg ulations, and the postexilic ideals, which made the law the expression of a purely spiritual and ethi cal intent, with ceremonial regulations merely as a medium for leading to the end in view, which was to refresh the soul, to make the simple wise, to re joice the heart, and to enlighten the eyes.

VII

The doctrine of personal retribution does not find its complete expression until within a century of the appearance of Jesus. The book of Job, receiving its definite shape about 400 B. C.,[1] may be instanced as a proof that we are still some distance removed from the period when the doctrine of retribution

---

[1] This is Budde's view in his commentary on Job (*Das Buch Hiob*, 2d ed., p. lv), which seems to me to best satisfy all conditions involved.

had acquired much force. Throughout the book the assumption is that the favour and displeasure of God are limited to this world, and that after life is over all lie down to the quiet of the grave with none to disturb them, but also with none to care for them. Forgotten they lie there, the good and the bad, food for worms. Even the three "friends" of Job, who in the philosophical discussions that form the purpose of the book[1] represent the conventional point of view in postexilic days that God rewards the pious and punishes the evil-doers, do not ex tend their horizon beyond this world; and though it is suggested that sometimes the punishment falls on the descendants of the wicked man in case the real culprit escapes it, even the corollary that the virtuous man who suffers in this world should be content in the consciousness that his offspring will reap the reward denied to him is not brought for ward, much less the thought that the good will be rewarded after death, if not in this world. The scepticism of the author of the philosophical poem —for the discussions are in poetic form—corre spondingly goes no further than to question the view that had become the current one by the fifth cen-

[1] The story of Job, the pious and patient sufferer to whom eventually all things are restored, is merely the medium for the introduction of Job and his three friends as the participants in a discussion of the problem of suffering and of evil. The story is used as a modern preacher might use a biblical story—as the text for a sermon suggested by the tale. The book of Job ended originally with chapter 31, where the closing words, "Ended are the words of Job," are still found intact. Chapters 32–42 : 6 represent further endeavours on the part of later writers to discuss the same theme, which is one of permanent human interest, and aroused as much attention then as it commands at the present time.

tury, whether the laws of justice and righteousness
ascribed by the Prophets to God as His weapons to
carry out His government of the world were actually
in force. The author, who is in sympathy with Job,
represents the latter as questioning the correctness
of the assumption that God punishes the wicked
only. Job's case is the unanswerable argument to
this, for the point of Job's sufferings is that he en
dures all kinds of misfortunes despite the fact that
he is, as the prose tale describes him, "perfect and
upright" (Job 1 : 1)—strong terms that are applied
to Noah (Gen. 6 : 9), and no doubt with a direct
allusion to the passage in the book of Genesis so as
to suggest the comparison between Noah and Job.
The Noah story is told to show that God saves the
righteous man even when all mankind, represented
as corrupt, is doomed to destruction. The point of
Job's speeches is to suggest that the righteous man
is not always saved, but, on the contrary, is tortured
and punished as though he had committed all the
sins and transgressions in the catalogue, whereas the
wicked often flourish and are saved while the just
perish. The book of Job is therefore of special in
terest in showing the opposition that the doctrine
of the Prophets encountered from those who main
tained a distinctly sceptical attitude, prompted, to
be sure, by a profound study of life as it is and
not by mere cynicism. But for the subsequent ad
dition of the speeches of Elihu (chapters 32–37) and
of God Himself, introduced in chapters 38–41, and
for the toning down of some of Job's speeches by

glosses and intentional changes, the book would never have been admitted into the Jewish canon.

The problem of unjust suffering and of the exist ence of evil in a world created by a beneficent Power enthroned in justice and righteousness is, in deed, a difficult one. Perhaps to seek an altogether satisfactory solution is a hopeless quest,[1] but it is significant that while Job in his speeches often ap proaches a denial of divine justice, not even a hint is thrown out in the book of Job in regard to a pos sible retribution beyond the grave.[2] Nor is there a suggestion that a distinction is to be made between the fate of the good and that of the wicked in Sheol, which, it will be recalled, is described in a manner closely parallel to the account of Aralu as a land of no return, a place of deep darkness (Job 10 : 21–22). "He that goeth down to Sheol shall not come up. He shall return no more to his house, neither shall his place know him any more."[3] On the other hand, in the book of Ecclesiastes, the scepticism of which is distinguished from that in the book of Job not only in being more pronounced but by its cynical flavour, we encounter by implication the ex istence of a belief that the fate in store for man is different from that of the rest of the animal world. For when the preacher (Eccles. 3 : 20–21), after stating

---

[1] The solution proposed by Mazdaism or Zoroastrianism, to use the more common term, that the power of evil is independent of Ahura-Mazda, the creator who has all attributes except that of unlimited power, is virtually an abandonment of the problem.

[2] The famous passage, 19 : 25–27—hopelessly corrupt through later contamination—cannot be used for this view.

[3] Job 7 : 9–10.

that "all go unto one place; all are of the dust and unto dust all return,"[1] adds, "Who knows that the spirit of men goes upward and the spirit of beasts downward," there is clearly implied a view which assumes a heavenly home for man as against Sheol —here reserved for the brute creation. In view of this we are also justified in assuming that when the cynic says that "there is one end to the righteous and the wicked, to the clean and to the unclean . . . as is the good, so is the sinner, he who swears is as he who fears an oath. This is an evil among the things under the sun, that there is one fate to all," he is polemicising against a view that differ entiated in some way between the fate of the just and that of the wicked.

Because of these implied teachings, the view of scholars who place Ecclesiastes after the composi tion of the book of Job seems to be correct, and, while we may not be justified in going far down into the second century before our era for the final shape of this remarkable philosophical work, as Pro fessor Haupt[2] and others propose, it can hardly be older than the third century,[3] and I am inclined to agree with those who see in the peculiar form of the preacher's scepticism—in its specific form as well as in its mundane tone—the influence of Greek philosophy which would oblige us to come well down into the third century as the probable date of com-

---

[1] In evident allusion to Gen. 3 : 19.

[2] *The Book of Ecclesiastes* (Baltimore, 1905), p. 1.

[3] See Barton in his Commentary on Ecclesiastes, p. 62; though Barton denies Greek influence, *ib.*, pp. 32 *seq.*

position.[1] If we had more literary remains of the fourth and third centuries preceding Christianity, we would be in a position to follow the development of beliefs regarding life after death in detail. As it is, we must be content with noting that the general tendency of religious thought which such produc tions as the books of Job and Ecclesiastes clearly antagonise did not proceed without counter-cur rents—on the one hand in the direction of a scepti cism about the practical workings of the theory of life as enunciated by the Prophets, on the other hand a questioning of the new doctrine that a dis tinction can really be assumed between the fate of the good and that of the bad after the reaper, Death, has gathered men in his embrace. Even in a book so late as the sayings of Ben Sira, Sheol is still the place of all the shades. As in the earlier Psalms, it is described as a place without delight, where there is no praise of God, and where man is plunged into eternal sleep; and, while the author, who wrote about the year 180 B. C., voices the coming of the Messianic kingdom when Israel will receive her retribution, he does not appear to hold out any such hope for the individual, and looks for the punishment of the evil-doer in the sins and mis fortunes that will be heaped upon his descendants.

---

[1] Many passages in Ecclesiastes have been retouched in the interest of orthodoxy to tone down their extreme sceptical tone, and many addi tions were made furnishing the counter-arguments of pious writers. As in the case of Job, it is because of these additions which covered the blunt scepticism and cynicism with a veneer of orthodoxy and conven tionality that the book—though not without a struggle—was admitted into the canon. See for further details Barton's Commentary, pp. 5 *seq.*

VIII

Such doctrinal expressions and literary contri
butions had by this time become much more the
expression of individual views than a few centuries
earlier.　Yet, for the very reason that they show
this individualistic character, we should be warned
against laying too much stress on them, as though
they represented the main currents.　The late
Psalms, in which it is often difficult to decide whether
the speaker is the individual or the community,[1] il
lustrate the close connection in the minds of the
writers between Israel as a community and the in
dividual members of the community, and it may well
be that it was the intention to apply the descrip
tions in such Psalms to both the community and
the individual.　If therefore the belief arose in a
retribution in the distant future for the sufferings
which Israel as a nation and as a religious commu
nity had to endure, we may feel certain that the
corollary was drawn applying the doctrine to the
individual.　It required only the further growth of
individualisation to bring about a complete corre
spondence between the hoped-for national retri
bution in a better age and the individual retribu
tion in a better state to be looked for after death.

About the same time as the composition of the
sayings of Ben Sira we find the oldest portion of

[1] See Coblenz, *Ueber das betende Ich in den Psalmen* (1907), which is
only one of many monographs discussing this question in regard to which
general agreement has not been reached.

the book of Enoch laying great emphasis on the
doctrine of individual retribution; and equally defi
nite is the book of Daniel, ascribed by the unani
mous verdict of critics to about the same period as
Ben Sira, in basing the hope that the pious who
sleep in the land of dust shall wake to share in the
eternal life, while the wicked will inherit shame.[1]
The conceptions in regard to this time of retribu
tion remain vague for a considerable period, but
despite this fact the feeling of confidence and of
trust in the goodness and righteousness of divine
government and in the ultimate compensation for
unmerited sufferings in this world grows apace.
Nowhere is this trust more emphatically and more
beautifully expressed than in many of the Psalms,
and it is because there does not seem to be any
other place for such strong sentiments of supreme
confidence in the power making for righteousness
that scholars have been led to place Psalms voic
ing this trust in the two centuries before this era.
Within this category fall such Psalms as the fa
mous twenty-third:

"Yahweh is my shepherd; I shall not want.
  He maketh me to lie down in green pastures:
  He leadeth me beside the still waters.   He refreshes my soul:
  He leadeth me in the paths of righteousness for His name's sake.
  Yea, though I walk through the valley of deep darkness, I will
    fear no evil: for Thou art with me;"

and the thirty-seventh, built up about pithy sayings
that indicate the popularity acquired by the new
doctrine:

[1] Chapter 12 : 2.

"Fret not thyself because of evil doers, neither be thou envious
  of them that work iniquity,[1]
For they shall soon be cut down like the grass, and wither as
  the green herb.
Trust in Yahweh and do good: dwell in the land and act
  with fidelity.
Delight thyself also in Yahweh,
And He shall give thee the desires of thine heart.
Commit thy way to Yahweh, trust in Him; He shall bring it
  to pass.
He shall make thy righteousness to shine forth as the light,
  and thy judgment as the noon-day."

Such Psalms, whether couched in the first person or
in the form of an address, are equally applicable to
the community or the individual. Again we have
late Psalms, like the one hundred and forty-fourth,
in which there is a transition from the individual's
concern to that of the community,[2] evidently again
from the point of view that trust in Yahweh is
equally applicable to both; and though I am in
clined to believe that in the latest Psalms, empha
sising absolute trust in divine righteousness, the
tendency is more distinctly individualistic, yet in
others, such as the second, also of late origin:

"Why do the nations rage,
  And the people devise what is vain?
  The kings of the earth set themselves,
  And the rulers take counsel together
  Against Yahweh, and against His anointed,"

[1] Parallel to Prov. 24 : 19; cf. also vs. 16 with Prov. 16 : 8, and vss.
23-24 with Prov. 20 : 24.

[2] Vss. 1-8, even if we accept Duhm's view (Die Psalmen, p. 295) that
these versions are an adaptation of Psalm 18—a national hymn—clearly
refer to an individual's distress, though the metaphors, such as in vss. 5-6,
"Touch the mountains that they smoke, hurl lightnings and scatter
them," etc.—an allusion to the revelation on Mount Sinai—are chosen
from the nation's experiences. On the other hand, vss. 9-15 are as dis
tinctly national in their import.

clearly the nation, not the individual, is meant. The combination of the two classes of Psalms, the expression of the individual's hopes and aspirations, and those of the nation, is characteristic of the religious thought during the two or three centuries before the advent of Christianity. The individual is moved into the foreground, his claims are dis tinctly recognised, in contrast to the earlier view of the solidarity of the family, tribe, or nation. On the other hand, the analogy between the life of the individual, with its hardships, its misfortunes, its varying conditions, and that of Israel during the centuries following upon the Exile, were so close as to suggest an almost complete assimilation of the hope in the Messianic kingdom with the time when the individual would also receive his reward. Israel as a people, and the people of Israel as individuals, represent, as it were, an equation. Israel as the servant of Yahweh, oppressed and despised of men as so powerfully portrayed by a later Isaiah, is the counterpart of "the poor and needy" who form the burden of so many Psalms[1] and by which des ignation the pious members of the postexilic com munity are meant, whose fidelity to the law entailed severe hardships and many deprivations. The fate of the individual was thus bound up with that of the nation. Both were encouraged to look for retribution at one and the same period of distant time, when the law of righteousness would be es tablished in the world, Israel restored to her posi-

---

[1] Notably Psalms 34, 70, 74, 86, and 109.

tion, and the individual rewarded for clinging to the law that is perfect and that refreshes the soul.

This identification of the individual with the peo ple represents, naturally, a limitation in the unfold ing of the ideals held up by the Prophets. The emphasis upon the virtues of the people was hardly consistent with the conception of a God of universal sway, not bound by any geographical jurisdiction or recognising any distinctions of blood. The con ception of Israel as a people was idealised, to be sure, in some of the more advanced exilic writings. Israel became a symbol of the ideal of righteous ness, and yet in the background, even in the minds of the best writers, the purely national aspirations and political hopes were ever present.

In judging of this combination of the individual with the people, we must make allowances for the temporary recrudescence of political activity as the result of the uprising of the so-called Maccabees, which occurred about the middle of the second cen tury before this era. For a time it seemed as though the nation would once more mount to a position of independence. The attempt to force upon the people Greek customs and to deal a fatal blow at the same time to the religion aroused the people to desper ate resistance; and, while the success was only tem porary, it led to a strengthening of the national con sciousness that had much to do with the opposition aroused when about a century, or a century and a half, later the attempt was made to bring about a complete break between national and religious ideals.

It is not accidental that in the book of Daniel, which reflects both the attempts to wean the people from adherence to the rites of their religion and the hopes awakened in the Maccabean age, we find the doctrine of individual retribution after death closely united to the portrayal of the ultimate salvation of the people. "At that time thy people shall be saved, every one that shall be found written in the book. And many of them that sleep in the dust of the earth shall awake, these to everlasting life and these to everlasting shame."[1] And yet there is evidence to show that even at this time the individualistic current was running ahead of the stream of national hopes. In Psalms 73 and 49, both dealing with the folly of relying upon riches which, it is assumed, are usually gained through iniquity and oppression, the hope is voiced that Yahweh will provide a better fate for the pure of heart and the clean of hands than for the wicked who prosper in this world and heap up ill-gotten gains. In the former Psalm this hope is represented as a mystery. The singer is in despair when contemplating the actual conditions in this world in which the innocent suffer at the hands of the wicked "until I penetrated into the holy secrets of God and noted their latter end—thou didst set them in slippery places, thou didst hurl them down to ruin (vss. 17–18) . . . But I am ever

[1] Dan. 12 : 1–2. The book of Daniel is a composite production, though the theme is the same throughout—God's providence for His people and the ultimate deliverance of the people from their enemies. In chapters 7–12, the visions of Daniel are made the medium of expressing the Messianic hope—the restoration of Israel to its place of superiority among the nations.

with thee. Thou hast taken hold of my right hand, with thy counsel thou guidest me and afterwards wilt receive me in glory" (vss. 23–24). More def inite is the hope expressed in Psalm 49 (vss. 15–16), that, whereas the ungodly "will sink like sheep to Sheol, with death as their shepherd. . . . God will redeem my soul from Sheol, for He will take me to Himself."[1] There is clearly an advance in the di rection of greater certainty over such a Psalm as the thirty-ninth in which the trust in God [2] goes no further than the prayer: "O! spare me that I may be gladdened before I go hence and be no more"— that is, to pass on to Sheol at the end of a happy life, and not to go down in sorrow as Jacob feared.[3] The significant feature in Psalms 73 and 49 is that hope of retribution beyond the grave is held out without any association with the Messianic age which is to bring about the restoration of the people—the new life of Israel through the resurrection of the national hopes.

IX

Many new aspects of the problem of life after death are brought forward in the course of the cen tury or century and a half preceding Christianity. The Messianic kingdom, instead of being looked upon as a permanent condition as in earlier writings, is portrayed as of temporary duration, to be sup-

---

[1] An allusion to Gen. 5 : 24, where it is said of Enoch "that God had taken him."

[2] Vs. 7. "And now what do I hope for, O Lord? My trust is in thee."

[3] Above, p. 222.

plemented by a final day of judgment. This is
the view set forth with more or less preciseness in
such works as Jubilees, Wisdom, the Assumption of
Moses, and by Philo of Alexandria—all dating from
about the beginning of our era. The advance of
individualism brings in its wake a sharper distinc
tion between the soul and the body; and, since phil
osophical speculations in regard to matter led to
the pessimistic view—based on the theological in
terpretation of the fall of man—that matter was
ineradicably evil and corrupt, the doctrine of im
mortality limited to the soul arose, and received
support through the influence of the book of Wis
dom and the works of Philo; while, concomitant with
this doctrine, the belief in a final day of judgment is
combined in such a work as the Apocalypse of Baruch—within the first century of our era—with ear
lier notions, which could not conceive of life with
out a material substance in which it was clothed.
As in the primitive phase of belief, which imagined
the dead in Sheol to continue a conscious existence
in the frame of mind in which they entered into the
nether world, so on the day of resurrection the dead
were supposed to rise with every defect and deform
ity they possessed at the moment of death.[1] The
bodies of the righteous, according to this writer, will
be transformed to conform to the reward assigned

[1] The Babylonian Talmud (Sanhedrin, 90b) even goes so far as to de
clare that the dead will arise in the very clothes in which they were
buried; and Jerome echoes an even more literal view, based on an er
roneous translation of the famous passage in Job 19 : 26. (See Charles,
Eschatology, Hebrew, Jewish and Christian, p. 281.)

to them of a spiritual existence of unending glory
and happiness. This view represents in its final
outcome a great advance over what we find in the
second Book of Maccabees (chapter 7), where retri
bution is not only limited to the righteous among the
people of Israel, but where Sheol is still an inter
mediate state, whereas the nations enter at once on
their eternal doom. The emphasis on the individ
ual's fate, in combination with the modification of
the Messianic hope, which led to the assumption of
a Messianic kingdom of temporary duration, had as
another significant outcome the rise of the belief in
a personal Messiah, who is to usher in the new era.
The book of Enoch may be instanced as a proof of
the prominence that this doctrine had acquired at
the beginning of the first century before this era,
for he describes the Messiah in such terms as "the
anointed one" (or the Christ), "the chosen one,"
and even "the son of man" [1] familiar to us from the
New Testament. We have in the apocalyptic writ
ings of this time the growing definiteness of the
universalistic view which included all nations—the
Gentiles therefore alongside of Israel, the elect—
in the visions of the Messiah and of the Messianic
kingdom, in the pictures of the lot of the pious in
heaven, and of the wicked in a special place of pun
ishment, and of the day of resurrection and final

[1] Whatever this designation may originally have connoted—on which
see Professor Nathaniel Schmidt's full discussion in *The Prophet of Naz
areth*, chapter V—there can be no question that it is used in a symbolic
and not in a literal sense, and therefore belongs properly to "Messianic"
terminology.

judgment. It was not easy for the Jewish nation alistic spirit to overleap the barrier marked by na tional hopes, for that is what the acceptance of the universalistic spirit expressed in the utterances of postexilic Prophets like Malachi[1] and in chapters inserted in Isaiah [2] and in some Psalms[3] involved. If Yahweh's temple is to be "a house of prayer for all nations," [4] and Jerusalem the holy city to which all peoples will flock, then the only special province left to Israel, the elect, is to be the leader of the new movement, but only at the sacrifice of all par ticularism and nationalistic aspirations. The Mac-cabean uprising brought with it a rekindling of na tional hopes and with this a reassertion of Israel's special prerogatives even in the days of the Messi anic kingdom which is pictured in such writings as Daniel, Enoch, the Psalms of Solomon (c. 70 B. C.), and Baruch as the time when the righteous among the nations will serve Israel, while the wicked, by whom are meant primarily the enemies of the chosen people, will not partake in the resurrection, but will remain in Sheol and there be subjected to tortures for their sins. Still, even in the writings be longing to the end of the second and to the first century before this era, notably in portions of the

[1] 1 : 11 : "From the rising of the sun unto its going down, my name is great among the nations; and in every place incense is offered unto my name and a pure offering."

[2] Isa. 19 : 24–25 : "On that day Israel shall be a third with Egypt and with Assyria, a blessing in the midst of the earth, which Yahweh of hosts has blessed saying, blessed be Egypt my people, and Assyria, the work of my hands, and Israel my inheritance." *Cf.* also Isa. 2 : 2–4 =Micah 4 : 1–3.

[3] *E. g.*, Psalms 22, 65, 86, and 87.   [4] Isa. 56 : 7.

book of Enoch—more composite in character than most of the writings of the period[1]—there runs the theme that all the righteous among the nations are to have a share in the blessings of the future, including the assignment to heaven and participation in the resurrection; and it is significant that this point of view finds an expression even in the Talmud,[2] despite the particularistic position which forms the very foundation-stone on which the structure of Rabbinical Judaism is erected. The upshot is a somewhat inconsistent and vague compromise, involving the theoretical acceptance of the universalistic spirit as a corollary of Prophetical Judaism, with an endeavour to retain the special position to be accorded to the Jewish people even in the Messianic age and on the day of final judgment. It is this conflict between nationalism and universalism that results finally in the divorce between Judaism and Christianity.

The complete break with the old conception of Sheol as a general gathering-place, and even as an intermediate sojourn for the righteous, which finds its literary expression in the book of Jubilees, in Philo, in the Apocalypse of Baruch, in Josephus, and more particularly, of course, in the Gospels and other writings of the New Testament, leads to the view of Sheol as the abiding-place of the wicked in contrast to the blessed immortality in heaven ac-

---

[1] See the introduction in Charles's *The Book of Enoch*, pp. xlvi–lvi (Oxford, 1912).

[2] " The righteous of all nations will have a share in the world to come " (Tosefta, Sanhedrin, xiii).

corded to the righteous immediately after death. A direct consequence of this distinction between heaven and hell, when once it assumed definite form, was to lead to pictures of torments for the wicked in Sheol, which form the basis for the lurid pictures in the theological treatises of mediæval Christianity.

X

The further development of views regarding life after death which lies beyond the scope of these chap ters, proceeded in part under Jewish and in part under Christian influences. Thus the differentia tion between the resurrection of the body and the immortality of the soul may be looked upon as a result in which both Jewish and Christian concep tions had about an equal share; but practically we have in the movements of thought regarding life after death during the two centuries preceding this era all the elements for the Pauline theology, which became the working hypothesis of Christianity down to the days of the Reformation—all the elements with the exception of the coping-stone of the struc ture, to wit, the wiping out of the original sin of mankind through the blood of the "anointed," the Christ. This carries with it as a logical corollary the doctrine of salvation for mankind through the acceptance of Jesus as the Messiah, and the sym bolical union with the son of God whose death becomes the vicarious sacrifice *par excellence*. The personality of Jesus in this system which represents the culmination of a long process of thought and speculation extending from the days of the pre-exilic Prophets impresses us sometimes as almost secondary, in comparison with the stress laid by Paul on the *theories* entwined around the name of the Christ. To be sure, the personality in all great religious as well as in political movements is essential, but it is not surprising that in our own days of rigid questioning of all traditions the question as to the historicity of Jesus should have arisen. The question lies outside of my field, but I trust that I may be permitted to express my own conviction that in the picture of the great teacher of Galilee drawn for us in the Gospels we have not only a real personality, but one who impressed himself so deeply on his surroundings—so much more so than his precursor, John the Baptist, with whom Jesus has much in common—that when the time came for summing up the religious movements that had so profoundly stirred the minds of men in Palestine and beyond the boundaries of this little land, Jesus became for Paul at one and the same time the exponent, the embodiment, the medium, and the illustration of the system so logically and impressively worked out by him. The teachings of Jesus as revealed in the Gospels are conceived in the spirit of the Hebrew Prophets. The bent of his mind, so far as we can detect it, is ethical rather than theological, though to be sure theological concepts are involved in his ethics. The Jesus of the Pauline system is primarily a theological concept attached

to the personality under the mysterious law of his
tory that brings about the inseparable bond between
great events and great leaders concerned in the
events. But while paying our homage to the Paul
ine system, we must not close our eyes to the fact
that corresponding to the national limitations of
Rabbinical Judaism remaining theoretically a uni
versal religion, yet practically confined to a single
group, we have in the case of organised Christianity
a growing differentiation between those who may
obtain salvation by the acceptance of Jesus as the
Messiah and Redeemer of mankind, and those who
persisted in remaining outside of the circle; and it
is just here that we touch once more upon the more
immediate problem of life after death with which we
are concerned. Despite the spiritual conception of
divine government in both Judaism and Christian
ity; despite the emphasis laid in both upon the jus
tice, mercy, and love of the Creator and Guide of
humanity, Judaism draws a sharp line of demarca
tion between Jew and non-Jew, while in Christianity
the doctrine of salvation, limited to those who ac
cept the Pauline system, led to an emphasis upon
the distinction between heaven and hell, the former
being reserved to the believers while unspeakable
tortures of eternal damnation were in store for the
unbelievers. This emphasis grew until in modern
days a reaction set in against this deduction from
the Pauline system.

We have thus followed in outline the remarkable
course of development to which the early Hebrew

traditions of views of life after death were subjected from the days of Moses to the times of Jesus. The point of importance for us is the evidence for a long process of spiritual growth as an outcome of the new spirit infused into old Semitic beliefs which may, indeed, be traced back to the period of Moses, but which found a more complete expression in the teachings of the pre-exilic and postexilic Prophets. Of such a development we find no trace whatsoever in the case of Babylonian and Assyrian traditions. So far as the views of life after death are concerned, these remained practically and essentially the same throughout all periods—marked by materialistic con ceptions that were in keeping with the limitations in the unfolding of the beliefs in the government of the universe through beings that remained on the level of personifications of the forces of nature. Among the Hebrews the introduction of the ethical element leads to the doctrine of individual retribu tion which steadily gathers strength through the ex periences of the Hebrew nation and is further rein forced through the speculations of leaders imbued with the ethical monotheism of the Prophets. It reaches its culmination in Jewish and Christian teach ings of rewards and punishments in a future existence, accompanied by such concomitant beliefs as the dis tinction between Paradise and hell, the resurrection of the body, the final day of judgment, and, as the flower of spiritual faith, the impressive doctrine of the immortality of the soul as the imperishable di vine element in man.

The gradual separation between Hebrew and Babylonian traditions is no less marked in the do main of ethics to which, in the concluding chapter, we now turn.

CHAPTER V

HEBREW AND BABYLONIAN ETHICS

I

It is not easy to fix upon a test by which to measure the ethics prevailing among a people, even when we are able to study and observe the life and customs of the people at first hand. To judge by the lowest level is manifestly unfair; to judge by the highest endangers the correctness of our conclu sions, and in striking an average, accidental factors, not to speak of the subjective element, may exer cise an undue influence in determining what this average is. The difficulties are increased when we come to measure the value of an ancient civilisation, known to us only from written sources, and which we must endeavour to reconstruct from material only partially preserved and in regard to which we can never be absolutely certain that the conclusions drawn may not be upset, or at all events interfered with, by future discoveries.

In the case of Babylonia and Assyria we are con fronted with the additional difficulty that for cer tain large periods our material is as yet very defi cient, and that we are in doubt in regard to the date of most of the religious literature, which naturally is of vital import in a study of Babylonian and Assyrian ethics. We are still far removed from the time when it will be possible to trace the devel opment of religious thought and of the relationship of the religion to the life of the people in detail. For the present we must content ourselves with gen eral outlines, which, however, for our purpose is quite sufficient.

My aim has been, as will have become evident by this time, to indicate not merely the points of divergence between the two civilisations that started out with much in common, but more particularly to indicate why, with important traditions and beliefs so close to one another as to be practically identical, we find the Hebrews proceeding along a line of de velopment which gradually transformed these tradi tions and beliefs into a medium for expressing the highest spiritual aspirations of the human race and led to one of the most impressive endeavours to find a solution for the mysteries by which we are surrounded—above all for that profoundest of mys teries, the relation of the individual to a universe assumed to be under divine government. I say, one of the most impressive attempts because we must never forget that in a district lying far beyond the possible scope of influences emanating from either Babylonia, Egypt, or Palestine, we find in the re ligious history of India another and totally different endeavour to penetrate into the secrets of the uni verse with an earnestness that challenges our ad miration, all the more because its outlook on life is dark and not hopeful, and because it appears to enthrone at the head of the universe blind chance. The question underlying the investigation which I have attempted in these chapters is why it hap pened, and how it happened, that the form taken on among the Hebrews of the account of the Crea tion of the world, of days set apart from others, of views of life after death, and of various other forms of traditions or expressions of beliefs have exercised so profound and wide an influence on the religious history of mankind, whereas the corresponding be liefs and traditions among Babylonians only pro ceeded up to a certain point and then disappeared in the political downfall of Babylonia and Assyria.

II

A study of the general character of Babylonian and Assyrian ethics will help us further to an under standing of the general purport of our investigation. A test which, it will be admitted, is a fair one in judging of the general ethical status of a people, albeit not the only test, is the relationship in which a people regards itself as standing to the powers upon which it feels itself dependent. Now, whether we turn to the first period of Babylonian history or to the last period of the Assyrian and neo-Baby lonian epochs, we find this relationship to the gods never rising above a materialistic level. It is true that with advancing civilisation the ethical stand ards conditioning social life lead to a modification

of the element of power which is the main char
acteristic of the gods, whether they be personifica
tions of the powers of nature or whether the activ
ity of the gods, disassociated from merely terrestrial
phenomena, is transferred to the heavens.

As laws developed for the regulation of the rela
tions between man and his fellows, with the funda
mental aim of dealing out justice within the limita
tions imposed by class distinctions which were never
set aside, the gods also are conceived as actuated
by a desire to wield their power in a just manner.
Perhaps the highest expression assumed by this tend
ency to temper mere strength with ethical consid
erations is the view taken as early at least as 2000
B. C., and probably considerably before this time,
of Shamash, the sun-god of Sippar, who, absorbing
the cult of numerous local deities, conceived as per
sonifications of the light and heat of the sun, be
comes the sun-god *par excellence.* The beneficial
power of the sun as the indispensable source of vege
tation and fertility forms the natural starting-point
for attaching to Shamash attributes of love and of
gracious consideration for the needs of mankind.
The sun is the power which dissipates darkness
and sends its rays into the remotest corners; the
sun rising above the horizon and spreading light and
warmth becomes the picture for bringing joy into
the hearts of men and for removing sorrow and
grief, associated by a perfectly obvious logic, with
crime and darkness. Shamash thus becomes the
guide of mankind, illuminating, as it were, the path

of life along which man is to proceed. Let us take as an example a passage from one of the hymns[1] addressed to Shamash in which this thought is beau tifully and poetically expressed:

"Oh, Lord illuminator of the darkness, who opens the face of
  heaven,
 Merciful God, who lifts up the lowly, and protects the weak,
 For thy light even the great gods wait,
 All the Anunnaki watch for thy face.
 Thou guidest all men as one group,
 Full of hope, they look with raised heads for the light of the
  sun.
 When thou appearest they rejoice and leap for joy.
 Thou art the lamp for the remotest ends of the heaven,
 Thou art the light for the wide earth.
 All nations look up to thee with joy."

It is an interesting touch, indicative of the pro found emotions aroused by the appearance of the glorious orb, that the gods join mankind in waiting for the moment when the first rays of the morning sun appear to dissipate the darkness that had reigned only a short time before. The hymn was evidently composed as a greeting to the rising sun. But there is a fervour in this greeting which raises it above the plane of a mere adoration of the power of nature. The poet's song becomes a symbol of the joy and hope in a guide directing man along the right path. The light of the sun is associated with purity, with justice, and with life. The great orb is invoked to remove impending catastrophe, to scatter wrong

---

[1] See Jastrow, *Religion Babyloniens und Assyriens*, I, pp. 426-436, for many specimens of hymns and prayers to Shamash.

and iniquity, to protect the weak against the strong, the just against the evil-doer. The power of the sun leads to a reign of justice and happiness.

"Thou guidest the lot of mankind,
Eternally just in heaven art thou.
The just ruler of the lands art thou.
Thou knowest what is right, thou knowest what is wrong.
Shamash anoints the head of the just.
Shamash binds the bad as with a leather strap.
Oh, Shamash, the power of Anu and of Enlil is thine,
Oh, Shamash, supreme judge of heaven and earth art thou."

It is this phase of the sun-god that is emphasised over and over again in the hymns and incantations, and that is revealed in incidental references in the historical inscriptions. The thought rises to an even higher expression in one of the finest of the hymns preserved to us,[1] and from which I should like to quote at least one passage.

"Him whose thought is directed to iniquity thou destroyest;
Him also who unjustly endeavors to alter boundaries.
The unjust judge thou restrainest through imprisonment.
The one who accepts bribes, who does not guide justly, on him thou imposest sin.
But he who does not accept bribes, whose concern is for the oppressed,
Is pleasing to Shamash, his life will be prolonged.
The judge who renders just decisions,
Will end in a palace, the habitation of princes will be his dwelling place."[2]

[1] The complete text, so far as preserved, in Jastrow, *Religion Babyloniens und Assyriens*, I, pp. 433–6, and Zimmern in *Der Alte Orient*, XIII, pp. 23–27.
[2] *Cf.* the similar thought in Prov. 22 : 29, "Seest thou a man diligent in his work, he will stand before kings."

We have the direct proof that this view of Shamash did not remain a merely ethical ideal, but that it entered into the practical life of the people. The great king Hammurapi (c. 2000 B. C.), who codified the laws of the land, places at the head of the large diorite stele on which he inscribes the laws, a design representing himself in an attitude of adoration before Shamash,[1] whom he invokes as the one who inspired him with the spirit of righteousness to rule his people according to the will of Shamash himself.

In the introduction to the laws,[2] Hammurapi declares that he was named by the gods as king of Babylonia, "To spread justice in the land, to destroy the wicked and the bad, so that the powerful may not oppress the weak, in order that I, like Shamash, may appear to mankind to illuminate the land, Anu and Enlil have named me for the guidance of mankind."

The common titles given to Shamash in all divisions of Babylonian and Assyrian literature are: "The Judge," "The Guardian of Justice," "The One Who Pronounces Just Decrees." In his name the laws of the land are executed. Now, fine and impressive as the sun-god is—and this represents the high-water mark of religious aspiration in Babylonia and Assyria—there is nevertheless a definite

---

[1] See the illustration in Jastrow, *Aspects of Belief and Practice in Babylonia and Assyria*, facing p. 392.

[2] See the English translation of the introduction and laws in R. F. Harper's edition, *The Code of Hammurabi* (Chicago, 1903), or C. H. W. Johns, *Oldest Code of Laws in the World* (Edinburgh, 1903), or a more recent German translation in Ungnad-Kohler's *Hammurabis Gesetz* (Leipzig, 1912). The spelling of the name with *p* is the more correct one.

limit set to the development of this view of divine
government which associates justice and righteousness
with the personification of a power of nature.   Let
me endeavour to make clear what I have in mind.

Neither Babylonians nor Assyrians, in attaching
justice and righteousness to Shamash, could lose
sight of the fact that the sun-god does not always
show his beneficent nature to man.   The heat of
the sun brings forth the produce of the earth, but
as his rays increase in intensity, the severe heat be
comes also a destructive force.   The sun of a spring
day, hailed with joy as putting an end to the cold
and the rain and the storms of winter, develops into
the sun of midsummer's torrid heat, bringing suffer
ing and disease and death.   It was all very well to
associate this aspect of the sun with a god known
as Nergal,[1] but that could not prevent the people
nor, for that matter also, the priests from overlook
ing the fact that Nergal represented precisely the
same power of nature as Shamash.   In hymns[2] in
which Nergal, precisely like Shamash, is praised as
the power without whom the earth does not bear
fruit, he is found occasionally referred to as merci
ful, but the general picture drawn of him is that of
"a destructive warrior," "clothed in terror," "of
mighty powers," "without a rival among the gods,"
"overthrowing the rebellious, and overwhelming the
powerful."   He is described as a mighty dragon
pouring venom over everything, as a mighty giant

---

[1] See above, p. 144.
[2] See specimens in Jastrow, *Religion Babyloniens und Assyriens*, I, pp.
467-480.

with a drawn sword, or, again, as prowling about at night and inflicting havoc on all sides. It will be recalled [1] that Nergal is transferred to the head ship of the pantheon of the lower world, as the power which forces the living to exchange this world for the eternal prison, gloomy and dark. If then the power bringing life and joy and cheer can be transformed through the natural course of nature into a destructive, cruel, and death-dealing force, it is evident that a definite limit is thus set to the development of ethical ideas in the relationship be tween man and the gods. The only outcome of the dilemma would be the assumption that the benefi cent power punishes evil and the wrong-doer. But this solution would not apply to the case in point, since the sun of midsummer strikes the just and the unjust alike, nor is there the slightest suggestion in the religious literature of Babylonia and Assyria that Nergal's wrath is due to the sins of mankind. He is a god without mercy, cruel by nature, who strikes whenever and whomsoever he can.

The problem of the existence of evil in a world supposed to be created by a power of goodness is difficult enough, as we have seen,[2] but when this power is conceived as a purely spiritual force, and not as a personification of some material phenomena, there is at least a possibility of reaching a solution which explains the sufferings and misfortunes as due either to man's sinful nature, or that such trials are sent to test the calibre of man's moral strength and

---

[1] Above, pp. 204 *seq.*   [2] Above, p. 235.

religious faith.[1]   We have, then, in the material as
pects of the relationship between man and the gods
definite limits set to the infusion of the ethical spirit,
nor are these limitations set aside by the tendency,
to be noted at a comparatively early stage in the
unfolding of the Babylonian and Assyrian religion,
to heap on some single deity the powers and attri
butes of all the others.   This tendency, despite the
assumptions of some scholars, never led to any real
monotheistic system of religious thought.   We find
at different times and in different centres deities
like Enlil, Ea, and Shamash, addressed in terms
which clearly indicate that quite apart from the
power of nature, which they orginally personified,
these gods became the embodiment of divine gov
ernment of the universe viewed as a unit.   This
tendency finds its most complete expression in the
case of Marduk, originally a sun-god, and who, from
being the patron of the city of Babylon, becomes, as
we have seen,[2] the head of the Babylonian pantheon,
upon the definite constitution of the empire that
had its seat in the city of Babylon.   Marduk not
only absorbs the powers of Enlil, Shamash, Ea,
Adad, and others, but he is even designated by the
names of these various deities.   A fragmentary
tablet[3] that has been the subject of considerable
discussion tells us that:

[1] Such are the conventional points of view urged by the friends of
Job in their speeches.

[2] Above, p. 67.

[3] *Cuneiform Texts from Babylonian Tablets, etc., in the British Museum,*
XXIV, Pl. 50.   The tablet was first published by T. G. Pinches in the
Journal of the Victoria Institute, 1896, pp. 8 *seq.*

"Ea is the Marduk of canals.
   Ninib is the Marduk of strength.
   Nergal is the Marduk of war.
   Zamama is the Marduk of battle.
   Enlil is the Marduk of sovereignty and control.
   Nebo is the Marduk of possession.
   Sin is the Marduk of illumination of the night.
   Shamash is the Marduk of justice
   Adad is the Marduk of rain," etc.

But this is far removed from any genuine mono theism. It may be designated as henotheism, to use the well-known term introduced by the late Max Müller. But the mere fact that the cult of the other gods with whom Marduk is identified proceeded undisturbed by this absorption of other roles is a sufficient indication that even henotheism was not consistently carried out. Even if it had been, Babylonia and Assyria would never have reached the point of conceiving divine government in terms of ethics pure and simple, as long as a chief deity was identified with a power of nature or projected on the heavens and identified with a star —the planet Jupiter in the case of Marduk. A theo logical system that cannot rid itself of a material istic conception of divine Power has definite barriers set to its growth. It must be remembered also that monotheism, viewed merely as a doctrine, does not necessarily lead to a higher form of religious aspira tion. The belief may be, and frequently is, the out come of purely philosophical speculation. Mono theism becomes religious only in proportion as there is infused into the one Power of the universe an ethical spirit free from all materialistic implications. The monotheism of the Hebrew Prophets is a relig ious doctrine, not because the Prophets made Yahweh the single source of all phenomena and occur rences, but because they conceived of Yahweh as a spiritual force ruling the universe by self-imposed laws of justice and righteousness. It is because of this element that the national Yahweh becomes the universal Jehovah.

III

The limitations of Babylonian and Assyrian eth ics show themselves also in what the Babylonians and Assyrians regarded as the real aim of life. Material blessings, prosperity, success in war and in private undertakings are emphasised in both the secular and religious literature. Perhaps we may add to these benefits also tranquillity of the soul, but even with this addition the aim of existence is far from impressing us as inspiring, or as bringing out the best elements in human nature. The scope taken by divination methods in everything pertaining to public and private life throughout all periods of Babylonian and Assyrian history is a sufficient proof for the thesis here maintained, that the aim of life was too closely associated with materialistic bene fits to furnish a stimulus towards higher things, or to become a force leading to nobility and to the exercise of the highest virtues. The main concern of the Babylonian and Assyrian religion, viewed from the practical side, appears to have been to

serve as a means of ascertaining the fate in store
for the country, for the king as the representative
of the gods, and for the individual so far as individ
ualism entered at all into the religion. Whether
through the inspection of the liver of the sacrificial
animal, or through the observation of the signs in
the heavens, or through unusual phenomena in the
case of new-born animals and infants, the priests
attached to the temples endeavoured to meet these
prime religious needs by making elaborate collections
of handbooks which, furnishing an interpretation
of all possible signs and symptoms in the case of the
three chief divisions of divination lore, might en
able them to give an answer to anxious inquiries.
The significant feature of these divination methods
is that the interpretations attached to the collec
tions of omens all bear on purely material benefits
or material ills. According to signs observed in the
liver, according to the phenomena and movements
of the heavenly bodies, or according to anomalies
noted in the case of the young of animals and of
infants,[1] a conclusion was drawn whether crops
would be favourable, whether rain would be abun
dant, whether a proposed military campaign would
be successful, whether disease would strike down or
life be prolonged, whether riches would be acquired
—all answers very much of the same nature that
those receive who consult the astrologers, the clair-

[1] For a full exposition of Babylonian-Assyrian divination, see the
second volume of the author's *Religion Babyloniens und Assyriens*, pp.
203-969. A brief survey will also be found in the author's *Aspects of
Belief and Practice in Babylonia and Assyria*, chapters III and IV.

voyants, and the fortune-tellers of our own days. It will be admitted that a religion which concerns itself so largely with a purely material aspect of life is not likely to furnish us with a very lofty aim of existence. Many people still consult astrologers and fortune-tellers, but it is safe to say that very few delude themselves into the belief that in doing so they are performing a religious function. We go to houses of worship and invoke the divine mercy, but we would not think much of the religious spirit of a preacher who would translate this appeal into purely materialistic terms. We all desire success. Many of us long for wealth. All people are grateful for health, and long for tranquillity of soul, but we look on religion not for the purpose of obtaining these needs but rather as a means of using them in the proper way when we secure them. That idealistic element is entirely lacking, in so far as our material enables us to judge, in the religion of Babylonia and Assyria, and it is only through the addition of such an element that we attain an aim in life worthy of the dignity of man.

The lack of any inspiring goal of life is illustrated in the case of the Babylonians and Assyrians in their attitude towards surrounding and distant nations. It is frequently maintained that the Babylonians were, on the whole, a peace-loving people, in contrast to the Assyrians to whom war seemed to be a nat ural exercise of power, as essential to them as breath itself. There is an element of truth in this general isation, but if pressed too hard the generalisation becomes false. In the earliest period of Babylonian history we find the Euphrates Valley divided into a number of states constantly at war with one another. The aim of each principality was to secure a control over the others, and as the rulers of one centre obtained a position of supremacy, their eyes were directed to conquest beyond the natural confines. To the east of Babylon lay Elam. Some of the earliest records that we have deal with the constant hostilities between Babylon and Elam, and some of the finest monuments furnish an illustration of this severe and bitter contest which continued for cen turies until Babylonia finally worsted her rival. The Babylonians themselves were obliged to submit for a period of over five hundred years[1] to a foreign people who came from the mountainous districts to the east and northeast of the Euphrates Valley.

These Cassites, as they were called, endeavoured to extend their rule into the north, into Assyria proper. Babylonia and Assyria became from about the eleventh century on, rival powers, and if the idea of world conquest originated with the north ern empire, it is largely due to the growing strength of the North, which placed Babylonia for many centuries on a defensive position against Assyria, until finally she was obliged to submit to the yoke imposed upon her by Assyrian rulers. Assyria car ried the disposition to exercise control over a large territory much further than Babylonia, but there is little reason to question that Babylonia would have

[1] From c. 1750 to c. 1200 B. C.

imitated the example of Assyria had she been able to do so. In fact, as we have seen,[1] Sargon, of Agade, founded an empire which was designated as embracing the "four quarters of the world." The higher culture of the south, and which gradually spread to the north, exercised, to be sure, a certain restraint, chiefly because with the growth of com merce wars became a much more serious menace to the prosperity of the country. But this restraint would never have been strong enough to overcome the ambition of Babylonia to rank as the mistress of the world had she been in a position to do so. Assyrian rulers, like Tiglath-Pileser I in the eleventh century, like Sargon and his successors in the eighth and seventh centuries, who were fired with the am bition to spread the power of Assyria on all sides, were merely carrying out the policy introduced by the older Sargon of the south, as early as the middle or the beginning of the third millennium before this era.

It cannot be my purpose to enter into a discus sion of the ethical justification of war. It may be that war represents a natural state of affairs among mankind, and that it corresponds, as some philos ophers tell us, to the struggle going on in all nature. Let us admit that up to a certain period in the de velopment of human civilisation war is the expres sion of the struggle for existence, and that for main taining one's possessions and defending them from attacks war is inevitable even in advanced stages

[1] Above, pp. 12 *seq.*

of culture.   But if human history impresses any les
son upon us, it certainly teaches that war is not a
factor in the progress of human culture, or in lead
ing to a higher development of the race.   Culture,
the advance of the arts, the rise of literature, a
growing sense of humanitarianism, all these achieve
ments have come not because of war but in spite of
it, and it is perfectly reasonable to assume that we
would be much further advanced on the highroad of
civilisation were it not for the ravages, the cruel
ties, and the misery inflicted on mankind through
endless bloody struggles.   The evils existing in the
world at the present time—the evils of poverty, the
oppression of the weak by the strong, the mischief
wrought through bitter hatred, through social and
religious prejudices—are to a large extent the direct
outcome of the desire for conquest, which at all
times has proved a serious check to the unfolding of
the highest ethics.

The cruelty of war increases as we go backward
in the track of time.   On old Babylonian monu
ments, as well as on more recent illustrations of
warfare with which Assyrian kings decorated their
palace walls, the element of cruelty is a strikingly
prominent feature.   Naram-Sin depicts himself in
the act of driving an arrow into the neck of a cap
tive pleading for mercy.[1]   As one of the wall dec
orations of an Assyrian palace we find the heads of
the slain enemy[2] heaped up before royal officers in

[1] See the illustration in Jastrow, *Aspects of Belief and Practice in Baby
lonia and Assyria*, facing p. 22.
[2] See Paterson, *Assyrian Sculptures*, Palace of Sinacherib, Pl. 52.

the act of counting them. With such examples, it was inevitable that the people in their relations to one another should have been actuated to a certain extent at least by the same spirit. The gods are invoked before battle is given. They are repre sented as being in the midst of the fray, and in their name and with their help not only is the enemy conquered but conquered towns are burned and pillaged, the men slaughtered, and the women and children captured.

IV

On the other hand, it comes as a surprise to us to find in another department of activity, which is sometimes looked upon as akin to war, namely commercial undertakings, a spirit of fairness prevail ing in Babylonia and Assyria which shows itself not merely in the numerous records of commercial trans actions but in the regulations embodied in the code of Hammurapi and on clay tablets furnishing legal decisions for the regulation of questions arising from the growth of business activity.[1] The rulers them selves furnish an example of respect for law which is all the more surprising when we consider how by their own confession they had so little respect for the life and property of those against whom they took up arms. Assyrian conquerors like Sargon mention with pride among their exploits the regu lation of the rights of citizens. Assyrian kings imi-

[1] Specimens from various periods will be found in Johns, *Babylonian and Assyrian Laws, Contracts, and Letters* (New York, 1904), pp. 80–115 and 227–303.

tate the example of Hammurapi in emphasising their
desire that their reigns should be marked by justice
to all, and in setting forth their aim to protect the
weak against the strong. The example set by the
rulers had its influence upon the people, so that we
find as a marked characteristic both of Babylonians
and Assyrians a respect for law, which carries with
it also the desire for fair dealings in business life.
A considerable portion of the statutes in Hammurapi's code is taken up with the regulation of com
mercial transactions. In their general spirit these
laws are humane and aim to secure an equal advan
tage so far as possible to two contending parties.
It is provided,[1] for example, that a person who takes
a field under contract to cultivate is responsible for
a produce equal in amount to that grown in a
neighbouring field. If he fails to carry out the
contract he must not only pay the amount of the
produce, but he must also undertake the cultivation
for the future produce. If a man lets a field for a
fixed sum he takes the risk of the failure of the
crop. If the proprietor of a tilled field has pledged
it to some one and then takes the produce (to which
he is not entitled), he must restore to the man to
whom the field has been pledged the capital, inter
est, and, as a fine, the cost of the maintenance of the
field. Any one who uses for his own purpose money
or anything given to him in trust must restore the
full amount, plus one-fifth of the value as a fine.[2]
A creditor who helps himself without legal author-

---

[1] §§ 42-47.　　　　[2] § 112.

ity to a possession of the debtor is obliged to restore what he has taken and forfeits his claim.[1]

The code of Hammurapi also throws a favourable
light on the ethical spirit in which relations between
husband and wife, and father and children were
regulated.[2] Infidelity on the part of the wife was
severely punished. True, the ordeal by means of
water to ascertain the guilt or innocence of the wife
is included in the regulations of the code, but a
paragraph is added which virtually abrogates this
primitive method of testing the guilt of the woman,
for it is stipulated that if she swears an oath attest
ing her innocence, she may return to her family. If
a woman, availing herself of her husband's impris
onment as a prisoner of war, marries without being
forced by stress of necessity she is put to death by
drowning, but if she does so under stress of neces
sity she is not punished. On the return of her
husband the first marriage regains its legality, and
the children of the second marriage belong to the
second husband.

Polygamy was recognised among the Babylonians
as it was among the ancient Hebrews, but it is in
teresting to note endeavours to regulate conditions
under which a concubine is to be admitted to the
household. In case the first marriage is without
issue a man can take a second wife, but she is not
given the privileges belonging to the first. If a wife
becomes an invalid the man may take a second wife,
but he is obliged to support the first one as long as

[1] § 113.   [2] §§ 118, 195.

she lives, and if the invalid wife so desires she may leave her husband's house and still claim support. The old law according to which wife and children are the property of the husband and father is the oretically recognised but practically abrogated, so that gifts made by the husband to his wife consti tute her property; nor can this property be claimed by the children as long as the mother lives.

Incest of all kinds[1] is severely punished—the intercourse of a father with his own daughter by the banishment of the father; of a man with his daughter-in-law by death; incest of a man with the betrothed of his son by a heavy fine and by the dissolution of the betrothal. A man may legit- imatise the children born to him of a maid, and such children have an equal share in the paternal estate. Even slaves were recognised as having the right to property of their own, a remarkable fact that practically changed slavery to an indenture, much as in the oldest of the Pentateuchal Codes slavery is recognised, but in being limited to six years of service is thereby similarly converted to mere indenture.[2] This method of changing the character of ancient laws without directly abrogating them is characteristic of legal procedure in antiquity. The theory underlying law among the Hebrews, the Baby lonians, and elsewhere was that a legal decision was a decree issued in the name of the deity. In other words, the law was an oracle, and it is signif icant that the Hebrew word for a legal decision,

---

[1] §§ 154–158.   [2] Ex. 21 : 2.

torâ, finds its equivalent in the Babylonian *tertu*, which is the common term for an omen or an oracle. The judge was a representative of the deity, and therefore it was held that a law as such could never be abrogated, but new decisions could be rendered which had the practical effect of replacing primitive law with one revealing a more advanced stage of understanding. I have just called attention to the fact that the Babylonian law still recognised the right of the man to sell his wife and children. The Hebrews, too, must have had a law of this kind, but in the so-called Book of the Covenant (Ex. 21 : 7 *seq.*) it is modified in a manner which converts the sale of a man's daughter into a hire of her services, with a view to her marriage with her new master.

The Hammurapi code is similarly full of exam ples of later modifications of legal decisions which, while maintaining the original principle, modify the method of applying the principle. Thus the primi tive *lex talionis*, or the law of retaliation, is found in the code,[1] couched in precisely the same terms as in the biblical codes, "eye for eye, tooth for tooth, bone for bone," but just as in the biblical codes[2] this principle is made the basis for a compensation equal to the value of the injured limb or organ, with a distinction, to be sure, between the two classes of citizens, the freeman and the dependent. In the case of injury to a dependent the valuation of the injury is imposed as a fine, but in the case of a free-

---

[1] §§ 196-201.

[2] See, *e. g.*, Ex. 21 : 26-27, which stipulates that the slave whose eye or tooth has been injured by his master is to be given his freedom.

man the old law is still literally applied, and eye for eye, tooth for tooth, bone for bone, is meted out as a punishment.

While fully recognising the limitations in the development of Babylonian ethics, due in no inconsiderable measure to this distinction between classes, we must not fall into the error of underestimating the extent to which ethical principles were recognised by the people as an ideal. We have, fortunately, preserved among the tablets of Ashurbanapal's library quite a number of texts furnishing ethical precepts not unlike the collections in the biblical book of Proverbs. On these tablets we find utterances like the following:[1]

> "Thou shalt not slander; speak what is pure.
> Thou shalt not speak evil; speak kindly.
> He who slanders and speaks evil,
> Shamash will visit recompense on his head.
> Let not thy mouth boast, guard thy lip.
> When thou art angered, do not speak at once,
> For if thou speakest in anger thou wilt repent afterwards,
> And in silence sadden thy mind. . . .
> To thy God come with a pure heart,
> For that is proper toward the Deity.
> Prayer, penitence, and prostration early in the morning render him,
> And with the god's help thou wilt prosper.
> In thy wisdom learn from the tablet.
> The fear of God begets favor, offerings enrich.
> Love and prayer bring forgiveness of sin. . . .
> Give food to eat, wine to drink,

[1] *Cuneiform Texts from Babylonian Tablets, etc., in the British Museum,* Part XIII, Pl. 29-30. Another text of this character is translated by Zimmern in *Der Alte Orient,* XIII, i, pp. 27-29.

> Seek what is right, avoid what is wrong,
> For this is pleasing to God.
> It is pleasing to Shamash;
> He will requite him."

Now we must, as a matter of course, make due allowance for a possibly wide gap between ideal and practice, but the existence of the ideal forms a means of estimating the height of the ethical aim. It would appear, indeed, that cruelty among Babylonians and Assyrians was largely exercised on the enemy, on those with whom one was engaged in a deadly contest. The limitations of Babylonian and Assyrian ethics are thus a reflection on the cruelty of war rather than on the character of the people. This defect in the ethical system of Babylonia and Assyria resolves itself therefore into a criticism of one of the distinctive features of the Babylonian and Assyrian civilisation, the insatiate thirst for conquest and for bringing neighbouring nations into a condition of subjection.

A more serious indictment may be made from the point of view emphasised at the outset of our investigations regarding the relationship between man and the gods. It is, perhaps, idle to speculate what course would have been taken by the Euphratean civilisation had the Babylonians and Assyrians abandoned the policy of conquest, but it is, I think, safe to assume that the general character of the ethics would not have been materially altered, unless the priests had imbued the people with a spirit which would have remodelled the materialistic conception

of the government of the universe through powers
not only beyond human control but outside the
province of any law.   So long as divine government
was interpreted in terms of power, and power of an
essentially materialistic character, we might have a
strong emphasis on fair dealings in business trans
actions, we might have an endeavour to regulate
family relationships in an equable spirit, rulers
might set an example of profound respect for law,
ethical precepts might be taught by the priests, and
yet so long as power was conceived of not merely
as an element in divine government but as its
supreme manifestation, the aim of life could never
have risen beyond a desire to secure material bless
ings.   This is well brought out in one of the episodes
of the Gilgamesh epic, in which the advice is given
to the hero to desist from the attempt to seek im
mortality and to content himself with the joys and
pleasures of this world.[1]

> "Thou, Oh, Gilgamesh, let thy belly be full.
> Day and night be merry,
> Daily celebrate a feast,
> Day and night dance and make merry.
> Clean be thy clothes, anointed be thy head;
> Be washed daily in pure water.
> Look joyfully on the child that grasps thy hand;
> Be happy with the wife in thy arms."

The passage reminds us of the spirit of the book
of Ecclesiastes which, in fact, gives the same advice
in almost the same words:[2]

[1] See above, p. 211.   [2] Chapter 9 : 7–9.

"Go thy way, eat thy bread with joy, and drink thy wine with
      a merry heart.
  Let thy garments be always white, and let thy head not lack
      ointment.
  Live joyfully with thy wife whom thou lovest,
  All the days of thy life of vanity which He hath given thee under
      the sun,
  For that is thy portion."

We will presently see that Hebrew ethics found a
corrective, or rather the answer to the implications
of such teachings. The fact that the advice is em
bodied in the epic of Gilgamesh—the most impor
tant literary achievement of Babylonia—may be
taken as an indication that for the Babylonians,
even for those who had attained the highest level,
the advice to the hero reflects the aim of life, which,
to be sure, includes acting fairly, dealing out justice,
fulfilling one's obligations towards men and towards
the gods, but all this in order that it might bring as
a reward the enjoyment of the material pleasures of
this world.

V

There is no warrant for assuming that the He
brews started out with a better equipment for the
development of ethics than the Babylonians, or than
any of the nations by whom they were surrounded
in their own country. The early traditions and
narratives show us the Hebrews living very much the
same kind of life as the other groups in Palestine.
The stories of the Patriarchs give us fascinating

pictures of conditions existing at the time when the Hebrews, or, at all events, when some of the Hebrew settlers led a nomadic life. The story of Laban's dealings with Jacob, and Jacob's success in getting the better of the tricky Laban, may be taken as characteristic of the ethics of the time. Laban makes various promises, to give Jacob his daughter Rachel, to compensate him for his labours, all of which promises he breaks. Jacob apparently submits, but at a critical moment when Laban agrees to a cer tain proposition that all speckled and spotted sheep born in the fold should belong to Jacob, the latter, by an ingenious device, brings it about that all the young lambs are speckled and spotted.[1] This strat egy is not only approved, but it is intimated that this success was due to the fact that Jacob was aided by Yahweh. Both Jacob and his mother deceived the enfeebled father, Isaac. Such stories were evi dently popular, and reflected at one time the general spirit of the people. To be sure, there were other narrators who felt that such stories were not alto gether edifying, and so we find one of the writers represented in the book of Genesis omitting the de tail of Rebecca's and Jacob's deception, and indicat ing as the reason why Rebecca urges Jacob to leave his home and why Isaac consents to this plan, be cause Esau had taken wives from the surrounding peoples and for fear that Jacob might do the same.[2] This motive reveals the opposition at a very late

[1] Gen. 30 : 31–39. Two versions of the story have been combined in the narrative.

[2] The little section, Gen. 27 : 46–28 : 9, is from the Elohist document.

period to mixed marriages, but the significant point of interest for us is that it is introduced to remove the bad taste left by the story of the deception practised on the husband and father.

The books of Joshua and Judges furnish various traditions of the conquest of Palestine by the He brews,[1] and are full of instances which show us that the Hebrews acted precisely as other groups did when engaged in bloody contests with enemies. The pages of the Books of Kings are stained with blood shed, with deeds of cruelty, tyranny, and dishonesty. The court of David is a hotbed of intrigue. Solo mon in introducing splendour and a degree of lux ury which contrasted so glaringly with the former simplicity of life, paved the way for corruption and for those internal dissensions that played havoc with the political fortunes of both the north and the south. What is it, then, that enabled the He brews eventually to rise superior to their surround ings and to come out of the ordeal of growing political weakness and of a national catastrophe that seemed to foreshadow the extinction of the people, with a spiritual power that found an expres sion in masterpieces of religious literature which, for a certain flavour of thought, have never been excelled in the history of mankind and remain up to the present time the basis for the ethical inter pretation of human life? I refer, of course, to the Prophets and to the Psalms.

[1] See the admirable analysis of the versions of the conquest by L. B. Paton in the *Journal of Biblical Literature*, vol. XXXII, pp. 1–47.

In saying this I do not wish to underestimate the force of movements in this direction prior to the appearance of the great Prophets of the eighth and seventh centuries. In a former chapter[1] I endeavoured to set forth the profound stimulus that must have been exerted by Moses, and we have seen that we are justified in attributing to him a more spiritual conception of the national deity, Yahweh, than was attached to the divine protectors of other Palestinian groups. True, Yahweh remains for Moses the God of Israel, but a deity who is no longer identified with any special personification of a natural power, though retaining traces of having been originally conceived as a god of the storm whose voice is heard in the crash of thunder and who manifests himself in the lightning flash, in fire and in smoke. The Yahweh of Moses is a deity whose seat is no longer confined to any particular place, who moves away from Mount Sinai with the wanderings of his people, and who follows them in their settlements in the agricultural districts and then adopts the old sacred site at Jerusalem as his main sanctuary.[2] A deity, moreover, who is not to be worshipped by any image is a national deity largely in name only. The limitations to his scope and jurisdiction become circumstantial rather than essential, so that the Prophets obeyed a correct instinct in attaching their conception of a universal power to the God of Moses. They were not conscious of having produced a new point of view; they merely drew corollaries from a view

---

[1] Above, pp. 175 *seq.*   [2] Above, p. 180.

of divine government outlined by Moses himself, and suggested by the national experience during the centuries intervening since the organisation of the tribes into a homogeneous group.

We have also seen that the conception of Yahweh as an ethical power may be traced to the Mosaic age, and this despite the unhistorical attempt of postexilic compilers of laws, narratives, and tradi tions to carry back the later aspirations to an ear lier and, indeed, to a remote age. The Decalogue, which in its original form bears the stamp of Moses' personality, contains the germ of the teachings of the Prophets that Yahweh is a God of justice and mercy who demands, as an absolute condition of his favour, obedience to laws that have a distinct ethical flavour. After Moses we have historical personages like Joshua, Gideon, Samuel, Elijah, and Elisha who, after making full allowance for the legendary accre tions to the accounts of their careers, stand out sharply against the horizon as leaders who were im bued with a higher spirit; they are not heroes who gain their leadership by force of arms, though heroic exploits are told of some of them, but by the ex ample they furnished of obedience and devotion to ideals which, however short they may fall of latei standards, were for their time essentially ethical and calculated to bring about in due course aspirations of a higher character. We must thus assume a steady stream of influences in the direction of the more spiritual conception of divine control of the nation's life till we reach the time of an Amos, a

Hosea, and an Isaiah, with whom the movement takes on definite shape.

It matters little for our purpose here whether we take up utterances of the Prophets, which by com mon consent are placed in the postexilic period— in many cases embodied in the orations of pre-exilic Prophets—or such as may be regarded as pre-exilic, the spirit throughout that portion of the Old Testa ment collection which is grouped under the names of fifteen Prophets is the same, with the single ex ception perhaps of Jonah, which stands by itself.[1] A number of the figures among the Prophets stand out as individuals. We can picture to ourselves Amos, a rustic, probably not very attractive in his exterior, but whose words gush forth with all the power of a mountain stream. We can picture the earlier Isaiah reared in a great capital, equipped with worldly knowledge to reinforce his spiritual faith. We can conjure up the picture of Jeremiah, severe and impetuous, but for the most part the individualism of the Prophets sinks into the back ground, and it is their message which like a single melody with many variations rings in our ears. Of

---

[1] The book of Jonah, if we exclude the Psalm inserted in the second chapter which is clearly of later origin, is a narrative aimed against the tendency of the Prophets to foretell disasters. The writer is a satirist who wishes to hold up these Prophets to ridicule by showing that they are more bent upon having their forecasts justified, than upon having their warnings heeded. Jonah is introduced as a type of the Prophet who regrets that Nineveh—a disguise for Jerusalem—repents of its deeds and is to be saved from the threatened destruction. The episode of the whale is in keeping with the satirical vein running throughout the nar rative. Jonah is thrown overboard as the cause of the storm—a sign of God's anger—but even the whale cannot endure the Prophet and accordingly spews him out after three days.

such little consequence was the personality of the preachers speaking in the name of Yahweh, even in ancient times, that later compilers did not hesitate to add to the utterances of a Prophet exhortations which seemed to breathe the same spirit, quite un concerned for the accidental circumstance of author ship.

Authorship, in fact, counted for little in the an cient Orient. It was the utterance or the statement or the compilation that was regarded as the essence, and it is not until we come to an advanced literary period that the question of authorship was a matter of any concern. Greek culture with its emphasis on individualism may be said to have invented the idea of authorship, so far as it involves the individual's claim to his mental product. We have no specific word for author in ancient Hebrew, but merely a term ordinarily rendered as "scribe" which may be used indifferently for a secretary who writes at dic tation, for one who copies or compiles what another has composed, as well as for the one who indites an original composition. A writer in ancient times was merely one who wrote, whether he composed what he wrote or wrote what others had composed. Hence, on the one hand, the circumstance of ano nymity in ancient literary productions applying to Egypt, Babylonia, and ancient India where authors are rarely if ever named, and, on the other hand, the promiscuous and unhistorical assignment of pro ductions to some name that had become prominent, whether a real or a traditional personage, at a time

when the individualistic character of literary com
position had become more pronounced. Because
Moses comes down in tradition as a law-giver, all
laws are ascribed to him; because David may have
written some martial poetry, all Psalms are attrib
uted to him;[1] because Solomon became the tradi
tional *grand monarque* under whom luxury spread
and who was noted for his wisdom, he becomes
the author of Ecclesiastes and of the book of
Proverbs.[2]

Another result of this method of literary produc
tion in the ancient Orient was that no book was pro
duced at one sitting, as it were. A book was always
a compilation; it grew from age to age, much as a
story grows with each repetition. It received its
final shape only when it had outlived its popularity,
or when the tendency of thought which had given
rise to it had exhausted its vitality and some new
movement had set in. A modern book begins its
life after the author has finished it in its entirety
and it has left the press; an ancient book lives and
grows as long as it is unfinished, and when it is fin
ished it may be said to be dead. Composition,
therefore, became essentially compilation. It may
safely be said that there is not a single book of the

[1] The headings to the Psalms are of course later than the compositions
themselves, and a comparison between the headings in the Hebrew text
and in the Greek version shows the existence of varying traditions. It
should also be noted that the Hebrew preposition translated "to" may
mean a variety of things. A psalm "to" David may indicate, indiffer
ently, a psalm ascribed to David, or about David, or in the manner of
David, or of the time of David as well as by David.

[2] Despite the fact that other authors or collectors of proverbial sayings are mentioned in the book.

Old Testament which does not contain portions be
longing to different periods, sometimes separated
from one another by centuries.   In the case of the
laws, in fact, almost every chapter represents a com
pilation of various sources or contains additions from
various hands, quite apart from glosses and com
ments and counter-utterances that any "scribe"
might add in copying or reading a chapter or sec
tion.   A modern almanac, such as is published an
nually by many newspapers, would form an analogy
to an ancient book, in so far as it is generally anon
ymous and its contents are a compilation from vari
ous sources, made by many hands.

In accordance with this method of book-making
we find attached to the book of the earlier Isaiah a
whole group of chapters that are generally regarded
nowadays as the work of a second Isaiah.   Within
both groups there are chapters or sections within
chapters that clearly betray the hand of later edi
tors,[1] who came across other published orations
which they added to the earlier collection, merely
because what they found seemed to fit in, not from
the point of view of historical sequence, but from
a similarity in spirit or style or the specific treat
ment of a theme.   The inserted chapters or sections
might also be intentional imitations of the earlier
Prophet written with a view of having them at
tached to some great name.   Pseudepigraphy, which
involved attaching to a composition some name, as

[1] See the introduction to Gray's Commentary on Isaiah, as an illus
tration of the complicated process which produced the book in its present
shape.

in the case of the book of Daniel, that had become
prominent or a name that had become a type for
a certain kind of writing, was merely another nat
ural consequence of the indifference to the question
of personal proprietorship in literary production.
In every one of the prophetical books, with the pos
sible exception of Ezekiel, who seems to have himself
compiled some of his utterances, there are certain
sections or whole chapters that are pseudepigraph-
ical. But as a result of this sinking of the individ
uality of the Prophet in the composition of the pro
phetical books a unity is given to this portion of the
Old Testament that is quite remarkable. Whether
we turn to Amos[1] and read his burning words:

"Seek good, and not evil, that you may live. . . . Hate the
evil, and love good, and establish judgment in the gate. Perhaps Yahweh, the Lord of Hosts, will be gracious unto the rem-
nant of Joseph. . . . Woe unto you that despise the day of Yahweh! What is the day of Yahweh for you? it is darkness and
not light. . . . I hate and I despise your feasts, and I will take
no delight in your solemn assemblies. . . . Take thou away from
me the noise of thy songs, for I will not listen to the melody of
thy viols. But let judgment roll down as waters, and justice
as a mighty stream;"

or again:[2]

"Behold the days are coming, says the Lord Yahweh, that I
will send a famine in the land, not a famine of bread nor a thirst
for water, but of hearing the words of Yahweh. And they shall
wander from sea to sea, and from the north to the east, and shall
run to and fro to seek the word of Yahweh, without finding it.
In that day shall the fair virgins and the young men faint for
thirst."

[1] Amos 5 : 14-24.   [2] Amos 8 : 11-13.

Or we turn to Isaiah and read:[1]

"When you come to appear before me, who hath required this at your hand, to trample my courts? Bring no more sinful oblations, incense is an abomination unto me; new-moon and sabbath and the calling of an assembly—I cannot endure iniq uity with a solemn meeting. . . . And when you spread forth your hands I will hide mine eyes from you. When you make many prayers I will not hear. Your hands are full of blood. Wash you, make you clean, put away the evil of your doings from before mine eyes. Cease to do evil; learn to do well, seek judgment, relieve the oppressed; judge the fatherless, plead for the widow."

Or Jeremiah:[2]

"As the thief is ashamed when he is found, so is the house of Israel ashamed; they, their kings, their princes and their priests and their prophets, saying to the wood, 'Thou art my father'; and to a stone, 'Thou hast brought me forth.' . . . Wherefore will you contend with me? You all have transgressed against me, says Yahweh. In vain have I smitten your children; they received no correction. Your own sword hath devoured your prophets like a destroying lion. . . . Also on your skirts is found the blood of the souls of the innocent poor. I have not found it at a place of breaking in, but on all these, and yet thou sayest, 'I am innocent, surely his anger is turned away from me.' Be hold, I will enter into judgment with thee, because thou sayest, 'I have not sinned,'"

or again:[3]

"Stand in the gate of the house of Yahweh, and proclaim there this word, and say, Hear ye the word of Yahweh, all ye of Judah that enter in at these gates to worship Yahweh. Thus says Yahweh of Hosts, the God of Israel: Amend your ways and your doings, and I will cause you to dwell in this place. Trust not in lying words, saying, 'The temple of Yahweh, the temple

[1] Isaiah 1 : 12-16.　　　[2] 2 : 26-35.　　　[3] 7 : 2-7.

of Yahweh, the temple of Yahweh.' For if you thoroughly amend your ways and your doings; if you thoroughly execute judgment between a man and his neighbor, if you oppress not the stranger, the orphan and the widow, and shed not innocent blood in this place, neither walk after other gods to your hurt, then will I cause you to dwell in this place, in the land that I gave to your fathers from of old, forever."

The message is everywhere the same. Justice and righteousness alone can save the people. The Prophets direct their denunciations against the conventional view held in reference to sacrifice, to prayer and all forms of worship, not that they opposed such forms, but because they realised that the cult was a hinderance to spiritual growth, unless carried on in a spirit of purity and unless the effect of the cult was seen in the conduct of the worshippers. To us all this, because familiar, may seem trite, but it is difficult to overestimate the revolution in religious thought brought about through the substitution of such ideals of justice, righteousness, kindness, mercy, purity of mind, for the incrustated view that God demanded worship, and that through offerings and the observance of festivals the Deity could be reached and brought into favourable accord with human desires and wishes. Small wonder that the Prophets aroused the most violent opposition, that their utterances frequently involved a risk of their life, for they appeared to their hearers to be violent revolutionists compared with which the anarchists of our days seem gentle and kind. They seemed to sweep away the entire fabric of the religious experience of the past. They boldly declared that the most glo-

rious period of Hebrew history, marked by an elab
orate temple organisation with daily offerings and
constant prayer, was to be brushed aside as contrary
to the will of Yahweh.   And what had these icono
clastic denunciators of the fashions of the day to
offer in place of the popular religion? A vague or
intangible conception of a spiritual Power enthroned
in righteousness, and demanding nothing of His wor
shippers but "to do justly, to love mercy, and to
walk humbly with thy God" (Micah 6 : 8).

VI

Yet this principle was to become the basis for a
faith destined to make its way throughout the world;
and with the new faith came the new ethical ideal,
marked by a complete harmony between the spirit
and the outward expression of the spirit in conduct,
in the attitude of mind, and in the view to be taken
of the cult. As a single illustration—and there is
no time for more—of the total change brought about
in ethical ideals through the influence of the Proph
ets, it is sufficient to refer to the Prophets' concep
tion of sin and atonement as expressed in its most
perfect form in many of the Psalms, and to contrast
this point of view with that which we find in Baby
lonian penitential compositions.[1]

These Babylonian hymns are full of reverence,
and are couched in beautiful language, picturing the

---

[1] See numerous specimens of such penitential hymns in Jastrow, *Religion Babyloniens und Assyriens*, II, pp. 65–132.

contrite heart bowed down through contemplation of its shortcomings.

> "Mine eye is filled with tears,
> On my couch I lie full of signs,
> Weeping and sighing have bowed me low. . . .
> Many are my sins that I have sinned.
> May I escape this misfortune, may I be freed from disease!
> Forgive me my misdeeds, let my appeal reach thee. . . .
> O my God, creator of my being,
> Protector of my life, producer of my posterity,
> My angered God, may thy heart be appeased.
> My angered Goddess, grant me grace!"

But what are the sins that this penitent has in mind? The answer is clearly indicated in almost every one of such compositions. The anger of a deity has manifested itself in some misfortune that has come, through sickness, through the death of a beloved member of the household, through failure of crops, through destructive storms, or through a national catastrophe. The sin implied throughout is the neglect of something demanded by a deity, and we are rarely left in doubt as to the nature of these demands. Some rite has not been performed, some gifts have not been presented at the temple, a festival has been neglected, a preference shown for some deity that has aroused the jealousy of another. The Babylonian conception of sin is well brought out in the frequent allusion to the unknown char acter of the transgression. "My sins I know not," is the refrain in several of these compositions, and what is more, the penitent is at times in doubt as to the god or goddess whom he has offended, and therefore frequently adds:

"O God, whether known to me or unknown;
  O Goddess, whether known or unknown, forgive me my trans-
    gressions."

Now we find many traces of this same conception in portions of the Old Testament, and it is rather significant that in the Pentateuchal Codes, despite the fact that they show the influence of the new ethical ideal, the general conception of sin still as sumes that it can be wiped out through some offer ing, or, at all events that the offering is essential to forgiveness. This limitation, for such it must be accounted, is perhaps inherent in a ritualistic code, which, after all, is concerned with externalities; but all traces of such a conception disappear in the Psalms.

"The wicked shall not stand in the judgment,
  No sinners in the congregation of the righteous,
  For Yahweh knows the way of the righteous,
  But the way of the wicked shall perish." [1]

"Yahweh, who shall abide in thy tent,
  Who shall dwell on thy holy hill?
  He who walks uprightly, and does righteousness,
  And speaks truth in his heart." [2]

The psalmist pleads,

"Give ear to my words, O Yahweh,
  Consider my meditation. . . .
  For Thou art not a God who takes pleasure in wickedness,

[1] Psalm 1 : 5.   [2] Psalm 15 : 1-2.

> Evil shall not sojourn with thee,
> The arrogant shall not stand in thy sight. Thou hatest
>   all workers of iniquity.
> Thou shalt destroy them that speak lies."[1]

Or again,

> "O Yahweh, rebuke me not in thine anger,
> Neither chastise me in thy hot displeasure.
> Have mercy upon me, O Yahweh, for I am wasted away.
> O Yahweh, heal me, for my bones are vexed. . . .
> I am weary with my groaning;
> Every night make I my bed to swim;
> I water my couch with my tears.
> Mine eye is consumed because of grief. . . .
> Depart from me, all ye workers of iniquity;
> For Yahweh has heard the voice of my weeping." [2]

> "Judge me, O Yahweh, according to my righteousness, and ac-
>   cording to my integrity that is in me. . . .
> My shield is with God, saving the upright in heart. God is a
>   righteous judge." [3]

> > "Guard me as the apple of thine eye
> > Hide me under the shadow of thy wings
> > From the wicked that oppress me,
> > From my deadly enemies that compass me about." [4]

> "With the merciful thou wilt shew thyself merciful,
> With the perfect thou wilt shew thyself perfect,
> With the pure thou wilt shew thyself pure,
> And with the perverse thou wilt shew thyself froward,
> For thou wilt save the needy[5] ones, but the haughty eyes
>   thou wilt bring down,
> For thou wilt light my lamp; Yahweh my God will lighten
>   my darkness." [6]

[1] Psalm 5 : 1-7.   [2] Psalm 6 : 1-4.   [3] Psalm 7 : 9-12.
[4] Psalm 17 : 8-9.
[5] On the application of the term "needy," see above, p. 241.
[6] Psalm 18 : 25-28. The composition though, according to the heading
assigned to David in thanksgiving for his escape from his enemies and

"Make thy ways known to me, O Yahweh,
Teach me thy paths,
Lead me in thy truth, and teach me;
For thou art the God of my salvation,
On thee do I wait all day.
Remember, O Yahweh, thy tender mercies,
For they have been ever of old.
Remember not the sins of my youth, nor recall my transgressions.
According to thy loving kindness, remember thou me." [1]

Rarely do we find any reference in the Psalms to offerings or to external means of appeasing the angered Deity. The thought throughout is that sin can only be forgiven if the disposition is there to lead a life pleasing to a righteous Power. The very emphasis on the justice of God furnishes the proof of the silent assumption, as a fundamental principle, that only the pure in heart, those who have cleansed their souls from evil and sinful thoughts, can venture to approach the throne of mercy. The essence of the cult thus becomes, un der the influence of the later Hebrew ethical ideal, the stimulus towards the higher life.

I have referred to the Pentateuchal Codes and pointed out that the ritual still shows traces of the earlier and materialistic conception of sin. An im partial consideration of these Codes forces on us the conclusion that while they are full of a humane spirit, particularly noticeable in the book of Deu-

from Saul, in reality reflects the political and religious conditions in the Maccabean days, as is generally agreed by scholars. See Duhm's Commentary, p. 59. The language, tinged with Aramaisms, is sufficient to prove the late age of the composition.
[1] Psalm 25 : 5-7.

teronomy, and the conception of the Deity is quite as sublime as that found in the utterances of the Prophets, yet the institution of an elaborate sacri ficial regulation is a step backward from the relig ious ideals of the Prophets. The problem involved is an intricate one and can only be touched upon here. We must, to be sure, bear in mind that the Prophets were not really opposed to sacrifices and ceremonial observances, but only to their abuse and to the assumption that the carrying out of the cult is what Yahweh above all desired. Some of the Prophets, like Jeremiah, show, indeed, a rather fa vourable attitude towards ceremonialism if combined with a pure heart and in conjunction with upright conduct. A large section in Ezekiel (chapters 40–47) is devoted to a plan for the rebuilding of the temple and the reorganisation of the cult with elaborate ceremonialism. For all that, the general trend of Prophetism is towards worship in spirit and not through external forms. The emphasis of their relig ious philosophy is on conduct and not on the cult —certainly not on ceremonialism as a means of approaching Yahweh and of securing his favour. We must remember also that these sacrificial regu lations which assume such huge proportions in the latest of the compiled codes, known as the Priestly Code, were intended to serve a practical end; namely, to constitute a source of income for the large priestly organisation needed in a large centre like Jerusalem. A revolution was effected through the Deuteronomic Code that was quite in keeping with the spirit of the Prophets, and which aimed at nothing less than to abolish the numerous sanctuaries scattered throughout the country in favour of a single sanc tuary for the legitimate cult in Jerusalem.[1] That was a bold step indeed, which was not actually carried out until the postexilic period. It was a great gain thus to demolish at one blow the rites observed in the sanctuaries outside of Jerusalem, and in which, we may be sure, many Canaanitish practices were maintained by the sheer force of tradition. We have seen, however, that this worship of Yahweh which extended throughout the country, though carried on at sites of original Baal worship, was an impor tant factor in leading to the belief that Yahweh was not, like other gods, confined to one centre. It was therefore from this point of view a step back to ear lier conditions to concentrate the cult in a single sacred site. Practical necessity, on the other hand, demanded that there should be a cult carried on by a priestly organisation and that such a central organisation, recognised as legitimate, should be supported by the populace. The compilers of the Priestly Code, attaching themselves, so far as pos sible, to existing practices and to deeply ingrained forms of worship, introduced merely such modifica tions in the older sacrificial regulations as were nec-

[1] This is emphasised over and over again in Deuteronomy and included the order to destroy all other sanctuaries, e. g., Deut. 12 : 1-5, 13-14; 14 : 25; 15 : 20; 16 : 2, and so in almost every chapter of the Code. Gressmann, in his recent work, *Mose und seine Zeit*, p. 466, shows that Deuteronomy in carrying the centralisation idea back to Moses followed a correct instinct, for in the wilderness, and during the nomadic period of the national life, there was only *one* sanctuary, though naturally only because there was no need for any other. See further on this point, above, pp. 181 *seq.*

essary to adapt them to the new conditions, in the belief perhaps that the ethical transformation of the idea of God, which meanwhile had been accom plished, was a sufficient guarantee against a return to the former materialistic view of the divine wor ship as a means to a more or less selfish end. The emphasis placed throughout all the Pentateuchal Codes upon the conception of Yahweh as a God who rejoices the heart, who is kind and merciful to those who act justly, but who is unrelenting to evil-doers, "visiting the iniquity of the fathers upon the children to the third and fourth generation"-— the emphasis placed upon this conception of Yahweh should indeed have been considered a sufficient pro tection against mistaking the form for the substance, against attaching an undue importance to sacrificial and other rites as a means of approaching the throne of grace. The danger, however, was not averted, and we have abundant evidence that during the two or three centuries preceding the final destruc tion of the little that was left of the national inde pendence of the Jews, the abuse of worship, against which the Prophets voiced their strong protest, had again crept in. There was, to be sure, no return to such conditions as prevailed in the pre-exilic period. For one thing, the Jews—as we should de nominate the people from this time on rather than as Hebrews, which designation should be limited to the pre-exilic period—were scattered not only over Palestine but also outside of the national home. Only a small proportion of the descendants of those who after the destruction of Jerusalem had settled

in Babylonia ever returned to their native country.
Extensive Jewish colonies and communities had
sprung up in various parts of Egypt, around Ele
phantine in the south[1] and around Alexandria in
the north.   To these, as to all Jews not settled in
Jerusalem, the central sanctuary became a symbol
rather than a reality, a symbol of the spiritual bond
uniting Jews everywhere, but hardly an effective
force in moulding the religious life of the people.
The sacrificial observances at the temple in Jeru
salem did not assume the importance and promi
nence that was hoped for by the compilers of the
Priestly Code; and the obligation imposed on every
Jew to come with his family to Jerusalem three
times a year must necessarily have remained a dead
letter to the vast majority.   At the old harvest fes
tival in the fall, the pilgrimage or *Hag*,[2] as it was
called, there appears to have been a considerable
gathering of pious worshippers in Jerusalem from
various parts of Palestine, but the number that came
from beyond the borders must at all times have been
small.   Such annual gatherings served to keep alive
the sense of unity and no doubt fostered the national
aspirations, but their influence hardly extended be
yond this point.   The Samaritan schism,[3] which had

[1] See Eduard Meyer, *Der Papyrusfund von Elephantine* (Leipzig, 1912),
—an admirable summary and discussion of the recent remarkable discov
eries of papyri dealing with the affairs of the Jewish colony at Elephan
tine.

[2] Identical with the Arabic *Hadj*, the term for the pilgrimage to Mecca.

[3] See James A. Montgomery's work on *The Samaritans*, chapters III–V,
for an account of the growth of the separation between Jews and Samari
tans in the postexilic period.

brought about a sharp separation between the cults
of Jerusalem and Samaria, was a further feature in
checking the influence of the Jerusalem priesthood.
The attachment of the Jews of Egypt to the cen
tral sanctuary was also lessened by the existence of
an independent "Yahweh" temple in Elephantine;
and there may have been such shrines at other
places. It was not therefore the sacrificial minu
tiæ observed at the temple in Jerusalem that con
stituted any serious menace to the growth of the
genuine ethical spirit independent of ceremonialism.
The movement towards the regulation of the details
of life by ceremonial observances began, curiously
enough, in lay circles quite outside of priestly influ
ences. The most characteristic feature of postexilic Judaism is the rise of combinations of laymen
for the study of the law. The synagogue appears
by the side of the temple[1] and becomes a much more
potent force than the official sanctuary in the devel
opment of the religious life of the people. Worship
in the synagogues makes its start as an appendix
to the study of the law and as a further means of
spreading religious teachings. It is in connection
with the synagogue that we find the tendency mak
ing itself felt of unduly emphasising the details of
ceremonial regulations. Pharisaism is the outcome
of this tendency, but we would be doing Pharisa
ism an injustice to assume that it ever went so far
as to utterly neglect the spirit in favour of the let-

[1] See Schurer's *History of the Jewish People in the Time of Jesus Christ*,
II, 2, p. 527.

ter.   The

checked the complete sway of the new ethical ideals,

. . . .

change wrought through the gradual spread of Prophetical Judaism that even the worship of the letter

. . . 1 . . . .

it shared with the other Jewish sects
of the time, the thought of Jehovah as the universal
power predominated over the conviction—a legacy
of the former national conception—that Jehovah
had a special concern for the people chosen by him
to proclaim his universal reign.   No doubt the average Jew, during the few centuries preceding the

was still under the influence of the time when Yahweh was conceived as limited in his jurisdiction to
a single group   But this influence did not extend

. . . .

. . . .

the universal father of
and the God of the Hebrew people
fathers.   The two conceptions b
other and gave rise to a deep religious spirit, which
actuated the Pharisees quite as much as the representatives of religious movements in Judaism away
from legalism.   Nor was there any danger of any
real conflict between these two . . . .
people needed as a supplement to the idea of a universal power the assurance that Jehovah was still
specially concerned with those who had chosen Him

and who, therefore, by virtue of a mutual relation
ship, regarded themselves also as specially chosen.
This need was supplied by the consciousness of an
identity of the universal Jehovah with the old na
tional Yahweh. But even what traces still remained
of the national conception of the Deity had become
so entirely synonymous with the Power making for
justice and righteousness as to counteract the tend
ency towards any artificiality of the religious life
through the growing complications of minute cere
monialism. Besides, the spirit of this ceremonial
ism, even though as a system it makes no appeal
to our sympathies, was thoroughly ethical. I hold
no brief for legalism in religion, but an impartial
survey of Rabbinical Judaism demands the recogni
tion that the ritual, particularly in the course of its
transference from the temple to the lay place of
assembly, the synagogue, became more and more
an expression of the attitude of the individual to
wards a Power conceived in spiritual terms, and one
whose chief concern is for the establishment of a
reign of love, justice, and righteousness in the world.
The Jewish prayer-book, which begins to make its
appearance at this time—a direct outcome of the
synagogue and not of the temple—voices this con
ception on every page. The universality of the
divine sway is emphasised, and the unity of the
human race held out as the ultimate goal of man
kind. A future is foreshadowed in which, to be
sure, national aspirations still play a part, but in
which they are completely overshadowed by the pic-

ture of all nations moving towards Jerusalem as the spiritual centre to usher in the Messianic age, por trayed as the triumph of love and justice in the world.

VII

Neither therefore on the side of ethics, nor in the conception of divine government as set up by the Prophets, did the later legalistic aspects of post-exilic Judaism seriously interfere with the further development of religious idealism or of ethical prac tices. Of more serious moment was the spirit of scepticism that had crept in and made considerable headway after the Exile, and which finds an expres sion in such productions as the books of Job and Ecclesiastes. The scepticism, particularly as set forth in Ecclesiastes, was a matter of deep concern, because the doubt as to the existence of a divine rule of justice in the world involved as a corollary a return to the materialistic conception of life. The book of Job, as we have seen,[1] is concerned prima rily with a purely philosophical discussion of the problem involved in assuming at the head of the universe a Power ruling in justice, contrasted with the actual state of affairs in this world, in which injustice and wickedness flourish, while the good and pious languish and receive punishment that be longs to the wicked. The conclusion that the ideal life is not worth living is suggested but not dis tinctly drawn. Job contents himself with giving

[1] Above, pp. 233 *seq.*

expression to his doubts as to a just Providence, and to pouring forth his pathetic complaints of the un fortunate condition in which he had been placed, ap parently without reason. The book of Ecclesiastes, on the other hand, boldly takes the step of suggest ing that the one thing to do in a world constituted as this one is, is to eat, drink, and be merry, and to endeavour to drive away the thought of "for to-morrow we die." The sceptical basis, however, in Ecclesiastes is of the same order as in Job, involv ing a doubt as to the real working of justice and righteousness in the world. Both productions must be placed in the postexilic period, and it is safe to take as the time limit of their composition in their present definite form the year 400 B. C., though it is likely, as pointed out,[1] that Ecclesiastes is to be placed almost two centuries later. This scepti cism was perfectly natural, and it is not necessary to assume outside influences as bringing it about, though contact with Greek philosophic thought, so predominatingly sceptical, must have been a feature in accentuating it. The difficulties that the He brews encountered in their political and social life after the partial reconstruction of the Jewish commonwealth necessarily had a depressing effect. There were no indications that a time was approach ing when power and strength would be checked in carrying out their purpose. There was suffering on all sides, there was injustice everywhere. The weak were being crushed by the strong, the poor were be-

[1] Above, p. 236.

ing trampled upon. Priests appeared to be worldly and rulers tyrannical. The books of Job and Ecclesiastes must therefore be taken as an expression of the spirit of pessimism that had entered into the minds of many of the thoughtful ones among the people. These productions represent unquestionably a counter-current against the religious ideals, and in so far as they involve a reaction against the sovereignty of ethics in the life of the individual and favour a materialistic aspect of human endeavour, they are symptomatic of a check encountered by postexilic Judaism in its endeavour to realise the hopes of the leaders for the establishment of a religion based on the Prophets' conception of a divine government of justice and mercy.

The corrective to a sceptical or materialistic tendency was, however, found in the growing strength of the conviction that man, limited in his intellectual powers and circumscribed even in his will, had to resign himself to a realisation that it was not given to him to penetrate into the ways of God. The deficiencies of the human intellect were frankly recognised, and the conclusion drawn that the finite mind could not be expected to understand the way in which the Infinite—infinite in spirit as well as in power—carries out His divine purpose in the world. Many of the Psalms reflect this answer given to those who voiced their scepticism as to the reality of the just government of the universe. The psalmist complains of his bitter fate in terms frequently as pathetic as those found in the book of Job, but, unlike Job, he almost invariably adds to his complaint his trust that in the long run, and on the whole, justice will triumph, and the Lord will save the pious.

"Yahweh is my rock, my fortress and my defender;
My God, my strong rock, in him will I trust." [1]

———

"My God, my God, why hast thou forsaken me?
Why so far from helping me, from the words of my complain-
ing?
My God, I cry in the daytime, but thou hearest not;
And in the night season I am not silent.
But thou dwellest in holiness,
The praises of Israel are (for thee).[2]

.   .   .   .

Our fathers trusted in thee.
They trusted, and thou didst deliver them.
They trusted in thee and were not ashamed." [3]

and, finest of all, in the Twenty-third Psalm:

"Yahweh is my shepherd. . . . He leadeth me in the paths of righteousness for his name's sake. . . . I will fear no evil for thou art with me . . . Thy rod and thy staff, they comfort me. . . ."

There is a sense in which this sublime and solemn trust may be looked upon as the last word of the religious and ethical ideals of the Hebrews.

It is not necessary for our purposes to enter fur ther into the details of Hebrew ethics resulting from the teachings of the Prophets. These teachings—

[1] Psalm 18 : 2–3.
[2] I follow Duhm's reading, favoured by the Greek version.
[3] Psalm 22 : 2–6. The Psalm has the earmarks of the Maccabean period.

let me emphasise the point once more—were not
seriously affected by the unfolding of a legalistic
aspect of the religious life in the centuries preceding
the rise of Christianity, even though we must regard
this movement, which culminates in Talmudic Juda
ism, as a reaction from Prophetical Judaism.   It is
sufficient in a general survey of Hebrew and Baby
lonian ethics to indicate the divergent lines of devel
opment taken by the course of ethics in the two
civilisations and which may be briefly summed up
in the statement that Babylonian and Assyrian
ethics, despite its many notable aspects, failed to
find the corrective to the materialistic conception
of life which is an unavoidable outcome of what
we ordinarily regard as the progress of civilisation.
Such progress manifests itself in an advance in the
arts, in the growth of commerce, in a more compli
cated political organisation, and in the elaboration
of the religious life, and it is accompanied by in
creasing wealth and by more luxurious modes of life.
The danger inherent, therefore, in any high form of
culture is an undue emphasis on material advantages
which, if unchecked, leads to effeminacy and ulti
mate degeneration.   Babylonian and Assyrian ethics
failed to check this tendency.   The advice given to
the favourite hero, Gilgamesh, "to eat, drink, and
be merry"[1] strikes a characteristic note, and there
are no indications of a counter-movement such as
we meet with in Hebrew literature, which by means
of interpolations and counter-comments actually

[1] Above, p. 278.

succeeded in converting the parallel teachings of Ecclesiastes into an argument for the vanity of the materialistic conception of life.[1] Prophetical Judaism discovered the formula that acted as the antitoxin to both the materialistic and sceptical in fection of advancing civilisation. That formula in volved the setting up of holiness and purity as the aim of life in keeping with the ethical conception of a Deity of universal scope, Himself enthroned in holiness and purity, but whose mysterious workings were beyond the reach of the finite human under standing. The solution, to be sure, involved diffi culties—difficulties which are keenly felt still in our own days—but the removal of all materialistic as pects from the conception of divine government of the universe, and the persistent maintenance of high ethical aims led to the strengthening of the element of faith—faith in the unseen, faith in the unknow able, faith in the midst of the mysteries of life.

VIII

There is, however, another side of the picture on which, before proceeding to the conclusion, we must briefly touch. As a result of the inevitable conflict between the materialistic currents of advancing civ-

---

[1] The book of Ecclesiastes, so frankly sceptical and cynical as we have seen (above, p. 235), is full of interpolations intended to soften down the extreme utterances of the preacher or to furnish the answer to his argu ments. Without these interpolations, on which Barton's *Commentary on Ecclesiastes*, pp. 43–46, may be consulted, the compilation would never have been admitted into the canon; even with them the admission was effected only after a prolonged struggle. See Barton, *l. c.*, pp. 2–7.

ilisation and the maintenance of ethical and religious ideals, we find throughout the pages of the Old Testament—saturated as they are with the spirit of the Prophets that led, as we have seen, to the more or less complete transformation of ancient traditions and to a recasting of the legendary lore, of the history and the laws of the people to conform to this spirit—an unfavourable attitude towards what we, from our point of view, would regard as prog ress. The disposition is to give the preference to the simple over the more complicated ways of existence, leading logically to an opposition to more advanced forms of political, social, and religious organisation. This tendency crops out in the tales of Genesis, embodying, as we have seen, traces of early myths and of popular traditions. In the story of Cain and Abel the preference is given to Abel, the shepherd, as against Cain, the tiller of the soil, who becomes in the course of tradition also the builder of cities.[1] The lower form of culture is thus given the prefer ence over the higher one. In keeping with this the Patriarchs are represented as shepherds. A necessary concession to later conditions is made in the Pentateuchal Codes which assume as the ordi nary mode of life that of the agriculturist, but agri culture in these codes is contrasted with commerce, the higher stage, and, as we have seen, commerce is looked upon askance.[2] Again, therefore, the lower form is preferred to the higher. The political ideal of the Pentateuchal Codes is a loose and simple

[1] Gen. 4 : 17.   [2] Above, p. 167.

organisation of the tribes; it frowns upon a king
dom as a departure from ancient ideals, and we
need only read the description, in a late addition to
Deuteronomy, of what kings may be expected to do
to their subjects[1] to realise the ingrained opposition
against taking the necessary step of a higher form of
tribal organisation. The bitter speech placed in the
mouth of Samuel,[2] denouncing the desire of the peo
ple for a king as disloyalty to Yahweh, shows how
pronounced the tendency was against the higher
form of political life. The ideal sanctuary for the
worship of Yahweh in the codes is the tabernacle,
and a protest is entered against a structure in which
iron is used, or an altar of hewn steps[3] as against the
primitive rough stone,[4] such as Jacob set up at Bethel.

The Prophets voice this same tendency in their
denunciation of wealth, extension of dominion, and
luxury. The ideal is essentially that of the simple
life—converting swords into ploughshares, and spears
into pruning-hooks, each one dwelling peacefully
under the shade of his vine and his fig-tree.[5] There
is, to be sure, also the counter-tendency which led
to glorifying David and Solomon as the ideal kings
and to making them the authors of some of the finest
portions of the Old Testament writings, but this is
the work of a later age, in which other factors are
involved, and one need only read the narratives
in which the exploits of these national heroes are
recounted to see the traces of the earlier opposi-

---

[1] Deut. 17: 14-20.   [2] I Sam. 8 : 7-18.   [3] Ex. 20 : 25.
[4] Gen. 28 : 18.   [5] Micah 4 : 3-4.

tion to them. Such stories as David's relations to Bathsheba[1] and Solomon's defection from Yahweh[2] would never have been recounted had there not existed an element in the populace which looked with disfavour upon the kingdom, and whose senti ments are voiced in tales that were intended to show the disastrous consequences of exchanging the simple life of the loose tribal organisation for the grandeur of a royal court and the other changes that came in the wake of the higher culture, marked by the development of the country into a military power. The Prophet Jeremiah[3] furnishes the direct proof of the existence even in his days of a group within the people, known as the Rechabites, who, in their protest against advancing culture, continued to live in tents, and not in houses, who even looked askance upon the agricultural stage, and remained faithful to the nomadic ideal. This rather austere attitude towards life had its natural outcome in a form of conservatism that is a characteristic feature of the Prophets—both those of the pre-exilic and those of the postexilic period—which shows itself not only in their disapproval of the ambition of the Hebrews to emulate the example of the flourishing civilisations about them—Assyria, Babylonia, and Egypt, and subsequently Greek culture—but in the emphatic manner in which they hold up the time of the tradi tional sojourn in the wilderness, at the very begin ning of the national life, as the ideal period when Yahweh's relations to his people were closest.

[1] II Sam. 11.　　　[2] I Kings 11.　　　[3] Chapter 35.

That period is pictured as the happy wooing-time, when Yahweh found Israel and made her his beloved bride, the golden age to a return of which the Prophets longingly looked forward as the only salvation of the nation. Hence the projection of the entire religious organisation, including the secular laws and the religious rites into the remote past, back to the period when Moses through direct converse with Yahweh gave his people the instructions which were to be their guidance for all times. The traditional assignment of the entire Pentateuch to Moses, which modern scholarship has shown to be untenable, is thus of value as representing the logical outcome of Prophetism. It would never have arisen had not the Prophets held up the Mosaic period as the golden age of the simplicity of life, free from worldly ambitions, the age of naïve, unquestioning faith in Yahweh, and of a just valuation of the aims of existence.

This feature of Hebrew ethics, thus impressed upon it through the direct influence of the Prophets, leads, as I have suggested, to a serious outlook on life that is not without its forbidding aspect. The attitude became a resisting force, a force suspicious of progress for fear of the evils that may be engendered, a force that prefers the old to the new, that is disposed to place life at its best in the past, to idealise that past, and seek in it the guidance for the present. This austerity clung to Judaism throughout the succeeding ages. It coloured its ideals and hopes and gave to Rabbinical Judaism

that ultraconservative character which necessarily
led to an overthrow of Talmudical authority when
the Jews, upon being politically rehabilitated, began
to commingle with their fellows and to enter actively
into a world organised on a totally different basis,
and whose watchword was "progress." The aus
tere side of the ethics of the Prophets gave to life
in general among the Jews down to the threshold
of modern days a somewhat sombre aspect that tem
pered even the festive occasions—an aspect that was
accentuated by the distressing experiences, the hard
ship, and persecutions through which the adherents
of Judaism were destined to pass; but it also gave
the people the strength to face these experiences;
it hardened their moral fibre, it made them capable
of withstanding the allurements of ease and luxury,
and was the chief factor in developing among the
Jews those virtues of home life for which they be
came noted, and which flourish best under a stern
conviction of duty. In short, the austere aspects
of Hebrew ethics, while they diminished the sense
of the pure *joie de vivre*, without by any means sup
pressing it entirely, developed among the people
the sense of the seriousness of life which is the basic
condition of firm attachment to ideals.

IX

The final point to which we are led in tracing the
unfolding of religious thought and of the aim of life
among the Hebrews, and which carried them so far

away from Babylonian views and traditions, deals with the rise of a new religion issuing out of the old one. With the appearance of Christianity a new factor makes itself felt in the ancient world. Jesus represents the complete break between nationalism and religious aspiration. The break, to be sure, was an inevitable and logical consequence of the posi tion taken by the Hebrew Prophets, but it never practically came about until the days of Jesus, when the conflicting currents of thought in Palestine reached their crisis. The ethics of Jesus as embod ied in the sayings and parables scattered through out the Gospels attach themselves directly to the spirit of the Prophets and the Psalms. He opposes the tendency to make legalistic requirements the test of the religious life. He finds the corrective to the sufferings, misfortunes, and evil in the world in a sublime feeling of trust, of the same order as that which we encountered in the Psalms, and it is not accidental that the last words attributed to him should have been a quotation from a Psalm that describes the man of sorrows and of suffering. In all this Jesus is simply the successor of the Proph ets and the psalmists. The point of departure in his ethics from older ideals is the complete divorce from a nationalistic conception of divine govern ment in practice as well as in theory. That, to my mind, is the real significance of the period ushered in through him and his followers. The sayings of Jesus, forming the basis of the gospel narra tives—the core around which the story of Jesus is

constructed—also reveal to us his real personality,
the true bent of his mind and the direction of
his thought; and even if all the sayings and para
bles attributed to him should not be genuine, they
are conceived in his manner and are true to his
spirit.   I have only time to call your attention to
the beatitudes[1] as an illustration of the closeness
with which Jesus attaches himself to the ethics of
the Prophets and the Psalms.   When Jesus says,

"Blessed are the poor in spirit; for theirs is the kingdom of
     heaven,"

the poor meant are the 'poor and needy" so fre
quently mentioned in certain groups of Psalms;[2]
they are the pious ones of the postexilic congrega
tion, who, without worldly ambition, seek to live a
life patterned after religious and ethical ideals.

"Blessed are they that mourn, for they shall be comforted,"

is paralleled by the thought so often expressed in the
Psalms that they who sow in sorrow shall reap in
gladness.   Similarly, the third and sixth beatitudes,

"Blessed are the meek,[3] for they shall inherit the earth,"

"Blessed are the pure in heart, for they shall see God,"

are reflections of the description of the pious and
the pure in the Psalms, while the fourth beatitude,

---

[1] Matt. 5 : 3–11 = Luke 6 : 20–22 (in extract).   [2] Above, p. 241.
[3] The term translated "meek" is the exact equivalent of the Hebrew
'ani, which is used in the Psalms to describe the pious members of the
congregation.

"Blessed are they which do hunger and thirst for righteousness,
for they shall be filled,"

follows the thought of Amos[1] of the time when
Yahweh will send "a famine in the land, not a fam
ine of bread nor a thirst for water, but of hearing the
words of Yahweh." In the last two beatitudes,
where Jesus calls those happy and blessed who are
persecuted and defamed because of their righteous
ness, he expressly refers to the Prophets,[2] "for so
persecuted they the Prophets who were before you."

In the three remarkable chapters of Matthew
(chapters 5, 6, and 7), which may be regarded as a
summary of the ethics of Jesus, there is scarcely a
suggestion of ceremonialism, except by way of a pro
test against the undue emphasis on the externalities
of religion, precisely in the manner and the spirit
of both pre-exilic and postexilic Prophets. The
ethics of Jesus thus represent the culmination of
the movement which, stretching from Moses across
more than a millennium, led to a view of life based
on a conception of divine government in which
righteousness and mercy have usurped the place
taken by power and arbitrariness, and formulating,
as the end of existence, the perfection of character
in place of the satisfaction of worldly ambitions.
Overthrowing the barriers marked by an undue em
phasis on ceremonialism towards a further develop
ment of religious idealism, and drawing from the
teachings of the Prophets the conclusion that relig
ion must be a bond uniting all mankind, unfettered

---

[1] Amos 8 : 11. Above, p. 288. [2] Matt. 5 : 12.

by national limitations, the new religion, which con
tained so much of the old, starts out weighted with
the rich legacy of the past.   Transcending the geo
graphical boundaries within which it arose, it passes
on to carry the message of the Prophets and psalm
ists throughout the world.

I have thus endeavoured, by choosing a number
of characteristic features of traditions covering the
religious views and the religious thought of He
brews and Babylonians, to illustrate the different
directions taken in the development of these views
and traditions.   It has been my aim to show that
the direction in each case is an expression of the pe
culiar spirit of each people.   Outwardly, on a mere
superficial view, civilisations arise in different parts
of the world that have much in common.   The out
ward form, following certain lines of development,
is frequently similar in countries separated by long
distances from one another, and in civilisations that
arose independently of one another.   The attention
of the student of history should be directed to the
attempt to find in each civilisation, and beneath
the outward resemblance, the expression of the
genius or spirit peculiar to the people.   To repeat
the thought that I have endeavoured to illustrate
throughout this work, the ultimate differences be
tween Hebrew and Babylonian traditions are of
far greater significance than the points of re
semblance which are due in part to a direct in-

fluence exercised by the one upon the other, and in part are to be accounted for through common origins. The Babylonian civilisation as expressed in the course taken by its traditions, in the development of religious thought and of the aim of life, betrays, despite its achievements, the limitations inherent in a materialistic conception of divine government, which shows itself both on the religious and on the ethical side—in the views taken of the gods as in the attitude towards life. It shows itself in the political course of Babylonia and Assyria and in their literature and art, while the Hebrew civilisation, inferior in achievement, insignificant from the point of view of political influence, is saturated with an idealism, religious and ethical, that represents its contribution to mankind, a contribution of lasting value and one that was destined to survive the magnificence of ancient empires. It is this idealism issuing from the direction taken by the religious thought and by the religious institutions of the Hebrews that eventually brings about the wide departure from Babylonian and Assyrian counterparts, which it has been my aim to explain in the case of the specific traditions chosen as illustrations.

At the close of my task I am even more painfully aware than at the beginning of the futility of the attempt to give an exhaustive treatment of this important and fascinating theme in a brief series of lectures; but since in the course of a somewhat extended experience I have found the exhaustive treatment also exhausting—at least to the hearer and reader if not to the author—I have no apology to offer, if I have succeeded in indicating correctly the point of separation between Hebrew and Babylo nian traditions, and have made clear the reason why the two civilisations that have occupied us have so much in common and why they have so much more *not* in common. I am well aware also, that in a course of this nature I may have given expression to opinions and conclusions with which you, or some of you, may not be altogether in sympathy. I trust, however, that I have at least succeeded in placing the results of my studies before you with a due consideration for your feelings and a full sympathy with your convictions so far as they differ from mine. The last word of true science should always be the emphasis on the open mind and the ex pectant disposition. The test of a genuine desire for truth is the willingness to reinvestigate our con clusions, the maintenance of a sympathetic attitude towards new light, in the firm assurance that the truth which is the goal of mankind, and which it should be the aim of each one of us to realise so far as possible in our own life, will also be the means of our salvation.

APPENDIX[1]

HEBREW AND BABYLONIAN ACCOUNTS OF THE DELUGE

I

THE Babylonian tale of a destructive and prolonged rain-storm which swept away the habitations of men ex ists in several versions, as is the case with the Babylo nian Creation myth.[2] There is, however, this difference between the versions of the Deluge story and those of the Creation myth, that, while local forms of Creation tales are due to the desire of the priests or worshippers of a deity in a particular centre to accord to their patron god the distinction of being the creator, this motive does not appear to enter as a factor in giving rise to various versions of a catastrophe brought about by some god con trolling the destructive forces of nature. Nor do we find in the Deluge versions of Babylonia, so far as recovered, indications of a rivalry among the gods for the glory of having saved a favourite individual and his family from the general destruction. In all versions this deed is ascribed to Ea, who is the god of humanity *par excel lence* throughout all periods of the Babylonian-Assyrian religion. It may be, therefore, that all the versions are to be traced back to Eridu, the seat of Ea's cult, at or close by the Persian Gulf,[3] which was the element sacred

[1] See Preface, p. xii. [2] See chapter II.

[3] At present, however, owing to the steady accumulation of soil through the deposits of the Euphrates River, proceeding at the rate of about ninety feet a year, Abu Shahrain, the site of ancient Eridu, is about ninety miles inland.

to Ea as a water deity.   Perhaps in the variant names of
the favourite who survives the Deluge we may see indi
cations of local rivalry, each centre ascribing the distinc
tion of being thus singled out to its special *heros eponymos*
—whether a purely legendary character, or one with a
substratum of historical reality.

The versions of the Creation and of the Deluge agree,
however, in this respect, that all are nature-myths, that
is to say, narratives in which gods conceived as forces
of nature are portrayed as bringing about a change of
seasons.   Creation and Deluge stories supplement each
other, the former symbolising the change from the rainy
and stormy season to the dry one when the spring-god
triumphs over the cruel god of winter, while the latter
marks the triumph of the storm-god, who destroys ver
dure and vegetation and puts an end to all growth.   The
Deluge represents, therefore, the change from the dry
season to the rainy one.   Since Babylonia has merely
two seasons, Creation and Deluge stories thus picture the
two chief scenes in the annual drama of nature.   It was,
as we have seen,[1] a natural thought that led the Baby
lonian priests to regard the rebirth of nature in the spring
as repeating annually in miniature form the act of Crea
tion at the beginning of time, to take the annual occur
rence as the basis for their theory of the beginnings of
things.   Correspondingly, the Deluge myth rests on the
annual decay and death of nature, and portrays such
an occurrence, only magnified to a universal destruction
which was suggested, perhaps, by the recollection of a
particularly violent rainy and stormy season, accompa
nied by destruction of cities and great loss of life.   Before
the perfection of a system of canals, which by controlling
the overflow of the Tigris and Euphrates and by directing
the waters through the canals into the fields, changed the
annual curse into a blessing that brought about the ex-

[1] Above, p. 96.

traordinary fertility for which the Euphrates Valley became famed,[1] each year brought with it a deluge—at least on a miniature scale. The Deluge story is, therefore, a myth of the annual change of seasons—writ in large letters; and the fact that we find deluge stories in all parts of the world[2] wherever similar climatic conditions with the divi sion into two seasons as in Babylonia exist is confirma tory of the view here proposed.

The main version of the Babylonian Deluge myth comes to us, like the corresponding Creation myth, from the great library gathered by Ashurbanapal. Its Babylonian origin is indicated by internal evidence, and its great an tiquity attested by being incorporated in the Babylonian Epic of Gilgamesh. The latter, as a favourite hero, be comes a peg to which a variety of myths and old tales and traditions are attached,[3] with which he originally had nothing to do, and which originated quite indepen dently of their present position in the Epic. The three episodes which alone appear to form part of the original traditions associated with the hero, and which rest upon some historical basis, though the recollections are obscured by legendary accretions, are: (1) Gilgamesh's control of the ancient city of Uruk, which, as an invader from Elam, he conquered and ruled with an iron hand; (2) his con flicts with Engidu (who afterwards becomes his friend and associate) and with the tyrant Khumbaba, which ap pear to rest on some genuine exploits. Engidu and Khumbaba, however, are not historical characters. The former is the type of primeval man, the latter a myth ical personage who plays a part in a nature-myth which is woven into the exploits of Gilgamesh. The other epi-

[1] See Herodotus, I, § 193.

[2] See Andree, *Die Flutsagen* (Braunschweig, 1891), for a convenient summary; and, also, Usener, *Die Sintflutsagen*, 2d ed. (Bonn, 1911).

[3] On the Gilgamesh Epic as a composite production, see Jastrow, *Reli gion of Babylonia and Assyria*, chapter XXIII, and Ungnad-Gressmann, *Das Gilgamesch-Epos* (Gottingen, 1911), pp. 84 *seq.*

sodes of the Epic, so far as recovered,[1] such as (1) Ishtar's wooing of Gilgamesh and her rejection by the hero,
(2) the conflict between Gilgamesh and Ishtar, (3) the
killing of the divine bull, and (4) Ishtar's revenge in smit
ing Engidu with disease, to which he succumbs, are in part
nature-myths, in part astral myths[2] which have been at
tached to Gilgamesh and Engidu. After the death of
Engidu, Gilgamesh is represented as deeply depressed,
seized by the fear that death, too, will soon overtake him.
The last four tablets of the Epic are taken up with this
theme of the sad end in store for man—death from which
there seems to be no escape. Gilgamesh undertakes a
series of wanderings in search of a remote ancestor, Utnapishtim, the son of Ubara-Tutu, who has escaped the
common fate and enjoys immortal life with the gods.
From him Gilgamesh hopes to wrest the secret of immor
tality. After many adventures—into which again astral
myths have been woven—he at last is face to face with
Utnapishtim, whose name conveys the idea of continu
ous life. Gilgamesh tells the purport of his quest, but
receives the sad answer in reply that death is the inexo
rable law imposed by the gods. It is the same answer
that the maiden, Sabitu, dwelling at the seashore, gives
to the hero.[3] Life and death are meted out to man by
the gods, but "the days of death are not fixed," *i. e.*,
death has no end; it is eternal.

Gilgamesh then asks Utnapishtim to explain how a mor
tal came to escape the universal destiny, for Utnapishtim
appears to be human, a man such as Gilgamesh is. In

[1] Large portions of the Epic, which is recounted in twelve tablets, are
still missing.

[2] By this is meant occurrences in the heavens that are given the form of
a narrative, with personifications of heavenly bodies and constellations.
See Kugler, *Die Sternenfahrt des Gilgamesch* (1904). This does not mean,
however, that we are to interpret the whole of the Epic as a series of
astral myths.

[3] See above, p. 211.

reply, Utnapishtim tells the story of the great Deluge
planned by the gods in council, and from which he was
saved by the intervention of the god Ea, who reveals
to Utnapishtim in a mysterious manner that the destruc
tion of the universe has been decreed, and that by build
ing a boat for himself and his belongings he can escape.
The plan is carried out, and after the Deluge is over
the gods become reconciled to Utnapishtim's escape and
agree to give him a place among them, to the extent, at
least, of granting him the privilege of the gods—immortal
life.

The story is related in the eleventh tablet of the Epic[1]
and begins as follows:[2]

> "Gilgamesh speaks to him, to Utnapishtim, the far-re-
>   moved:
> 'I gaze at thee, Utnapishtim.
> Thy appearance is not different. As I am, so art thou.
> And thou are not different. As I am, so art thou.
> Thou art completely ready for the fray.
> . . . thou hast placed upon thee.
> (Tell me) how thou didst enter into the assembly of the
>   gods and secure life.'"

[1] That the twelve tablets correspond to the twelve months of the year,
suggested many years ago by the late Sir Henry C. Rawlinson, is indi
cated by the narrative of Gilgamesh's rejection of Ishtar's offer of mar
riage in the sixth tablet, corresponding to the sixth month (counting
from the spring in which the Babylonian year begins) as the time of
nature's decay. Ishtar, the goddess of fertility and vegetation, loses
her beauty and charm as the winter season approaches. Gilgamesh,
assimilated to the sun-god, separates himself from nature. By a simi
lar association, the Deluge story is related in the eleventh month, when
the winter storms reach their climax. At the same time we may ques
tion whether this plan of the Epic in its final form was consistently car
ried out. Certainly in the case of some of the episodes the connection
with the month corresponding to the number of the tablet in the series
in which the episode is recounted is not obvious.

[2] A translation of the larger portion of the tablet, that deals with
the Deluge, was made by me about a year ago for Professor Fowler's
work, *A History of the Literature of Ancient Israel* (New York, 1912),
pp. 80–84. Portions of it are here reproduced by permission of the

After this introduction, which reveals the seam intended to attach an originally independent tale to the adventures of Gilgamesh, Utnapishtim proceeds to tell his story.

> "I will reveal to thee, Gilgamesh, a secret story,
> And the decision of the gods I will tell thee.
> The city Shuruppak,[1] a city which thou knowest,
> (The one that) lies on the Euphrates,
> That city was old, and the gods thereof
> Induced the great gods to bring a cyclone over it;
> It was planned(?) by their father Anu,
> (By) their counsellor, the warrior Enlil,
> (By) their herald Ninib,
> (By) their leader En-nugi.
> The lord of brilliant vision, Ea, was with them.
> He repeated their decision to the reed-hut.
> 'Reed-hut, reed-hut, wall, wall,
> Reed-hut, hear! Wall, give ear!
> O man of Shuruppak, son of Ubara-Tutu,
> Break up the house, build a ship,
> Abandon your property, seek life.
> Throw aside your possessions, and preserve life,
> Bring into the ship seed of all living things.
> The ship that thou shalt build,
> Let its dimensions be measured, (so that)
> Its breadth and length be made to correspond.
> On a level with the deep, provide it with a covering.'"[2]

Towards the close of the story the name of Atrakhasis, meaning "the very wise one," is introduced as the name of the one who escaped the Deluge, and we have a fragment of a second version of the story[3] among the tablets of Ashurbanapal's library in which this name oc-

Macmillan Company. The latest editions of the text are Rawlinson, IV (2d ed.), Pl. 43–44, and Haupt, *Das Babylonische Nimrodepos* (Leipzig, 1891), pp. 134–149.

[1] Now identified as the site of the mound Fara. The name also appears as Shurippak, but the spelling with *u* is more correct.

[2] The first part of the line is obscure. I believe that the covering here meant is the deck to the framework.

[3] See below, p. 343 *seq*.

curs, and which is, moreover, identical with the name given to the hero of the Deluge in the account that has come down to us through Berosus.[1] In an old Baby lonian version of the same Deluge story[2] the hero's name is likewise Atrakhasis, and we are fortunate in having fragments of a tale of Ea and Atrakhasis,[3] from which it appears, indeed, that in a certain centre the latter was regarded as the favourite of the god of humanity, who succeeds with the help of Ea in warding off several times the threatened destruction of mankind through Enlil, the god of storms. Apparently, the Deluge finally comes de spite the efforts of Ea and Atrakhasis.

Now, at the close of the story where we encounter the name of Atrakhasis, Ea, who is endeavouring to reconcile Enlil to the escape of a single human being, says:

"I did not reveal the oracle of the great gods
  I sent Atrakhasis a dream, and so he understood the oracle
    of the gods."

We may therefore divide the speech of Ea in which he warns his favourite into two parts, assigning the mys terious words, which are just the kind that would be re vealed in a dream,

"Reed-hut, reed-hut, wall, wall!
Reed-hut, hear! Wall, give ear!"

to the Atrakhasis version, and the remainder of the speech, in which the oracle of the gods is manifestly and unmis takably revealed, and which contains no suggestion of a dream, to the Utnapishtim version. This single example

---

[1] Embodied by Eusebius in his chronicle (ed. Schoene), I, pp. 19–24. See Cory, *Ancient Fragments*, p. 60. The name here appears as Xisu-thros, which is merely the inverted form of Atrakhasis = Khasis-atra.

[2] See below, p. 340 *seq.*

[3] See the latest translation by Ungnad, in Gressmann's *Altorienta-lische Texte und Bilder*, pp. 61–65.

will suffice for our purposes to show that in this main version of the Babylonian Deluge stories two forms of the story have been combined, just as in the biblical tale we shall find[1] two versions dovetailed into each other. Utnapishtim continues:

> "I understood[2] and spoke to Ea, my lord.
> (The command) of my lord which thou hast commanded,
> As I have understood (it), I will carry out.
> (But what) shall I answer the city, the people, and the elders?
> Ea opened his mouth and spoke:
> Spoke to me, his servant.
> (As answer) thus speak to them:
> (Know that) Enlil has conceived hatred towards me,
> So that I can no longer dwell (in your city).
> (On) Enlil's territory I dare no longer set my face.
> Therefore, I go to the 'deep' to dwell with Ea, my lord.
> Over you he will cause blessing to rain down.
> (Catch of) bird, catch of fish,
> And . . . . . rich crops."

The following lines are badly preserved, as are also those which begin the description of the building of the ship, in which Utnapishtim is assisted by a body of work men. It would appear that the construction is carried out according to a plan drawn by Utnapishtim—an inter esting allusion to the architectural methods of Babylonia.

> "On the fifth day, I designed its outline.
> According to the plan (?), the walls were to be ten gar high.
> Correspondingly, ten gar the measure of its width.
> I determined upon its shape (and) drew it.
> I weighted it six-fold.[3]
> I divided (the superstructure?) into seven parts.
> Its interior I divided into nine parts.

[1] See below, p. 348 *seq.*

[2] Referring, evidently, to the mysterious warning, and not to the ex plicit command, which is so clear that it could not be misunderstood.

[3] A difficult line, which was perhaps intended to convey the thought that the substructure, or hull, was to be made very strong, so as to hold the house of seven stories, with nine inner divisions, to be built upon it.

Water-plugs I constructed in the interior.
I selected a pole and added accessories.[1]
Six[2] sar of asphalt I poured on the outer wall.
Three sar of pitch (I poured) on the inner wall.
Three sar the workmen carried away in their baskets.[3] Of oil,
Besides one sar oil which was used for the sacrifice,
The boatman secreted two sar of oil."

Obscure as some of the building terms occurring in this description are, the general character of the structure is clear. It is a house-boat with a hull or substructure the walls of which were ten gar high. It was provided with a strong deck, and we may assume that the interior of the hull was to be hollow, to be used as a "hold" for stores. The upper structure consists of a seven-storied building, divided into nine compartments. If this means that each story had nine divisions, we would have sixty-three rooms—a fair-sized apartment-house. Great care is taken to make it water-tight. It is plugged up and coated on the inside and outside with asphalt and pitch, and, if the interpretation suggested be correct, the workmen "grafted" a large quantity of oil intended, perhaps, for the hold. After the structure is completed, Utnapishtim celebrates the event by offerings of must, oil, and wine, "like on the New Year's festival," and then proceeds to load the boat.

"All that I had I loaded on her.
All that I had of silver I loaded on her.

[1] Another obscure line, setting forth, as I believe, the tools used for coating the exterior and interior of the house-boat with asphalt and pitch to make it absolutely water-tight.

[2] According to a duplicate fragment, "three."

[3] Strange as it may seem, the narrator seems to imply that the workmen appropriated three sar of asphalt and pitch, just as in the second following line it is intimated that the boatman secreted two sar of oil—his share of the "graft," which is thus shown to have a venerable origin. References to graft and bribes are not unusual in the reports of Babylonian officials—as far back as the days of Hammurapi.

> All that I had of gold I loaded on her.
> All that I had of living beings of all kinds I loaded on her.
> I brought to the ship all my family and household;
> Cattle of the field, beasts of the field, all the workmen I
>   brought on board."

The ship draws water to two-thirds of its bulk, and all is ready for the approaching storm.

> "Shamash had fixed the time,
>   'When the rulers of darkness(?) at evening time shall
>   cause a terrific rain-storm,
>   Step into the ship and close the door.'
>   The fixed time approached,
>   When the rulers of darkness(?) at evening time were to
>   cause a terrific rain-storm.
>   I recognized the symptoms of (such) a day
>   A day, for the appearance of which I was in terror.
>   I entered the ship and closed the door.
>   To steer the ship, to Puzur-Kurgal, the boatman,
>   I entrusted the palace[1] together with its cargo."

Then follows the description of the storm, which constitutes one of the finest passages in the narrative.

> "As morning dawned,
>   There arose on the firmament of heaven black clouds,
>   Adad thundered therein;
>   Nebo and Lugal marched in advance,
>   Ira[2] tears out the ship's pole.
>   Ninib marches, commanding the attack,
>   The Anunnaki lift torches,
>   Illuminating the land with their sheen,
>   Adad's roar reaches to heaven,
>   All light is changed to darkness.
>   .   .   .   .   .   .
>
>   One day the hurricane raged . . .
>   Storming furiously . . .

[1] Note this designation given to the structure—an indication of its large size, with its many stories and compartments.

[2] "God of pestilence."

Coming like a combat over men.
Brother sees not brother:
Those in heaven[1] do not know one another.
The gods are terrified at the cyclone,
They flee and mount to the heaven of Anu;[2]
The gods crouch like dogs in an enclosure.
Ishtar cries aloud like one in birth throes,
The mistress of the gods howls aloud:
'That day be turned to clay,[3]
When I in the assembly of the gods decreed evil;
That I should have decreed evil in the assembly of the
    gods!
For the destruction of my people should have ordered a
    combat!
Did I bring forth my people,
That like fish they should fill the sea?'
All of the Anunnaki weep with her.
The gods sit down, depressed and weeping.
Their lips are closed . . .
Six days and nights
The storm, cyclone (and) hurricane continued to sweep
    over the land."

The storm thus exhausts its force in six days, and with
the approach of the seventh the worst is over. The deso
lation wrought, the description of which is most effective
and pathetic, was complete.

"When the seventh day approached, the hurricane and
    cyclone ceased the combat,
After having fought like warriors(?).
The sea grew quiet, the evil storm abated, the cyclone was
    restrained.
I looked at the day and the roar had quieted down.
And all mankind had turned to clay.
Like an enclosure . . . had become.
I opened a window and light fell on my face,
I bowed down and sat down (and) wept,
Tears flowed over my face.
I looked in all directions of the sea.

[1] I. e., the gods.   [2] The highest part of heaven.
[3] I. e., be cursed with destruction.

> At a distance of twelve (miles)[1] an island appeared.
> At Mount Nizir the ship stood still.
> Mount Nizir took hold of the ship so that it could not
>   move."

The name of the mountain on which the ship rests sig
nifies "salvation," or "protection," and is evidently chosen
with symbolical intent.   At Mount Nizir the house-boat
remains for seven days, after which Utnapishtim sends
out in succession a dove, a swallow, and a raven to ascer
tain whether the waters have abated.

> "One day, two days, Mount Nizir, etc.[2]
> Three days and four days, Mount Nizir, etc.
> Five days, six days, Mount Nizir, etc.
> When the seventh day arrived,
> I sent forth a dove, letting it free.
> The dove went hither and thither;
> Not finding a resting-place, it came back.
> I sent forth a swallow, letting it free.
> The swallow went hither and thither.
> Not finding a resting-place, it came back.
> I sent forth a raven, letting it free.
> The raven went and saw the decrease of the waters.
> It ate, croaked, (?) but did not turn back.
> Then I let (all) out to the four regions (and) brought an
>   offering.
> I brought a sacrifice on the mountain top.
> Seven and seven *adagur* jars I arranged.
> Beneath them I strewed reeds, cedarwood and myrtle.
> The gods smelled the odor,
> The gods smelled the sweet odor.
> The gods like flies gathered around the sacrificer."

The reaction among the gods is inaugurated by Ishtar, the goddess of vegetation, who, when she saw the dis
astrous consequences it entailed, had already regretted

---

[1] Or after a space of twelve double hours.
[2] Sign of reduplication, *i. e.*, "Mount Nizir took hold of the ship so
that it could not move."

the decision in which she had acquiesced, and who now boldly denounces Enlil, the god of storms, as the instigator.

> "As soon as the mistress of the gods[1] arrived,
>> She raised on high the large necklace(?) which Anu had made according to his art.
> 'Ye gods, as surely as I will not forget these precious stones at my neck,
> So I will remember these days—never to forget them.
> Let the gods come to the sacrifice,
> But let Enlil not come to the sacrifice.
> Because without reflection he brought on the cyclone,
> And decreed destruction for my people.'
> As soon as Enlil arrived,
> He saw the ship, and Enlil was enraged.
> Filled with anger at the Igigi.[2]
> 'Who now has escaped with his life?
> No man was to survive the destruction!'
> Ninib opened his mouth and spoke,
> Spoke to the warrior Enlil,
> 'Who except Ea can plan any affair?
> Ea indeed knows every order.'
> Ea opened his mouth and spoke,
> Spoke to the warrior Enlil:
> 'Thou art the leader (and) warrior of the gods.
> But why didst thou, without reflection, bring on the cyclone?
> On the sinner impose his sin,
> On the evil-doer impose his evil,
> But be merciful not to root out completely! be considerate not (to destroy altogether).
> Instead of bringing on a cyclone,
> Lions might have come and diminished mankind.
> Instead of bringing on a cyclone,
> Jackals might have come and diminished mankind.
> Instead of bringing on a cyclone,
> Famine might have come and overwhelmed the land
> Instead of bringing on a cyclone,

---

[1] Ishtar.

[2] Here a collective name for the gods, though generally designating, like Anunnaki, a lower group of divine beings; see above, pp. 331 *seq.*

Ira[1] might have come and destroyed the land.
I did not reveal the oracle of the great gods,
I sent Atrakhasis a dream and he understood the oracle
    of the gods.
Now take counsel for him.'"

Enlil is swayed by this appeal and blesses Utnapishtim and his wife.

"Enlil mounted the ship,
Took hold of my hand and led me up,[2]
Led me up and caused my wife to kneel at my side,
Touched our foreheads, stepped between us (and) blessed us.
Hitherto Utnapishtim was a man;
Now Utnapishtim and his wife shall be on a level with the
    gods.
Utnapishtim shall dwell in the distance, at the confluence
    of the streams.
Then they took me and settled me at the confluence of
    the streams."

The rest of the tablet[3] does not concern us here. It
is taken up with Gilgamesh's sojourn with Utnapishtim
and his wife. This lasts for a week, after which he begins
the journey to his home. Gilgamesh has learned the se
cret of Utnapishtim's preservation, but his quest for life
has not met with success. Utnapishtim can hold out no
hope. He and his wife care for Gilgamesh kindly, who,
worn out with fatigue, falls into a deep sleep. After he
has awakened they provide for his safe return across the
waters of death, which he had to cross to reach the dwell
ing of Utnapishtim. Just as the boat is leaving the shore,
Utnapishtim tells Gilgamesh of a plant which has the power
of restoring the aged to youth. He secures it, but a ser
pent robs him of it, and naught is left but to return to
Uruk with his purpose unfulfilled.

The last tablet takes up another phase of the same

---

[1] God of pestilence.   [2] *I. e.*, brought me on land.
[3] Lines 206–326, or one-third of the whole tablet.

problem—the mystery of death and the search for immortality, but without reaching any encouraging solution.[1]

Before passing on to a consideration of the biblical counterpart, let me briefly summarise the other Babylonian versions known to us.

II

The oldest and most important of these versions is the one found by Arno Poebel among the tablets from Nippur in the Museum of the University of Pennsylvania.[2] The significant features of this version are, first, that it is written in Sumerian, which in itself points to its high antiquity,[3] as against the one in the Gilgamesh Epic which is in Semitic (or Akkadian), and, secondly, that it occurs as part of a continuous narrative which, like the group of narratives and traditions forming the first eleven chapters of Genesis, begins with the Creation story, passes on to the Deluge story and embodies chronological lists furnishing the names and length of reigns of early rulers and dynasties that appear to represent the source whence Berosus obtained his remarkable array of early Babylonian rulers with their amazingly long reigns.[4] We are not concerned here with these lists which involve problems of a most puzzling character, and we have already referred to the essential features of the order of Creation in this early version so far as preserved.[5]

[1] See above, pp. 211 *seq.*

[2] See the Preface and above, p. 95, where the title of Poebel's forthcoming publication is given.

[3] Poebel dates the tablet on which the story is recounted at about 1850 or 1900 B. C.

[4] See Cory, *Ancient Fragments*, pp. 51–54 and 85–86; Zimmern, *Keilinschriften und das Alte Testament*, pp. 531 *seq.;* or Rogers, *Cuneiform Parallels to the Old Testament*, pp. 78–79.

[5] Above, pp. 95 *seq.*

Unfortunately only the lower portion of the tablet, which consisted of three columns each on obverse and reverse, is preserved. Poebel's estimate is that about three-fourths of the text is missing, and he is in hopes that missing portions may yet be found either in the University Museum or in the Imperial Ottoman Museum of Constantinople, where many of the tablets from Nip pur have been retained. Corresponding to the role played by the goddess Ishtar in the Gilgamesh version, we find the goddess Nintu or Ninkharsag lamenting the destruc tion of mankind—her offspring. The centre of worship of Ninkharsag appears to have been the ancient city of Adab,[1] but as a chief goddess she becomes identical, as do all the goddesses of important centres, with the great mother-goddess, the source of all fertility and vegetation —the progenitor of mankind. As such she appears in the new Sumerian text and is directly identified with Innanna, which is one of the designations of Ishtar. Nin kharsag, however, is present when the gods decide to bring on the destructive Deluge. Her regret, accordingly, comes too late.

> "At that time Nintu . . . like[2] . . .
> The holy Innanna (i. e., Ishtar) wailed on account of her
>   people.
> Enki (i. e., Ea) in his own heart held counsel."

This line furnishes the key-note to the situation. It is evident that Ea as the god of humanity plays the same part as in the main version of the Deluge, and as he does in other Babylonian myths. It is he who reveals to Ziu-

---

[1] Represented by Bismya, where Dr. E. J. Banks, acting for the Uni versity of Chicago, conducted remarkably successful excavations which, it is to be hoped, will some day be continued. See Banks, *Bismya, or the Lost City of Adab* (New York, 1912).

[2] Poebel ingeniously completes the line: "screamed like a woman in travail," as a parallel to the passage in the Gilgamesh Epic, above, p. 331.

giddu, described as "king and priest," the intention of the gods, whose gathering is expressely referred to:

"The gods of heaven and earth invoked the name of Anu (and) Enlil."

Alas! that the name of the place over which Ziugiddu rules is broken off, but it is a reasonable conjecture of Poebel's that since Shuruppak is the last of the cities to be named in the concluding portion of the Creation account[1] in our text, this city represents the capital of Ziugiddu's district. Now Shuruppak (or Shurippak), it will be recalled, is also the home of Utnapishtim, and it is against that place that the Deluge is primarily sent; though this would mean no more than that a particular version of the Deluge was associated with Shuruppak, just as Berosus's account is linked with the city of Sippar.[2] Ziugiddu[3] would appear then to be identical with Utnapishtim, to which the element Zi in the name which has the value of *napishtu* "life" directly points.[4]

Ziugiddu is described as piously devoted to the worship of the gods:

"In humility prostrating himself reverently.
Daily and perseveringly standing in attendance."

The dependence of the version in the Gilgamesh Epic upon the new version is unmistakably indicated in the

---

[1] See above, p. 96.　　　　　[2] See below, p. 346.

[3] Written with four signs Zi-u-gid-du, of which the last, however, is merely a phonetic complement.

[4] The two signs, U-Gid, convey the idea of "long," or "continuous," so that Utnapishtim would be a Semitic rendering of the idea conveyed by Ziugiddu, though not perhaps a literal translation. The equation between the two names is confirmed, as Poebel in his comments points out, by the important passage, *Cun. Texts*, Part XVIII, Pl. 30, 9, Zi-gid-da = *Ut-na-pa-(?)ash(?)-ti*, followed in the next line by Engidu, the companion of Gilgamesh whose name occurs in line 6. Poebel renders Ziugiddu as "who made life long of days." I should be inclined to say "whose life is long of days," *i. e.*, one who has continuous life.

manner in which the decision of the god is communicated
to Ziugiddu. A deity, whose name is not preserved but
who can be no other than Ea, addresses Ziugiddu as
follows:

> "At the wall at my left side stand and . . .
> At the wall I will speak a word to thee.
> O my holy one, listen to me;
> By our . . . a cyclone . . . will be sent.
> To destroy the seed of mankind, to . . .
> Is the decision, the oracle of the assembly of the gods.
> The command of Anu (and) Enlil . . .
> His kingdom, his rule . . .
> To him . . ."

Clearly, this address is the prototype to the address of
Ea to Utnapishtim.[1]

> "Reed-hut, reed-hut, wall, wall!
> Reed-hut hear!   Wall, give ear!"

The new version gives the situation in a more precise
form. Ea reveals himself at the wall of some structure
—presumably a sanctuary—indicated by a term[2] which
has hitherto been translated reed-hut. The decision of
the gods is thus announced in a somewhat mysterious
manner which, however, must have contained the in
structions to Ziugiddu to save himself and probably his
family and belongings by taking refuge on a boat to be
constructed by him. This portion of the fourth column
of the text is lost. At the beginning of the fifth column
we have the description of the storm and of the sacrifice
offered by Ziugiddu at the reappearance of the sun, which
reads as follows:

[1] Above, p. 326.
[2] *Kikkishu*, which is a synonym of *tarbasu*—"enclosure" (*Cuneiform Texts*, Part XIV, Pl. 48 [No. 36331], rev. lines, 8–9). The word may revert to primitive days when the shrines of the gods were built of reeds, as were the human habitations.

"All the windstorms with tremendous force together came.
The cyclone[1] . . . raged with them.
When for seven days, for seven nights,
The cyclone in the land had raged,
The large boat[2] on the great waters by the wind storm
    had been carried along.
Shamash came forth, shedding light over Heaven and Earth.
Ziugiddu (opened) . . . of the large boat.
The light of the hero Shamash shone on the (interior) of
    the large boat.
Ziugiddu, the king,
Before Shamash prostrates himself.
The king sacrifices an ox, (offers up) a sheep."

The descriptions appear to be much briefer in this
version than in the Gilgamesh narrative. Such episodes as
the sending out of the birds may, therefore, be due to
that steady growth and elaboration which is the char
acteristic trait of popular tales everywhere. In its gen
eral outlines, however, the older version tallies with the
later one, including the very important removal of Ziu
giddu to a distant place there to enjoy eternal life like
that of the gods. Anu and Enlil, who are the chief in
stigators of the Deluge, are apparently reconciled.

"Ziugiddu, the king,
Before Anu (and) Enlil he prostrates himself.
Life like that of a god he (*i. e.*, probably, Enlil) gives him
    (*i. e.*, to Ziugiddu).
An eternal existence like that of a god he grants to him.
At that time Ziugiddu, the king,
The name of . . . 'Preserver of the seed of mankind.' . . .
In a (distant?) . . . land,[3] the land of . . . they caused
    him to dwell.
(After) . . . they had caused him to dwell,"[4]

[1] The Sumerian term A-Ma-Ru is the equivalent of *abubu* (Meissner, *Seltene Assyrische Ideogramme No.* 8909), used in the Gilgamesh Epic.

[2] Ma-Gur-Gur—the same term as in another version referred to below, p. 342.

[3] Poebel reads "mountain," but I am inclined to believe that an island is meant like in the Gilgamesh version.

[4] The text now passes on to some other episode.

There can be no question that we have in this "Nip
pur" version[1] the prototype of the Utnapishtim episode
in the Gilgamesh Epic. The setting is the same, the
chief actors are identical, and the narrative follows the
same general course in both versions. Such variations
as a seven days' duration of the Deluge, as against six
days in the Gilgamesh Epic, are too slight to merit atten
tion. The number seven, no doubt, represents the older
tradition. Incidentally, this Sumerian version confirms
the thesis that the Deluge myth arose independently of
the Gilgamesh Epic, as also that in its later form it con
tains accretions due to the steady growth of the story,
as indicated by other versions that were once current and
that are in part known to us. The story is told in the
third person, whereas in the Gilgamesh Epic Utnapish
tim himself is the narrator. Moreover, Anu and Enlil
are introduced as the heads of the pantheon, while in
the Gilgamesh version Enlil receives the first mention,
though other gods are also associated with him. There
are indications, however, in this oldest Sumerian version
of a transfer of the role of chief instigator to Enlil, as the
storm-god *par excellence.*

Another version also reverting to a very early period,
but written in Semitic (or Akkadian), is represented by
a tablet which is fortunately dated in the 11th year of
King Ammisaduka on the 28th day of the 11th month,
corresponding to about 1800 B. C.[2] The name of the
hero is here given as Atrakhasis. The fragment was pub
lished by Professor Vincent Scheil[3] and is now in the Pier-

---

[1] Since Ziugiddu does not belong to Nippur, but in all probabilities—
like Utnapishtim, to Shuruppak, the tale must have been brought to
Nippur and did not originate there. The point of view, however, in
both the oldest and latest versions is limited to the Euphrates Valley
—to the "black-headed" people, as the Babylonians called themselves—
and for whom Babylonia constituted *tout le monde.*

[2] According to Ungnad, who accepts a higher chronology for Hammurapi, *c.* 1973 B. C.

[3] *Recueil de Travaux, relatifs a la Philologie et l'Archeologie egyptienne
et assyrienne,* vol. XX, pp. 55–61.

pont Morgan collection. It forms the second tablet of
a series known, from the opening words, as "When the
man had laid himself down to sleep." We fortunately
know the opening lines of the Gilgamesh Epic, so that
we can say definitely that this Babylonian version was
embodied in a different tale. It probably belonged to
a group of stories dealing with Atrakhasis and the god
Ea,[1] who is the protector of Atrakhasis, as in the Gilga
mesh Epic he is the protector of Utnapishtim. Unfor
tunately the fragment consisting originally of eight col
umns is very badly preserved, and since no portion of the
first tablet nor of any of the succeeding ones has been
found, it is idle to speculate on the character of the pro
duction in which Atrakhasis was introduced as the hero
of the Deluge. From the small portion preserved we
obtain a description of the storm and the cry of despair
of the people threatened with destruction. A dialogue
ensues, in all probability between Ea and Adad, the
storm deity, in which the former reproaches the god of
storms, thunder, and lightning for having superinduced
the Deluge, which is here designated by the same term[2]
that appears in the Gilgamesh Epic. Ea declares man
kind to be his creation and protests against the destruc
tion of his creatures. A portion of a ship is referred to,
and the fragment breaks off at the beginning of an ad
dress of Atrakhasis to "his lord," by which designation,
no doubt, Ea is meant.

We may, therefore, conclude that we have here the
Atrakhasis version of the Deluge and that the general
setting is about the same as in the main version, with
perhaps this difference, that Adad as the god of storms
is the instigator of the catastrophe overwhelming man
kind instead of Enlil, though it is, of course, possible
that Adad is merely acting on the command of the head
of the old Babylonian pantheon.

[1] See above, p. 327.   [2] *Abubu;* see above, p. 339, note 1.

The popularity of the story is further illustrated by a fourth version which we owe to Professor Hilprecht,[1] al though his interpretation of it is open to question. It ap pears to be much later than the one just discussed—proba bly by five centuries. Only portions of fourteen lines are preserved,[2] but these suffice to show that some deity—no doubt either Enlil or Adad—is about to instigate a catas trophe involving all mankind. The portion preserved con tains an address by some deity announcing the coming de struction[3] and advising or ordering some one to build a ship. The speaker is without question Ea,[4] and the person ad dressed is the favourite who is permitted to escape—Ut-napishtim or Atrakhasis—more likely the latter than the former. The command is fortunately clearly put, "Build a great ship," and the detail of providing it with a "strong covering" is also explicit and forms a parallel to the corre sponding passage in the main version, from which it ap pears that a deck for the hull and not a covering for the superstructure is meant. The large size of the construc tion is indicated by a term[5] which also occurs in the old

---

[1] Babylonian Expedition of the University of Pennsylvania, series D, vol. V, 1 (Philadelphia, 1910); also in German, *Der Neue Fund zur Sintflutgeschichte* (Leipzig, 1910). The fragment, according to Hilprecht, comes from Nippur. There is no internal evidence in the few lines preserved to this effect. The real Nippur version is represented by Doctor Poebel's text, and even this one, as pointed out, did not originate in Nippur. If Hilprecht's fragment was really found in Nip pur, it is a very late version and considerably modified from its original form.

[2] The restorations of these lines by Hilprecht have not been accepted by scholars; they appear to be somewhat arbitrary.

[3] The same word for Deluge, *abubu*, as in the other versions.

[4] According to Hilprecht's restoration of lines 2–3, the speaker de clares that he is about to bring on the Deluge, which would make Enlil the speaker, but this is most unlikely. The word *apashshar* in the second line means "I will unfold." As in the Gilgamesh version, Ea reveals the *pirishti ilani*, "oracle of the gods." The end of the third line reads "all men he will seize." Ea is describing what some other god proposes to do.

[5] Ma-Gur-Gur, correctly explained by Poebel as "large boat."

"Nippur" version. As in the main version, cattle[1] and beasts of the field are to be brought into the ship as well as workmen,[2] but a new detail is furnished in the specific reference also to "birds of heaven," assumed, of course, in the main version as occupants of the ship, since birds are sent out, but not *specifically* mentioned in the passage describing the loading of the ship.

The few lines of this fragment read as follows:

> ". . . I (*i. e.*, Ea) will reveal.[3]
> . . . all men together he (*i. e.*, Enlil) will seize.
> . . . before the deluge comes.
> . . . whatever there be, I will bring about
> overthrow, destruction, annihilation.
> . . . build a large ship, and
> . . . total be its construction.
> . . . a large boat carrying what is to be saved of life.
> . . . with a strong covering cover it!
> . . . . . . thou shalt make.
> (cattle of the field), beasts of the field, birds of heaven,
> . . . . workman,
> . . . . . and family (?) . . ."

This fourth version, therefore, adds little to the main one, and is of interest chiefly as showing the various forms under which the tale, recounted independently or woven in with composite productions, was circulated.

Lastly, we have in Ashurbanapal's library indications of still another version,[4] which, so far as preserved, differs

---

[1] I venture to restore the beginning of line 11 in accordance with the Gilgamesh Epic, XI, 86—the parallel passage.

[2] *Um-mi-ni* in line 12 corresponds to *um-ma-a-ni* in the Gilgamesh Epic, XI, 81. Hilprecht's restoration of the line in order to force a paral lel to the biblical statement in Gen. 6 : 20 is quite out of the question.

[3] The line is perhaps to be completed, "The decision of the great gods, I will reveal" (*pirishti ilani rabuti apashshar*).

[4] See Haupt, *Das Babylonische Nimrodepos*, p. 131, for the text; Ungnad, *Das Gilgamesch-Epos*, p. 19, for a recent German translation; for an English one, Rogers, *Cuneiform Parallels to the Old Testament*, pp. 103–4.

from the main one in again naming Atrakhasis as the
hero of the Deluge. It belongs, therefore, to the same
category as the third version and, indeed, it is not im
possible that it represents in fact a part of the fourth
version, just discussed.[1] It contains the close of Ea's
command to Atrakhasis in regard to the building of the
ship and the beginning of Atrakhasis's reply. It thus
joins on to the fragment published by Hilprecht. So far
as decipherable,[2] it reads as follows:

> "When the time that I shall indicate to you (arrives),
> Enter (the ship) and close the door of the ship.
> (Bring) into it thy grain, thy possessions, and thy goods,
> (Thy wife (?)), thy family, thy household and workmen.
> (Cattle) of the field, beasts of the field, all kinds of
>   herbs . . .
> I will indicate (?) to thee to preserve (thy) door." [3]

The address amplifies in some respects the parallel
passage in the main version,[4] but omits the specifications
in regard to the ship. Atrakhasis asks for these in his
answer to Ea, pleading his inexperience in ship-building.

> "Atrakhasis opened his mouth and spoke,
> Spoke to Ea, his lord.
> I have never built a ship . . .
> Draw (its design) on the ground.
> Let me see the design, and (I will build) the ship.
> (Ea) drew (its design) on the ground.
> . . . which thou commandest (I will build)."

The passage helps us to understand the description of the
construction in the main version[5] where Utnapishtim is
portrayed as himself making the design and building ac-

---

[1] The Assyrian copy is, of course, the copy of an older Babylonian
original.

[2] Only seventeen lines are preserved and some of them in part only.

[3] The line is obscure. The sense seems to be that Ea will indicate to
Atrakhasis how he will be able to keep food during the time of the
Deluge.

[4] Lines 25–27; above, p. 326.   [5] Lines 58–60; above, p. 328.

cording to it. The touch of having the god Ea, *show* Atra-khasis the plan of the house-boat, which was certainly an unusual construction, may strike one at first as naïve, but is in reality rationalistic to explain how any one could have thought of building a house-boat of such strange design and such huge proportions. The sceptic has ap peared on the scene and has begun to ask questions. It is in this way, as well as through the inherent interest of people for spinning out favourite tales by further de tails, that popular stories grow from generation to gen eration. This second version in Ashurbanapal's library is clearly more prolix even than the main one, and there fore in all probabilities of later origin.[1]

We have still to consider briefly an account of the Babylonian Deluge as given by Berosus in his lost his tory of Babylonia, but which has been preserved to us in the form handed down by Alexander Polyhistor and em bodied in the chronicle of Eusebius.[2] The name of the hero is Xisuthros (more accurately Xisouthros),[3] which, as already stated,[4] is an inverted form of Atrakhasis. The identification is confirmed by the name of Xisu-thros's father which appears in Alexander Polyhistor as Otiartes and is clearly identical with Ubaru-Tutu, the father of Utnapishtim. In the Gilgamesh version, there fore, Atrakhasis has been amalgamated with Utnapish tim and the former name was probably regarded by the compiler as merely an epithet ("the very wise one"),

---

[1] It may be well to remind the reader once more that although the texts in Ashurbanapal's library are all copies made in the seventh cen tury, the age of the originals naturally varies. Old and new are com mingled in this collection, and to complicate the situation the old is modi fied in being handed down from age to age before it is given its final form.

[2] Schoene's edition, *Eusebii Chronicon Libri duo*, I, pp. 20–24 (Ber lin, 1875). See Rogers's *Cuneiform Parallels to the Old Testament*, pp. 109–112, and Cory, *Ancient Fragments*, pp. 60–63; also p. 54 for an extract from Berosus preserved by Abydenus. Berosus flourished in the days of Antiochus Soter (281–262 B. C.).

[3] Variant forms are Sisouthros and Sisithros. [4] Above, p. 327, note 1.

given to Utnapishtim. Xisuthros appears as a king in Berosus's version, precisely as Ziugiddu is a king, and in the same author's list of ten antediluvian rulers,[1] he is named as the last one before the Deluge. Kronos, who for Berosus represents the equivalent of the god Ea, reveals the decision of the gods to bring on a deluge to Xisuthros by means of a dream. A reference to Ziugiddu's ability to interpret dreams occurs in the Sumerian version, though it is not clear that the mysterious revelation of Ea to Ziugiddu is made in a dream. A new touch in Berosus's account is the mention of Sippar as the home of Xisuthros, pointing to that place as the source of the Atrakhasis version. The hero is instructed to write down "the beginning, middle and end of all things" —an allusion, perhaps, to the long chronological lists of early rulers which had been handed down in Babylonia from older days. After writing his history, Xisuthros is to build a ship and to bring his relatives and friends into it, as well as winged creatures and four-legged animals and plenty of provisions. As in the Gilgamesh version, the hero is instructed to give an answer if he is plied with questions. He should say that he is sailing "to the gods to see that things may be well with men." The boat is specified as five stadia long and two stadia wide. "Wife, children and close friends" are placed on board and the storm breaks loose. Its duration is not indicated, but when all is over birds are sent out which at first return, "finding neither food nor a place to rest," but upon their being sent out a second time come back with clay on their feet, and when let forth a third time do not return to the boat. The ship had grounded on a mountain, and Xisuthros, having satisfied himself that the waters had abated, "removed a part of the side of the ship," went out with his "wife and daughter and the pilot," erected an altar, and brought a sacrifice. After

[1] See the references above, p. 335, note 4.

that he vanished with those who had come out of the
ship. Those who had remained in the ship landed and
sought in vain for Xisuthros, "calling him by name."
Xisuthros did not return, but a voice came from heaven
announcing that Xisuthros had gone to dwell with the
gods, and calling upon people to pay reverence to the
gods. Wife, daughter, and pilot are to share the hon
ours accorded to Xisuthros. The voice also called upon
those seeking for Xisuthros to return to Babylon from
Armenia, where the ship had landed, to recover the
writings left by Xisuthros at Sippar and to share them
with men. They did so, and "founded many cities and
thrones and again repopulated Babylonia."

The variations in this account from all of the versions
considered are for the most part slight but significant
as showing that new touches were constantly being added.
The story became increasingly composite in character,
the general tendency being to combine the existing ver
sions into one. In the process, however, details were also
lost. So Berosus omits to tell us how long the storm
lasted. No figures are mentioned by him at all except
in the case of the dimensions of the ark. No birds are
specified; the scene between Enlil and Ea is omitted, and
the close, introducing the voice from heaven, is tinged
with rationalism, though of a naïve type. A moral is
attached—to worship the gods, and an obscure tradition
of the recovery of lost writings[1] also incorporated with

[1] In the Jewish Midrash there are interesting allusions to lost writings
which Noah recovers, and from which he learns how to build the ark
and how to gather the animals. In fact, he obtains from the book which
was given to Adam by the angel Raziel a knowledge of all secrets and
mysteries so that he becomes a veritable Atrakhasis, "the very wise one."
See Ginzberg, *Legends of the Jews*, vol. I, pp. 154-7. The Midrashic
division of Rabbinical literature represents this same popular process of
spinning out popular tales. Despite its late origin, therefore, the Jew
ish Midrash retains many old touches. There is, no doubt, some direct
connection between the account of a recovered book from which Noah
derives his knowledge and the references in Berosus to hidden writings.

the tale. The specification that the ship landed in Ar
menia impresses one as a later addition, reflecting, per
haps, the identification of the biblical Ararat (Gen. 8 : 4)
with a mountainous district of Armenia.

The account of Berosus, on the other hand, shows that
the substantial character of the Deluge as a nature-myth
remained unchanged. The myth, to be sure, is somewhat
obscured and the attempt is made to give it the aspect
of a story with a moral. Although it is a weak attempt,
yet it points to the beginning of the process which, com
pletely carried out among the Hebrews, transformed the
nature-myth as it did the Creation myth into an ethical
parable. Let us now turn to the biblical account of the
great Deluge.

III

Corresponding to the two versions of the biblical
Creation story we have two accounts of the Deluge,[1]
but while the versions of the Creation follow each other
the two records of the catastrophe that wiped out all
mankind are combined and so skilfully dovetailed into
each other that until a few generations ago biblical schol
ars had failed to notice the composite character of the
four chapters of Genesis in question.

Both accounts strike the characteristic ethical note of
the transformed traditions of the remote past by empha
sising the corruptness of man as the cause of the Deluge
as against the Babylonian versions, none of which assigns
any cause whatsoever for the catastrophe. Of the two
versions the one forms part of a series of narratives run-

[1] Gen. 6 to 9, vs. 17; vss. 18–19 and 28–29 of chapter 9 form an
introduction leading to chapter 10, while the little section, verses 20–27,
is recognised by critics as an independent tale, and is introduced at this
point as a protest against viniculture. See the author's paper, "Wine
in the Pentateuchal Codes," in the *Journal of American Oriental Society*,
vol. XXXIII, pp. 180–192.

ning through the book of Genesis ascribed to the Yahwist, the other is embodied in the Priestly Code. We have, therefore, the same conditions that we encountered in the case of the Creation narrative.[1] The Yahwist is the older of the two, and, though pre-exilic, his account shows traces of having been subsequently worked over. The Priestly Code is a considerably later compilation, and belongs to the postexilic period, while the combination of the Priestly Code with the Yahwist document carries us down to a still later date. In the combination of the two the dividing-lines have in some instances become so faint as to be barely distinguishable, though, for the most part, the separation can be made with tolerable certainty.

The proof for the existence of the two versions in the present form of the biblical narrative is to be found in the many repetitions, the double records of such incidents as (1) the declaration of God of the wickedness of man and the corruption of the earth as the reason for the catastrophe,[2] (2) the double address of God to Noah to enter the ark,[3] in the one case to take in seven pairs of each clean animal species and a pair of the unclean, in the other case a pair of each animal species, (3) the double record of the entry of Noah and his family and of the animals into the ark,[4] (4) the double statement of the rising of the waters, of their covering the mountains, and of the floating of the ark on the waters,[5] (5) the double decla-

---

[1] See above, pp. 98 *seq.*
[2] Gen. 6 . 5-8 (Yahwist); 6 : 11-13 (Priestly Code).
[3] Gen. 7 : 1-6 (Yahwist); Gen. 6 : 18-22 (Priestly Code).
[4] Gen. 7 : 7 (Yahwist); 7 : 13-16 (Priestly Code). Note also such variations as the mention of the three sons of Noah in the Priestly Code while the Yahwist (or P and J, as we may briefly designate the two documents) simply says "his sons." The abbreviation J stands for Jahwist, which is the German spelling for Yahwist.
[5] Gen. 7 : 18 and 23 (Yahwist); 7 : 17; 19 : 20-22 (Priestly Code). The distribution between J and P in such instances of a complete dove tailing can no longer be determined with absolute certainty, but an approximate division is quite sufficient.

ration at the close of the narrative of God's resolve not to bring on such a catastrophe again.[1]

As an illustration let me place side by side the state ment of J and P regarding the reason for the Deluge and the announcement of its coming.

J

Gen 6 : 5–8:

"And Yahweh saw that the wickedness of man was great in the earth and all the inclina- tion of the thoughts of his heart[1] continuously evil. And Yahweh repented that he had made man on the earth, and it grieved him at his heart; and Yahweh said, 'I will blot out man whom I have created from the face of the earth,[2] for I re- pent that I have made him.'[3] But Noah found grace in the eyes of Yahweh."

[1] "Heart" used, as consistently in Hebrew, for "mind."

[2] Subsequent addition "from man to beast, even to creeping things, even to the birds of heav- en" to explain the universality of the destruction which was intended to strike at man first of all.

[3] So the original reading of the text which is changed to "I have made them" to conform to the in clusion of all animals, through the subsequent addition referred to in the preceding note.

P

Gen. 6 : 11–13:[1]

"Now, the earth was cor- rupt before Elohim, and the earth was filled with violence. And Elohim saw that the earth was corrupt, for all flesh had corrupted his way upon the earth. And Elohim said to Noah, 'The end of all flesh is come before me, for the earth is filled with violence through them. Therefore, I will de- stroy the earth.'" [2]

[1] Vss. 9 and 10, forming an intro duction to the P document, are given below, p. 352.

[2] This appears to have been the original reading, which is also the logical one. The addition of the suffix "them" to the participial form of the verb "destroy" was probably superinduced through the combination of the P document with J, and which, therefore, at this point assumes, as indicated in the addition in Gen. 6 : 7, that all liv ing creatures and not merely man are to be destroyed. The Hebrew construction in the present form of the text at the close of vs. 13 is awkward and necessitates the addi tion of the conjunction and (as is done in the Greek translation) in order to give any meaning.

[1] Gen. 8 : 21–22 (Yahwist); 9 : 8–11 (Priestly Code).

Such "doublets" can only be satisfactorily accounted for on the assumption that some redactor, following what we now know to have been the regular method of composition in the ancient Orient, combined at least two accounts of the same event into one continuous narrative. I say at least two, for there are indications that one of the documents so combined is itself the result of a composite process, namely, the P document, which embodies the narrative of the Elohist with additions that point to a third version.[1] As an illustration of complete dove tailing we may instance the account of the building of the ark,[2] in which statements from both documents have been so combined as to make it impossible to say which is J and which is P.

Gen. 7 : 14-16:

"Make for thyself an ark of gopher wood;[3] and thou shalt coat it on the inside and outside with pitch. Thus shalt thou make it: Three hundred cubits shall be the length of the ark, fifty cubits the width thereof, and thirty cubits the height thereof. A deck[4] of a full cubit thou shalt make for the ark,

[1] The detailed proof for this thesis must be reserved for a special article on the subject.

[2] Gen. 6 : 14-16. There is only one account of the building of the ark, which is, therefore, an indication that the three verses in which the ark is described represent the combination of both documents. It is, therefore, immaterial whether we put it on the J or on the P side, if we only bear in mind that both documents are represented in the account.

[3] "Make the ark in compartments" is apparently an addition by some redactor but which appears to be out of place. It fits in as an explanatory note at the end of vs. 16.

[4] The word that occurs here, sohar, cannot be a "window," as it was translated in the authorised version, for a different term is used to indicate a window in chapter 8 : 6. Nor can it very well be a "light," as the revised version renders it, since the ark consisted of three stories, one above the other, and there would be little use for a skylight. The addition of "above" points to a covering and, since in two Babylonian versions a covering is particularly referred to and its strength emphasised, it seems more plausible to assume that, however sohar is to be explained etymologically, it designates a deck in this passage. In the Tell el Amarna Letters (ed. Knudtzon, No. 233, 11), ṣuhru or zuhru

and a door to the ark on the side thou shalt make;[1] a lower
story, a second story and a third story thou shalt make it."

If we make the attempt to take the narrative as a
unit, it is quite impossible to thread our way through the
jungle in Gen. 7 : 12 to 8 : 19, which comprises the chief
details in the story, whereas if we distribute among the
two documents the figures giving the duration of the
Deluge and of Noah's stay in the ark, all becomes per
fectly clear. The Priestly Code, always distinguished by
its interest in genealogies and by its detailed figures, gives
us the genealogy of Noah (Gen. 6 : 9-10) as follows:

"These are the generations[2] of Noah. Noah was a righteous
man, perfect in his generation. Noah walked with Elohim.[3]
And Noah begat three sons, Shem, Ham and Japheth."

Wherever, therefore, these sons are named (e. g., Gen.
7 : 13; 9 : 18) we may be sure of having the P document

which comes close to our word, is introduced as a Canaanitish gloss to
Assyrian ṣiru, the ordinary word for "back," which would be an ap
propriate term to designate a deck or "covering" for the hull on which
the superstructure was to be erected. It would hardly be in place to
speak of the roof before mentioning the three stories. The words
"to a cubit thou shalt make it" would be intended to indicate the
thickness or solidity of the deck so as to hold the superstructure,
corresponding to the "six layers" of which the deck was to consist ac
cording to the main Babylonian version (above, p. 328). I take the
word "above" as an explanatory gloss to the rare term sohar which
occurs in the Old Testament in this single passage only.

[1] I. e., an entrance into the hull or hold. One is reminded of Berosus's account (above, p. 346), who refers to Atrakhasis "removing a part
of the side of the ship" as a means of exit.

[2] Of such genealogical lists we have ten in Genesis, all introduced by
the phrase "These are the generations," etc. (Gen. 5 : 1; 6 : 9; 10 : 1;
11 : 10, 27; 25 : 12, 19; 36 : 1, 9; 37 : 2), exclusive of Gen. 2 : 4: "These
are the generations of heaven and earth."

[3] The redundancy in the description of Noah as (1) righteous, (2) as
perfect in his generation, (3) that he walked with Elohim points to a
combination of several documents in P, to which reference was made
above, p. 351. There are many more instances of this in P's account
of the Deluge.

before us.   Similarly, figures giving the age of Noah (Gen.
7 : 6) at the time of his entering the ark, together with
the mention of the month and day—the 17th day of the
2d month—when the Deluge began (Gen. 7 : 11), the
period during which the waters increased (Gen. 7 : 24; 8 :
3), 150 days—the date when the ark rested on the moun
tains of Ararat (Gen. 8 : 4)—the 17th day of the 7th
month—the decrease of the waters till on the 11th day of
the 10th month the tops of the mountains were seen
(Gen. 8 : 5), and finally the period when the waters had
dried up, the 27th day of the 2d month (Gen. 8 : 14)—
all these numerical details are the earmarks of the Priestly
Code.   According to this document, 12 months and 10
days elapse from the time that Noah enters the ark till
he leaves it, or, since the basis of calendrical calculation
is the lunar month of alternately 29 and 30 days, this
gives us a lunar year of 354 days plus 10 days to round
out a solar year of about 365 days.[1]

By way of contrast we have in the Yahwist version
general and round figures, like seven and forty, repeated
several times, but which taken altogether give us a con
siderably smaller total for the stay in the ark.   Seven
days after Noah enters the ark (Gen. 7 : 4) the rain
begins.   It lasts forty days and forty nights (Gen. 7 : 4
and 12).[2]   After forty days (Gen. 8 : 6) Noah opens a
window and sends forth a dove (Gen. 7 : 7).   This dove
is sent forth twice again (Gen. 7 : 10, 12), at intervals
of seven days, so that when Noah prepares to leave the
ark only 108 days have passed since the time that he
entered it[3] as against a full solar year according to the

[1] This exact calculation, assuming a scientifically ordered calendar in
which the lunar months are taken as a basis but accommodated to make
the lunar year accord with the apparent annual revolution of the sun
along the ecliptic, points to the very late date of the final redaction of
the P version.

[2] In vs. 4 the duration is announced and in vs. 12 stated as a fact.

[3] Eighty days plus 4 times 7 days equal 108 days.

Priestly document. To bring out the main contrasts be
tween the two accounts, let me put side by side the state
ments of J and P in regard to the animals entering the
ark and the duration of Noah's stay.

(1) The command to enter the ark.

<table>
<tr><td>

J

Gen. 7 : 1-6:

"And Yahweh said to Noah,
'Enter thou and all thy house
into the ark, for I have seen
thee righteous before me in this
generation.

"'Of all clean beasts take
thou seven each, male and fe
male,[1] and of beasts which are
not clean two each, male and
female,[2] also of the birds of
heaven seven each, male and
female,[3] to keep seed alive on
the face of the earth. For
after seven days I will cause
it to rain on the earth forty
days and forty nights, and
blot out all creatures which I
made, from the face of the
earth.' And Noah did accord
ing to all that Yahweh com
manded him."

</td><td>

P

Gen. 6 : 18-22:

"'But I have established my
covenant with thee.[1] There
fore, enter thou into the ark,
thou and thy sons and thy wife
and the wives of thy sons with
thee, and of all living things,[2]
two of each shalt thou bring
into the ark to keep alive with
thee, male and female shall they
be.[3] Of birds after their kind,
of beasts after their kind, of all
things creeping on the ground
after their kind, two of each
shall come to thee to keep them
alive.[4] But thou take for thee
of all food that may be eaten
and store it, that it may be for
thee and for them as food.' And
Noah did according to all that
Elohim had commanded him.
So he did."[5]

</td></tr>
</table>

[1] Literally, "*man and his wife*"
which is the phrase characteristic
of J, whereas P uses the ordinary
Hebrew words for "male and female." (Gen. 6 : 19; 7 : 16.)

[2] See preceding note.

[3] In this instance the terms
"male and female" are the same
as in P, but the entire verse 3 is
under suspicion of being a later in
sertion in J to make the narrative
conform to Gen. 6 : 20.

[1] The reference to the covenant
is characteristic of the Priestly
Code.

[2] Gloss "of all flesh."

[3] Note again the redundancy of
phrases at the beginning of this
verse, "all living things," "all
flesh," "of all," again pointing
to a combination of a number of
sources.

[4] The Greek translation omits
the words "of cattle according to
its kind," but adds at the close of

the phrase once more "male and
female shall they be." Such vari
ations point to considerable manip
ulation of the text.
⁵ Again a redundant phrase.

(2) The entry into the ark and the duration of the Deluge.

J

Gen. 7 : 7, 10, 12, 16b, 18, 23:
"And Noah and his sons and
his wife and the wives of his
sons with him entered the ark
because of the waters of the
flood.[1] (And Yahweh shut him
in.[2]) And after seven days (the
waters of the flood were on
the earth and) the rain[3] was on
the earth for forty days and
forty nights. And the waters
prevailed and increased ex
ceedingly upon the earth, but
the ark moved upon the face
of the waters and (Yahweh)
blotted out all creatures which
were on the face of the earth.[4]
And Noah alone was left alive
and those with him in the ark."

[1] Vss. 8 and 9 are again later ad
ditions to J to bring about a con
formity between the two docu
ments. They read as follows:
"Of clean cattle and of cattle not
clean and of birds and all that
creepeth on the ground, in pairs
they came to Noah into the ark,
male and female, as Elohim had
commanded Noah." The state
ment that they came in pairs
agrees with P, but is against J,
which says distinctly in the case
of clean beasts that there were
seven pairs and of unclean two.

P

Gen. 7 : 6, 11, 13–16a, 17,
19–22, 24:
"And Noah was six hundred
years old when the flood of
waters came over the earth.
In the six-hundredth year of
the life of Noah, in the second
month on the seventeenth day
of the month, on that day all
the fountains of the great deep
were broken up and the win
dows of heaven opened. On
that very day Noah and (Shem
and Ham and Japheth),[1] the
sons of Noah and the wife of
Noah and the three wives of his
sons with them entered the
ark. They and every beast
after its kind, and all cattle
after their kind and every
creeping thing that creeps upon
the earth after its kind, and
every bird after its kind.[2] And
they came in unto Noah into
the ark in pairs, of all flesh that
had in it the breath of life;
and those entering were male
and female of all flesh that
went in, as Elohim commanded
him."[3]

("And the flood was forty
days on the earth).[4] And
the waters increased and lifted

The use, moreover, of the words *male and female*, as in P, against *man and his wife*, which is characteristic of J, shows that vss. 8 and 9 did not belong originally to the J document. On the other hand, since we have, in vss. 14 and 15, P's description of the entrance of the animals into the ark, we must assume that vss. 8 and 9 represent a third version—perhaps one allied to the Elohist document, but which was inserted by some redactor into J or added to P, though this is less likely.

[2] This statement, corresponding to the statement in the Babylonian versions of Utnapishtim's "closing the door" after entering the boat, now stands at the end of vs. 16, at the close of P's description of the entrance into the ark. Its original place in J is, however, after vs. 7, the transfer being due to the combination of P with J.

[3] The word for rain (*geshem*) is the term characteristic of the Yahwist version. The P document speaks of a flood (*mabbul*) which continues for 150 days and causes a rise of the waters to 15 cubits and upward. According to J, the Deluge is a violent storm of 40 days' duration, but the compiler of P and J has thrown the two terms "flood" and "rain" together as synonyms. Hence he introduces the term "flood" (*mabbul*) also into J, vss. 7 and 10. The redundancy of the style points to a combination of various sources.

[4] Amplifying addition, "From man to cattle, to creeping things and the birds of heaven, and they were blotted out from the earth," to conform to the addition in Gen. 6 : 7. See above, p. 350, note 2.

the ark which (thus) rose above the earth. And the waters continued to prevail exceedingly upon the earth until all the high mountains under the heavens[5] were covered. Up wards of fifteen cubits did the waters prevail,[6] and all flesh perished.[7] All that had the breath of life in its nostrils, all that were on the dry land died.[8] And the waters prevailed upon the earth for one hundred and fifty days."

[1] The names in this passage may be a subsequent addition taken over from Gen. 6 : 10.

[2] Two explanatory glosses are added, (1) every bird, (2) every winged thing. The Greek trans lation omits the second gloss.

[3] The construction in vs. 16 is exceedingly awkward, and since it is a repetition of what has already been said in vs. 15, it furnishes another piece of evidence that P is a combination of several sources.

[4] The first part of the verse is a repetition (taken from J) to connect the second account of the entrance into the ark with the beginning of the Deluge. The omission of "forty nights" (which the Greek translation, however, adds) shows that the words are merely added as a necessary link to what follows.

[5] The tops of the mountains ac cording to the view prevailing in antiquity reached to the heavens; these tops are, therefore, directly "under" the heavens.

[6] Repetition, "and the mountains were covered."

[7] Addition, "that creepeth on the ground, of bird, of cattle, and of

beast and of all that swarms on
the earth and all mankind."

[8] Note again the redundancy,
pointing to the composite charac
ter of the P account.

(3) The receding of the waters and the departure from the ark.

J	P
Gen. 8 : 2b, 3a, 6, 8–12, 13b, 18:	Gen. 8 : 1–2a, 3b, 4–5, 13a, 14–17, 19:

J

"And the rain was restrained from heaven and the waters re ceded gradually from the earth. And after forty days Noah opened a window[1] of the ark which he had made.[2] And he sent forth a dove to see if the waters were abated from off the face of the ground, but the dove found no rest for the sole of her foot and she returned unto him to the ark, for the waters were on the face of the whole earth; and Noah put forth his hand and took her and brought her back unto him into the ark. Then he stayed yet other seven days and again sent forth the dove out of the ark, and the dove returned unto him at eventide with a freshly plucked olive leaf in her mouth. So Noah knew that the waters were abated from off the earth. Then he stayed yet other seven days and sent forth the dove, which did not again return unto him. Then Noah removed the covering of the ark and saw that the face of the ground was dried. And Noah and his sons

P

"And Elohim remembered Noah and all the beasts and all the cattle that were with him in the ark, and Elohim made a wind to pass over the earth to dry the waters. And the fountains of the deep and the windows of heaven were stopped. And the waters de creased after one hundred and fifty days. Then on the seven teenth day of the seventh month the ark rested, on the mountains of Ararat. And the waters continued to decrease until on the first day of the tenth month the tops of the mountains were seen.

"And it was in the six hun dred and first year, on the first of the first month, that the wa ters were dried up from off the earth. And on the twenty-sev enth day of the second month the earth was dry. And Elo him said to Noah as follows: 'Go forth out of the ark, thou and thy wife and thy sons and the wives of thy sons with thee, every living creature that is with thee,[1] of birds, of cattle, of every-

and his wife and the wives of his sons went forth."

[1] The "window" in J corresponds to the "door" (Gen. 6 : 16) in the combined narrative, which shows that the latter term belongs to the other document.

[2] A later insertion in J (vs. 7) reads as follows: "And he sent away the raven which went forth hither and thither until the waters were dried up from off the earth." See the explanation for this addition on p. 361.

thing that creeps on the earth bring forth with thee that they may swarm in the earth and be fruitful and multiply upon the earth.'[2]   Every beast, every creeping thing and every bird, everything that creeps upon the earth after their species,[3] went forth out of the ark." [4]

[1] Gloss 'of all flesh.'

[2] This verse again forms a good illustration of the composite character of the P document, which becomes redundant because of the combination in it of at least two sources.

[3] Literally, "their families."

[4] This entire verse, with its awkward construction and its repetition of "creeping things," may be a later insertion.   It is certainly superfluous.

(4) The declaration that there will not be another Deluge.

J

Gen. 8 : 20–22:

"And Noah built an altar unto Yahweh, and took of every clean beast and of every clean bird and offered burnt offerings on the altar.   When Yahweh smelt the sweet savour, Yahweh said in his heart: 'I will not again curse the ground for the sake of man, for the inclination of the heart of man is evil from his youth, and I will not again smite all living creatures as I have done.   While the earth remaineth, seed-time and harvest, cold and heat, summer and

P

Gen. 9 : 8–11:[1]

"And Elohim spoke to Noah and his sons with him saying: 'I have established my covenant with thee and with your seed after you and with every living creature that is with you, of birds, of cattle, and of every beast of the earth with you, all that have gone out of the ark.[2] And I will establish my covenant with you that all flesh shall not again be cut off [3] (by the waters of the flood and there shall not again be a flood to destroy the earth).[4]'"

winter, day and night shall
not cease.'"

¹ The P document does not contain any account of Noah's sacri
fice, presumably because it was
identical with that in the other
document. It is, of course, pos
sible also that some of the phrases
in J's account belong to P.

The first seven verses of chapter
9 have nothing to do with the
Deluge. They embody a blessing
of Elohim upon Noah and his sons
and certain precautions regarding
the enlargement of man's diet by
permitting him to eat the flesh of
animals and not merely herbs and
vegetables as in the case of Adam
(Gen. 1 : 29); and adds certain
precautions regarding the eating of
blood, which was to be prohibited.

² The text adds redundantly
"every living creature of the
earth," which the Greek transla
tion properly omits.

³ The declaration ended here.
The remainder of the verse (11b) is
a subsequent addition, marked
again by a redundancy of expres
sion.

⁴ Vss. 12–17, forming the closing
episode of the Deluge, represent a
second address of Elohim, convey
ing the impressive explanation of
the rainbow after a storm as a sign
of God's covenant.

IV

If we now compare the two biblical accounts with the
main Babylonian version, which alone is sufficiently well
preserved to admit of a comparison, it will be seen that
the Yahwist document bears more resemblance to the
tale in the Gilgamesh Epic than does the other document.
Indeed, if we only had the version of the Priestly Code
before us, with its bare statement of a complete destruc-

tion of all life on earth, a stay of one year in the ark, and the escape of a favourite individual and his family in a ship, it might not be regarded as sufficient to assume a direct relationship to the Babylonian narrative. The numerous traditions of a Deluge known to us are by no means related, even when we can detect points of resem blance. Professor Usener, *e. g.*,[1] questions whether the Greek tale of Deukalion is dependent upon Babylonian traditions, despite the fact that the hero escapes a gen eral destruction of mankind by taking refuge with his wife, Pyrrha, in an ark constructed by him on the advice of his father Prometheus, who as the benefactor of hu manity reminds us forcibly of the role played by the god Ea in Babylonian mythology. If, however, we turn to the Yahwist version with its moderate figures, with its emphasis on the number seven, the sending out of a dove three times, and the making of an offering upon leaving the ark, the parallels to the Babylonian counter part are too numerous and too close to be accidental; and this, notwithstanding that in the Babylonian tradi tion the storm lasts only six or seven days as against forty in the Yahwist document, and that instead of a dove sent out three times, we have in the Gilgamesh Epic three different birds, and also that in Genesis we have an ark[2] instead of a ship. Such variations are just of the kind that will arise in the case of traditions which start from a common source, but then develop independently of each other. That is the assumption upon which we have proceeded throughout this investigation of the He-

---

[1] *Sintflutsagen*, pp. 31 *seq.* The case is different with the form given to the tale in Lucian, *De Dea Syria*, 12 *seq.*, which Usener shows is a combination of the Greek and Babylonian tales, localised at a sanctuary in Syria.

[2] *Tebah*—literally "box" used only in the Deluge story and in the narrative of Moses (Ex. 2 : 3–5). The Hebrew tradition recalled the peculiar character of the construction on which Noah takes refuge and, therefore, with intent avoided the term ship. It will be recalled that in the Babylonian versions the boat is also called a "palace."

brew and Babylonian traditions. The mere existence of two or more versions among the Hebrews is sufficient to attest the antiquity of the tradition itself as well as its popularity among the Hebrews. So, *e. g.*, the distinction between clean and unclean animals is a touch inserted into the Yahwist version at a time when the taboo on certain animals regarded as unclean as set forth in Deuteronomy, chapter 14, and Leviticus, chapter 11, was in force.[1] The little insertion about the raven who is immediately dismissed[2]—not sent forth as a messenger— is also added with intent, for the raven is specifically enumerated among the unclean animals (Lev. 11 : 14). Some pious redactor, aware presumably of the part played by the raven in the Babylonian tale,[3] where it is given the distinction of furnishing the sign that the waters had dried, inserted this gloss as a tribute to Noah's piety, who, becoming a type of an observant Jew, is thus pictured as getting rid of the unclean, and therefore obnoxious, bird at the first opportunity.[4]

Significant in the biblical version is also the delocalisation of the story. In the main Babylonian version the

---

[1] It is not, of course, necessary to assume that the laws were as explicit and as detailed as set forth in the Pentateuch. The chapters in Deuteronomy and Leviticus betray evidence of a gradual expansion from some very simple distinctions between clean and unclean animals. See above, p. 165, note 1, for the author's view of the regulations in the Priestly Code, many of which have all the earmarks of a high antiquity.

[2] Gen. 8 : 7. See above, p. 358, note 2.

[3] We must beware of the error of assuming that the Hebrews—at all events in exilic and postexilic days —were ignorant of Babylonian-Assyrian literature. The fourteenth chapter of Genesis is not improbably based in part on some cuneiform sources that the Hebrew compiler had before him. See above, p. 13, though we must not go as far as to assume the chapter to be a translation of a cuneiform historical document. The late Professor D. H. Müller in his *Ezechiel-Studien*, pp. 56 *seq.*, has also made it probable that Ezekiel made use of cuneiform literature to a certain extent.

[4] Midrashic tales about the raven emphasise this point of the raven which, as an unclean animal, is represented as being hated by God as well as by Noah. See Ginzberg, *Legends of the Jews*, I, pp. 163-4.

Deluge centres around Shuruppak and thus betrays its
local origin.   In Berosus, who hands down the Atrakhasis
version, it starts at Sippar.   Other versions may be found
which will name other centres.   The annual overflow
takes place throughout the Euphrates Valley, and so every
large centre could have its Deluge story, as it had its
Creation myth.   The biblical outlook is far wider—upon
mankind in general in the Yahwist document and upon
the entire earth in the Priestly Code.   The occurrence in
nature is entirely kept out of view in both.   The biblical
Deluge is no longer a magnified natural event, but a special
act of the Almighty, comparable in grandeur to the process
of Creation.   God himself is about to destroy what He
has brought into being.   The Hebrew point of view does
not even hesitate to represent God as regretting the crea
tion of man, so supreme is the ethical motive that has
been infused into the old nature-myth, and which accounts
for the features that separate it so completely from the
Babylonian counterpart from which at one time it could
hardly have been distinguished.

The absolute sway of ethical ideals is to be illustrated
by an awful example.   The world, made by God for the
sake of man, has failed to be guided by the dictates of
righteousness.   The principle of justice is carried still
further in the Priestly Code which assumes that the
whole earth and not merely man is corrupt.[1]   To be sure,
a discordant pessimistic note is sounded at the close[2] that
it is not worth while to destroy the world for man's sake
because man's inclination is towards evil.   Wickedness is
inherent in man, but this sad admission is merely an
evidence of the desperate dilemma with which the pious
Jew of later days found himself confronted, when brought
face to face with the question why a God of justice allows

[1] The Midrash, taking up this thought, says (Ginzberg, *ib.*, I, p. 160)
that the animals were as wicked as men.
[2] By the Yahwist.   See above, pp. 102 *seq*.

wickedness to reign in the world. The example, however, was furnished at one time that if wickedness passes be yond a certain level, God does not hesitate to undo His own handiwork.

Fiat justitia, et pereat mundus! It is as an illustration of this doctrine that the old nature-myth is retained— delocalised, stripped of all suggestions of its association with the annual change of seasons, with touches added to it that make it conform to specific Hebrew regulations such as the distinction between clean and unclean animals. The myth becomes a parable, the force of which is height ened by the poetic subscript to the tale[1]—the interpre tation of the rainbow as the symbol of God's covenant with the righteous. Noah—however we explain the ori gin of the name[2]—is a type. As such he is regarded by the Prophet Ezekiel by the side of Daniel and Job [3] who are likewise merely types and not real personages.

In the Babylonian tale Utnapishtim, Atrakhasis, and Ziugiddu are saved because they are favourites. Of Ziugiddu, to be sure, it is said that he was a reverent wor shipper of the gods, but the implication is not of an es sentially ethical character. The pious here is he who brings sacrifices to the gods and carries out prescribed rites. The biblical story furnishes the crumb of comfort for the pious members of the postexilic Jewish commu nity, the "poor" and humble ones of the Psalms,[4] that even in a universal destruction the righteous need not fear. He will find favour in the eyes of God, as did Noah. The waters that engulf the world will not touch him. The ark in which he finds refuge will rise on the waters, even though the waters mount above the highest peaks.

---

[1] Gen. 9 : 12–17.

[2] The explanation of the name, Gen. 5 : 29, as the one who "will com fort us," rests on assonance and is not a genuine etymology of the name. The explanation is in the style of the Jewish Midrash.

[3] Ezek. 14 : 14, 20.   [4] See above, p. 241.

Not only is the righteous saved, but he also saves the world. Because of Noah, Yahweh makes a covenant not to destroy the world again. He sets the rainbow in the sky, which will appear even while the rain pours and the storm rages as an assurance that Yahweh will remem ber Noah, the righteous man, and for Noah's sake re strain his anger at the ineradicable wickedness of man. The pessimistic note is thus changed into one which, though still in the minor key, yet is relieved somewhat of its hopeless outlook. If only ten righteous be found, Abra ham is assured,[1] Sodom and Gomorrah will be saved be cause of the righteous. The biblical Deluge story thus becomes another powerful sermon like the story of the Fall,[2] emphasising the central lesson of the Hebrew Proph ets—obedience to divine behests, even as Noah obeyed, and setting up righteousness as the supreme goal of life, even as Noah was righteous. It is a sermon that illus trates also the two aspects of the Hebrew faith in the postexilic period when the early narratives in Genesis received their definite shape, on the one hand, the attach ment to the aims of the Prophets on the part of the minority of the community, who, resigned to their hum ble position by virtue of their unworldly ambitions, sadly realised the lesson of Job—that the good often suffer while the ungodly flourish. But, on the other hand, while not closing their eyes to the fact that man's inclination is towards wickedness, and that as it had been before the Deluge so it was after the Deluge, and perhaps will long continue to be, they comforted themselves with the re flection that it is the righteous who will eventually save the world.

Recognising unreservedly the common origin of the Babylonian and biblical traditions of the Deluge—as a nature-myth picturing the annual change, and based per haps on a recollection of some particularly disastrous

[1] Gen. 18 : 32.   [2] Above, p. 61.

season,[1] the tradition gives rise among both Babylonians and Hebrews to various versions, differing from one an other in details. The development proceeds along inde pendent lines among the Hebrews from a certain time on, and under the influence of the teachings of the Prophets the emphasis comes to be laid on the wickedness of man and the corruption of the earth as the cause of the catas trophe, and on the righteousness of Noah as the reason for his escape. The story is retained like the Creation tale, because of its popularity, but is completely transformed in the long process which changed a nature-myth into an ethical parable. It received its final shape well along in the postexilic period, and was made the medium of im pressing upon the people the underlying principles of Prophetical Judaism.

[1] I do not believe, however, that the Babylonian or biblical Deluge recalls a violent geologic subversion in the region of the Persian Gulf in prehistoric days, as Eduard Suess, *Die Sinflut* (1884), would have us suppose. It is most unlikely that people living many, many thousands of years after such an event should have any recollection of it, however dimmed. The localisation of the Deluge in the Babylonian versions to which the biblical accounts, as we have seen, revert, is a sufficient ar gument against such a proposition.

INDEX

Asherah, symbol in Canaanitish cult, 31, 182, 183.
Ashurbanapal, King of Assyria, 68, 276, 323, 326, 344, 346.
Assumption of Moses, 245.
Assyria as warlike nation, 267 *seq.*, 277.
Astral theology, 71, 119 *seq.*, 143, 200, 264.
Astral worship, 32.
Astrology, 32, 81 *seq.*, 139, 141 *seq.*, 154, 171, 266 *seq.*
Astronomy, 144, 160.
Asushu-namir (created by the god Ea), 208.
Atonement, 291 *seq.*; day of, 171 *seq.*
Atrakhasis, hero of the Babylonian Deluge, 326 *seq.*, 334, 341, 344 *seq.*, 346 *seq.*, 354, 364, 365.
Atrakhasis version of Deluge, 341 *seq.*
Auspicious days, see Days.
Authorship, 285 *seq.*

Baal, 28, 179, 182.
Babylonia, influence on Palestine, 19, 32, 193; as early home of Hebrews, 5 *seq.*, 21 *seq.*; polygamy in, 273 *seq.*; warlike proclivities, 267 *seq.*, 277.
Babylonian-Assyrian civilisation, see Euphratean Culture.
Bad-nagar-dish (city), 96.
bamoth (high places), 29.
Banks, E. J., 337.
Baptism, 146.
Barton, George A., 236, 237, 308.
bâru (diviner), 150.
Barzilai, 55.
Bathsheba, 311.
Beatitudes, 315.
Beer-Sheba, 27.
Behemoth (monstrous creature), 115.
Belili (goddess), 71.
Ben Sira, 237 *seq.*
Berosus, 68, 73 *seq.*, 85 *seq.*, 100, 129, 327, 336, 338; version of Deluge, 346 *seq.*, 354, 364.
Bethel, 24, 310.
Birth, 146.
Birth-omens, 141, 266.
Bismya, site of ancient city of Adab, 337.

Black-headed people, 341.
Blood, as source of life, 129; eating of, prohibited, 361; in creation of man, 84 *seq.*, 128 *seq.*
Boat, see Ship; Ark.
Booths, festival of, 158 *seq.*
Bosheth, disguised form for Baal, 29.
bubbulu (disappearance of moon), 135.
Budde, Karl, 179, 232.
Bull, divine, 324.
Burial, 197 *seq.*, 213, 223.
Burning bush, 169.

Cain, 309.
Calendar, 82, 119, 159, 355.
Canaanites, influence on Hebrews, 28, 31 *seq.*, 182.
Canals, 214, 264, 322.
Cassites, 268.
Chaos, 72, 83.
Charles, R. H., 245, 248.
Child sacrifice, 182.
Christ, 249 *seq.*
Christianity, 43, 193, 248 *seq.*, 314 *seq.*
Christmas, 146.
Circumcision, 146.
Cities, founding of, 89 *seq.*
Clay, A. T., 10, 16.
Clean and unclean, 44.
Clean and unclean animals, 363, 365.
Coblenz, 238.
Code of Hammurapi, 271 *seq.*
Commerce, 167, 228, 269, 271 *seq.*, 307, 309.
Concubines, 273.
Confirmation, 146.
Confusion of languages, 6.
Consciousness after death, 196 *seq.*, 212.
Cory, I. P., 73, 85, 327, 336, 346.
Creation, Babylonian-Assyrian accounts, 7, 21 *seq.*, 37 *seq.*, 68 *seq.*, 89 *seq.*, 95 *seq.*; biblical accounts, 24, 37 *seq.*, 60, 80, 98 *seq.*, 116 *seq.*; Hesiod's theogony, 70 *seq.*
Creation of man, 83 *seq.*, 91, 100, 104, 128 *seq.*
Cremation, 198.
Culture, attitude towards, 309 *seq.*

Made in the USA
Lexington, KY
27 January 2014